Praise for **A Place at the Table**

"COURAGEOUS AND THOUGHT-PROVOKING." •
—Margaret O'Brien Steinfels, *The New York Times Book Review*

"If there is one book about homosexuality and gay rights that everyone should read, it is probably this one."
—John Fink, *Chicago Tribune*

"The most significant book on gay politics and culture that I've ever read."
—Gregory King, communications director, Human Rights Campaign Fund

"Powerful and important . . . the blockbuster of the season."
—Steven Petrow, *The Advocate*

"Bawer's well-reasoned, articulate arguments are of inestimable value."
—*Publishers Weekly*

"Challenging and compulsively readable . . . tightly reasoned and responsible . . . with a provocative viewpoint that has rarely, if ever, been so effectively in print."
—Bob Summer, *Lambda Book Report*

"COURAGEOUS."
—Jonathan Yardley, *The Washington Post Book World*

"A quiet, dispassionate voice trying to be heard above the din."
—John Heidenry, *The New York Daily News*

Books by Bruce Bawer

A Touchstone Book

Published by Simon & Schuster

New York • London • Toronto • Sydney • Tokyo • Singapore

Bruce Bawer

·

A Place at the Table

The Gay Individual

in American Society

·

TOUCHSTONE

Rockefeller Center
1230 Avenue of the Americas
New York, New York 10020

First Touchstone Edition 1994

TOUCHSTONE and colophon are registered trademarks
of Simon & Schuster Inc.

Designed by Karolina Harris

Manufactured in the United States of America

10 9 8 7 6 5 4 3

Library of Congress Cataloging-in-Publication Data

Bawer, Bruce, 1956–
    A place at the table : the gay individual in American society /
Bruce Bawer.
       p.   cm.
    1. Homosexuality—United States.   2. Gays—United States.
3. Subculture.   I. Title.
HQ76.3.U5B39   1993
305.38'9664—dc20   93-5798
                                                                CIP

ISBN: 0-671-79533-3
       0-671-89439-0 (pbk)

FOR CHRIS

Contents

Let us build an American home
for the twenty-first century where
everyone has a place at the table and
not a single child is left behind.

—President-elect Bill Clinton
  January 17, 1993

Author's note

This book is a reflection on the theme of homosexuality. I have written it because the current debate on homosexuality and gay rights has generated a lot more heat than light. Most of what is being said on the subject seems to me terribly wrong, and many of the people who are doing the loudest talking appear to have a vested interest in perpetuating discord and misunderstanding.

Because my sense of what it means to be gay derives largely from my own experience, this book is, in part, autobiographical. Furthermore, since it is essentially an attempt to correct the misperceptions that underlie certain widely held beliefs and oft-repeated arguments, it contains many quotations from recent magazine articles, newspaper op-eds, and television interviews in which those attitudes and arguments have been presented.

The book's first section offers an overview of recent social and political developments relating to homosexuality and gay rights, and puts those developments in historical and moral perspective. The second section scrutinizes the positions of those who criticize homosexuality or gay rights; the third examines the gay subculture and its premises; the fourth considers the dilemma of the gay individual and his problematic relation to both the mainstream culture and the subculture.

What word to use? If to many gays "homosexual" sounds like a clinical diagnosis, to many heterosexuals "gay" sounds like a political statement. Simply for variety's sake, I've chosen to use the two words interchangeably, both as nouns and adjectives. When speaking of homosexuality in pre-modern times, however, I'm inclined to refrain from using the word "gay," because it reflects a contemporary awareness of sexual identity that seems anachronistic when one is referring to, say, Socrates or Caravaggio or Richard the Lion-Hearted. I also tend to favor "gay" when discussing subculture-oriented individuals and "homosexual" when discussing individuals who are more mainstream-oriented. I've chosen not to use the word "queer," which is favored by some gay activists and academics but turns off almost everybody else, gay and straight.

Though much of this book will be seen to apply equally to gay men and women, a great deal of what I have to say will not strike many lesbians as being particularly relevant to their lives. This can't be helped. One reason is that there are, I think, innate differences between male and female sexuality, and consequently innate differences between male and female homosexuality; another reason is that for many lesbians the issue of homosexuality is tangled up with the issue of feminism, which is another ball game entirely. In any event, my emphasis on male homosexuality certainly shouldn't lead anyone to think that I don't feel lesbians also deserve places at the table.

Nor, in criticizing the monolithic aspects of the gay subculture and pointing out that the most easily identifiable gays are not representative of the homosexual population at large, do I intend to suggest that those particularly visible and identifiable gays are any less deserving than anyone else of respect and equal rights or to suggest that those who conform in one way or another to the subculture's prescriptions should be considered thereby to have forfeited *their* places at the table.

For their advice and moral support, I am grateful to several friends: David and Linda Attoe, Gloria and Will Brame, Stephanie Cowell, Rhoda Croft, Marge Danser, Tom DePietro and Dorothy Heyl, Dana and Mary Gioia, Lenny Hort and Laaren Brown, Brendan McEntee, Sally McGaughey, Carol Saltus, Judy White, and Harriet Zinnes. Thanks also go to these family members: Charlotte Davenport, Carol Bawer, Marsha and Aldo Greco, Ruth Cook, and Helen Sicora. I am fortunate to have had the opportunity to work with an extraordinarily gracious and sensitive editor, Elaine Pfefferblit; with her delightful assistant, Laura Demanski; with a marvelous agent, Molly Friedrich; and with Seale Ballenger, to whom I am indebted for his valuable comments and suggestions. My greatest debt is to my companion, Chris Davenport. This book grew out of countless conversations that we've had over the last few years and is almost as much his as it is mine. Finally, I thank my parents, Ted and Nell Bawer, for their unwavering interest in this project and their envelopes full of clippings. More than anyone or anything else, their love and support have animated my hope in the ultimate triumph of reason over irrationality, acceptance over estrangement, love over loathing.

1

"A sea of homosexuals"

One day a few years ago, when I was in my mid-twenties, I walked into a bookstore in midtown Manhattan. Though it has since been sold by one nationwide chain to another, the store is still there, one side of it facing Forty-second Street and the other opening into a cavernous stone passageway that in turn feeds into the main concourse of Grand Central Terminal. Near the store's street entrance in those days was a large magazine section. A wall rack about ten feet wide displayed hundreds of periodicals, from *Glamour* to the *Washington Monthly;* at the rack's base ran a foot-high counter containing tabloid-sized publications like the *New York Review of Books* and *Screw*, stacked in overlapping fashion so that only their titles showed.

Standing at this wall of magazines, when I entered the bookstore that day, was a tall boy of about fifteen. Lean and handsome, he looked, if anything, rather more shy and sweet-natured than the average New York City teenager; he radiated wholesomeness and sensitivity, and his neat dress and good posture suggested that he was well taken care of. This was, clearly, the much-loved son of a decent family.

To the average bookstore browser who glanced his way, he might have appeared to be an ordinary kid, spending an idle hour riffling aimlessly through *Motor Trend* and *Sports Illustrated*. But the moment I saw him, I knew this wasn't the case. The boy was nervous—anxious, even—as he carefully returned a magazine to its place on the rack and glanced furtively to his left and right.

What was going on? Why was he so distressed? My eyes surveyed the hundreds of magazines, and suddenly—to my astonishment—I realized that I knew exactly what was happening.

I forgot immediately about the book I was after and instead walked over to the rack. Taking a magazine, I positioned myself half a step behind the boy and pretended to read. As I stood there unnoticed by him, he reached out, slipped a magazine from its holder, glanced at it absently, then neatly put it back. Again looking to his left and right, he took a couple of steps along the wall, pulled out another magazine, glanced at it in the same cursory way, and returned it to its proper place.

This went on for about five minutes. I had other things to do, but I couldn't bring myself to leave. The boy was trying to work up his courage, and I wanted to see if he would.

He did. As I'd anticipated, all his shuttling back and forth brought him right back to where he'd begun. Standing there, he reached down to the foot-high counter, slipped out from under some other periodical a copy of a gay weekly called *New York Native,* and, trying to appear casual, opened it to the first inside page. If he'd barely glanced at the other magazines (in which, I knew, he'd only been feigning interest), he devoured this one. He stared at that first inside page in desperate bliss, gaped at it, ran his eyes down the columns of print as if he couldn't really believe it existed, drinking in its prose in great huge gulps like a downed airman quaffing water after straggling across a desert. He finished that page and went on to the next, and the next, and the next. All the time the expression of sublime amazement never left his face— although every so often his eyes darted about fearfully to see if anyone was watching. It didn't cross his mind, I'm sure, that he was being observed by me, directly behind him. Certainly it would never have occurred to him that I knew exactly what he was going through and was proud of him.

Proud? Yes. For when I looked at him, I felt as though I were seeing myself a few years earlier—confused, scared, reaching out tentatively for something that would explain to me who I was, and hoping no one would notice until I had something like an answer. In the same way that gay men can often recognize one another at a glance, so I'd known immediately not only that this boy was gay but also that he was just beginning to recognize his homosexuality, that he didn't yet fully understand what that meant, and that there was nobody in his life—no parent, sibling, teacher, friend, or minister—to whom he felt he could turn. And so he'd brought his questions to this bookstore. I knew how difficult it had been for him to come here and to reach for that copy of the *Native;* I was proud of him for having worked up the courage.

As I stood there behind him, I looked over his shoulder at the pages of the *Native.* I don't remember the specific contents: there were, I suppose, the usual articles about AIDS research, gay bashings, and recent gay-rights advances and setbacks, as well as the weekly statistical roundup of reported AIDS cases and deaths. But what leapt out at me, and stayed in my mind for some time afterward, were other things: a photograph, probably accompanying a review of some cabaret act, of a man in drag; photographs of black-clad men in bondage, presumably in advertisements for leather bars and S&M equipment; and photographs of hunky, bare-chested young men, no doubt promoting "massages" and "escort services" and X-rated videotapes.

These pictures irked me. The narrow, sex-obsessed image of gay life that they presented bore little resemblance to my life or to the lives of my gay friends—or, for that matter, to the lives of the vast majority of gay Americans. Yet this was the image proffered by the *Native* and other such magazines. For most of the editors and regular readers of these magazines were not simply gay; they were people whose lives revolved around—and who saw virtually everything else in their lives as relating directly to—their sexual orientation. The image of gay life promulgated in these publications did not reflect actual gay life in America; rather, they presented a picture of gay identity as defined by a small but highly visible minority of the gay population. There was, objectively, nothing wrong with this; these people had their own tastes and interests, their own way of viewing the world and themselves. Fine; that was their right. What *was* wrong was that the image that they projected had, for decades, strongly influenced the general public's ideas about homosexuality. Thanks to their extraordinary visibility—and to the fact that gay men like me, who might serve as alternative role models for such a boy, kept their homosexuality largely to themselves—many heterosexuals tended to equate homosexuality with the most irresponsible and sex-obsessed elements of the gay population. That image had provided ammunition to gay-bashers, had helped to bolster the widely held view of gays as a mysteriously threatening Other, and had exacerbated the confusion of generations of young men who, attempting to come to terms with their homosexuality, had stared bemusedly at the pictures in magazines like the *Native* and said to themselves: "But this isn't *me.*"

As I looked at those photographs over the boy's shoulder, then, my pride became mixed with concern. It disturbed me to think that those pictures should shape his notion of what it meant to be gay. I wished I could tap him on the shoulder and introduce myself and say—well, something more or less like this:

"Don't think those pictures of leathermen and cross-dressers and nipple clamps are what gay life is all about. They're *not*—no more than a *Penthouse* centerfold is what straight life is all about. There are hundreds of thousands of homosexuals in New York, and only twenty thousand subscribe to the *Native:* far more of us read *Time* or *Newsweek* than read the *Native* or anything like it. Gays are liberal and conservative, attractive and homely, smart and stupid. Some wear earrings and some wear three-piece suits. Some you couldn't imagine having anything in common with—and some are very, very much like you.

"So don't let this magazine disturb you. Don't let it add to your confusion about your sexuality. Don't let it make you think, *Well, if that's what it means to be gay, then I guess I must not be gay.* Don't let it make you think, *Well, I'm gay, so I guess I'd better try to become like that.* And don't let it make you think, *Well, I'm gay, but I refuse to become like that, so I guess the only alternative is to repress it and marry.*

"Wrong, wrong, wrong. Being gay doesn't oblige you to be anything— except yourself. Don't let *anyone*, straight or gay, tell you who you are. You're *you*. You're the boy you've always been, the boy you see when you look in the mirror. Yes, you've always felt there was something different about you, something you couldn't quite put a name to, and in the past few months or years you've come to understand and to struggle with the truth about that difference. You're beginning to realize that the rest of your life is not going to play out quite the way you or your parents have envisioned it. You didn't want to accept this at first, but now you know you have no alternative. And you want to be honest with yourself and your parents about this; more than anything else, you want to talk to them about this momentous truth you're discovering about yourself. But you can't bring yourself to do so, since you're pretty sure they'd be angry. You resent them for this. And on top of that you despise yourself, because even though you've always talked to them about everything, you're hiding from them a very important part of who you are, and because—even though you didn't choose to be gay (who, after all, would choose to experience the fear and loneliness and be-

wilderment you've known?)—you feel as if you've done something awful
to them by being this way.

"Well, don't feel guilty. Don't hate yourself. And don't hate your parents. When you tell them about your homosexuality, give them time to
understand, the same way you've had to give *yourself* time to understand.
As you know, it's not easy to understand. And above all, be true to
yourself, your good and decent self, and understand that there's no
inherent conflict between homosexuality and decency. Don't let anyone,
straight or gay, tell you any different."

I wanted to say all this to the boy—all this and much more. Of course,
it was a foolish thought: the boy needed to be listened to more than
lectured. Besides, it was hardly as if I had my own act together: not that
many years had passed since I'd accepted that I was gay. I'd still never
had a steady relationship, or discussed my homosexuality with some of
my friends or with the editors of the monthly review *The New Criterion*,
for which I wrote regularly. I'd never been rejected by a friend or relative
for being gay, and hadn't yet suffered a professional setback on account
of it. I was still figuring out how my homosexuality fit into my life, still
trying to figure out how to deal with it on a daily basis. I considered it
wrong to lie; I also considered it inappropriate to discuss it under, well,
inappropriate circumstances. But which circumstances were *appropriate*? The more I thought about it, the blurrier the line seemed to be
between what some homosexuals (and my own conscience) would consider dishonest concealment and what some heterosexuals might consider flaunting my sexuality.

I'd made one rule for myself: if someone asked me point-blank "Are
you gay?" I would answer honestly. But that was a relatively easy rule,
and didn't begin to speak to the variety of situations that cropped up.
Part of the problem, I realized, was that most heterosexuals are constantly alluding to their personal relationships without even realizing it,
let alone considering it inappropriate; they only notice it, and consider
it inappropriate, when a homosexual does the same thing. Married people have pictures of their spouses on their office desks; they wear wedding rings to work; in conversation with clients and co-workers, they
mention their wives or husbands without giving it a thought. Assuming
a gay co-worker to be straight, they make friendly jokes about "you single

people" and suggest teasingly that he or she is romantically interested in this or that member of the opposite sex.

Can a heterosexual reader understand how this feels? Imagine, if you're a straight male, working in an office where everyone else is gay. They all have pictures of their lovers on their desks, but you don't feel free to display a picture of your wife. Their lovers drop by at the end of the day and kiss them and drive them home, but you can't let your wife come to the office, because it might create discomfort and ill will, if not endanger your job. Your co-workers chat openly with their lovers on the phone, calling them "honey" and saying "I love you!" before hanging up; when you phone your wife you assume an affable but not intimate tone, as if she were just a casual friend. Occasionally your employer holds a party to which all employees' lovers are invited, but your spouse is not invited and stays home. At the party your co-workers and their lovers chat about their home life and you listen quietly, trying to smile when one of them tells you congenially: "Hey, we'll have to find you a boyfriend one of these days!" For it doesn't even occur to them that you might have a wife at home—they assume you're gay, same as them. After all, they like you; you get along; of *course* you're gay. You want to correct their impression, but you can't quite bring yourself to do so: your heterosexuality might be all right with them, but it might not. Being honest with them about your heterosexuality would doubtless force some of them to rethink their prejudices about heterosexuals and help them to see heterosexuals as human beings just like themselves. But at the same time your disclosure would almost certainly cause a change in the tone that some of them take with you; at the very least, there'd be a noticeable awkwardness, a stilted quality, a hint of condescension in their relations with you, as if you'd suddenly turned into another person. You know this because it's happened before, with other people in other offices.

Try to imagine how you would feel in this position, and you'll begin, perhaps, to understand what most gay people go through. How does one deal with such circumstances? The most radical elements of the gay population have their answer: hurl your sexuality in their faces, mention it constantly, return rancor for rancor. At the opposite end of the spectrum, completely closeted gays have another answer: don't rock the boat, turn the other cheek, lie. Neither approach satisfied me. The right answer, it seemed, lay somewhere between these two poles. But where? The more I lived as a self-acknowledged gay man in a straight world, the more I sensed that there was no perfect middle, that there were no cut-and-dried answers, that every situation was somewhat different from the next, and that for a gay person each human encounter posed a new moral and social challenge.

Perhaps, in retrospect, what I had to offer the boy in the bookstore was not my certainties but my confusion. How helpful it might have been to him—and, yes, to me—to talk about the challenges we both faced! But naturally this was impossible. A tap on the shoulder, a man's voice saying, "Excuse me"—it would have scared the hell out of him. He probably would have thought I was making a pass and raced out of there, his heart pounding. And what an accomplishment *that* would've been. I'd have succeeded only in reinforcing for him the most offensive myth of all about gay life: that every gay man is a would-be molester, on the prowl for teenage boys to "recruit."

What did I do, then? Nothing. I stood there silently as the boy finished reading the *Native*. I watched him slip it neatly back into its place on the counter. I watched him leave.

As he stepped out into the dark interior of Grand Central Terminal, I wondered when he would come out to his family and friends. In a week? A year? Twenty years? Never? I hoped that he would take care of himself, and that his parents, if and when he did come out to them, would be kind. And I wished that somewhere in the store there had been a book for me to press into his hands, a book that would have helped him to understand and accept himself—and that might even have helped his loved ones to understand and accept, too.

This book is for that boy.

It's also for the homemaker and mother who phoned the *Donahue* show during a discussion of gay issues to say in a sympathetic voice that she didn't know or understand much about homosexuality, and was in fact confused about it, but wanted to learn about it.

It's for all the heterosexuals who have complained at some time or another that they're "sick and tired of these gays pushing their sex lives in our faces."

It's for the woman who stood up at a 1992 meeting of the anti-gay Oregon Citizens Alliance and wept about the "spread" of homosexuality in America. To quote Robert E. Sullivan Jr.'s report in *The New Republic*: " 'I think of the kids, and in twenty years from now, how it will all be,' she says, her eyes welling up. 'And I just. I just . . .' The woman can't go on."

It's for the audience member who said on the *Jackie Mason* show that "teaching that homosexuality is normal . . . you twist a child's mind."

It's for the straight woman who, on a TV news report about gays in the military, was seen confronting Margarethe Cammermeyer, a former army colonel and Vietnam vet who had been dismissed for being a lesbian. Her voice quavering, the straight woman shrieked that gays and lesbians posed a threat to her family and to America, a country for which she would gladly give her life. Cammermeyer turned to her and replied in a polite, calm voice, "I almost did give my life for it." In sincere terror, the woman barked back, "I wish you had!" and stalked away.

It's for a friend of mine, a gay conservative writer, who, when I ranted over dinner about the anti-gay rhetoric at the 1992 Republican convention, said quietly, "It's best not to talk about these things."

It's for the kind, soft-spoken member of the radical direct-action group Queer Nation who said to me over another dinner, "I wish I could burn down every church in America."

It's for Bill Clinton, whose support for gay rights as a presidential candidate inspired countless American homosexuals, and whose backing away from that support in the months after his inauguration strongly disheartened them. Three days before becoming president, Clinton said, "Let us build an American home for the twenty-first century where everyone has a place at the table and not a single child is left behind." The vision lives, even if Clinton's dedication to it has seemed to waver.

It's for the children of people like Dan Quayle and Pat Buchanan. For those children's sake, I hope they're not gay: homosexuality is not an easy row to hoe, especially when you've got parents like Quayle and Buchanan. For the country's sake, I sometimes wish those kids *were* gay: it might help their fathers to understand how needless are the divisions they promote, how false the myths they perpetuate, and how unwittingly cruel their casual condemnations.

For the present divisions *are* needless. Especially at a time when the nation and the world face crucial problems, arguing about homosexuality and gay rights is a waste of time, energy, money, and emotion. To many heterosexuals, such as that bemused *Donahue* caller, homosexuality is a new and peculiar issue. But homosexuals have always been here. The chief difference is that in earlier times homosexuals led more or less secretive personal lives. Many were married and satisfied their sexual longings on the sly, with strangers. Often driven to severe neurosis by society's opprobrium, they lived in terror of arrest, exposure, disgrace. Today homosexuals are increasingly honest with themselves and others about their sexual orientation. As a consequence of this openness, heterosexuals are gradually becoming aware of the large numbers of homosexuals living among them. For many heterosexuals, especially those who have been touched closely by it—who have learned, in other words, that a friend or relative is gay—this openness has resulted in increased understanding and tolerance. For others, who may have experienced this openness only at a distance—that is, by seeing TV news stories about gay protesters or AIDS patients—it has been a cause of discomfort and confusion.

This discomfort and confusion have been exploited by certain reactionaries, notably leaders of the so-called religious right, who have spread lies about what homosexuality is and about what the gay-rights movement seeks to achieve. What it seeks, quite simply, is to abolish the inequities that homosexuals have to live with and that make it difficult and dangerous for them to live honestly. The point that has been lost amid all the rhetoric is that whatever anti-gay reactionaries may do, whatever laws they manage to enact or block or repeal, they cannot keep a single gay person from being gay; they can only keep him from being honest about it. And that dishonesty is not in *anyone's* interest, no matter what they may think. Dishonesty about homosexuality only breeds ignorance—and as a result of that ignorance, hate is sown in places where there might be love, distrust where there might be understanding, antagonism and violence where there might be harmony and peace. It is, indeed, dishonesty—both on the part of professional bigots who deliberately misrepresent homosexuality and on the part of the majority of gays who, feeling compelled by the ubiquity of prejudice to hide their homosexuality, have rendered themselves powerless to challenge those false representations—that has kept most Americans confused and ill-informed about the basic truths of homosexuality and gay life.

I wrote this book because I am the last homosexual who I ever thought would write a book about homosexuality. I'm a poet, usually classified as an elitist practitioner of "New Formalism," and a literary critic, generally lumped together with certain neoconservative intellectuals. I'm a monogamous, churchgoing Christian. I wrote this book, in short, because I am a member of what must be called—much as I hate to borrow a phrase from our thirty-seventh President—the "silent majority" of homosexuals. One of the things that characterize us silent gays is that, unlike the more visible minority of gays, we tend not to consider ourselves "members" of anything. Some of us are thoroughly closeted; others, though fully open about our homosexuality, simply don't think of it as defining us, as explaining everything about us. Yet as the debate over homosexuality has escalated, some of us have grown increasingly impatient—impatient with the lies that are being told about us by anti-gay crusaders; impatient with the way in which TV news shows routinely illustrate gay-rights stories by showing videotape of leathermen and drag queens at Gay Pride Day marches; and impatient with the way in which many self-appointed spokespeople for the gay population talk about the subject. (These "professional gays" often describe homosexuality in such a way that I, for one, can hardly recognize it.) Some of us silent gays have been so vexed by all this, in fact—and have, frankly, grown exasperated at ourselves for failing to contribute to the public dialogue on homosexuality and gay rights and, through our silence, making possible that dialogue's ugliness and fatuity—that we have stopped being silent. For to some of us, it has seemed increasingly clear that we have an obligation—to ourselves, to the general public, and to the young people whose personal discoveries will begin tomorrow and next year and the year after that—to stand up and speak our minds and correct the false images, even at the risk of seeming to become "professional gays" ourselves.

Yet most mainstream gays have remained silent. A gay acquaintance who is active in conservative politics recently described to me the panel discussion on sexuality that he'd attended at the 1993 *National Review* conference in Washington, D.C. On the panel was Andrew Sullivan, the gay editor of *The New Republic*, who had spoken up for tolerance, gay marriage, and so on. "How did the audience respond?" I asked. "They were hostile," my acquaintance replied. "There were a lot of negative remarks." "Didn't anybody agree with him?" I asked. "Well, of *course*," my acquaintance said, shooting me a look to indicate that plenty of gay conservatives had been in attendance. "But they didn't say anything."

They didn't say anything. In recent years, I've worked up the nerve to complain to associates of mine when they publish things I consider homophobic. A favorite way of responding to such complaints is to contrast my objections with another gay writer's acquiescence: "Well, X is gay and he doesn't seem to have a problem with this article." What they don't know, and what I'm not free to tell them, is that I've just spent the better part of an hour on the phone with X, listening to him gripe bitterly about the article in question and bemoan his own cowardice.

"You're braver than I am," said a gay conservative writer who has composed some of the boldest critical essays of our time, but who, he confessed to me, was too scared to mention the subject of homosexuality to an editor with whom he'd worked, and had a very friendly relationship, for decades. The editor in question had recently published an article on homosexuality and gay rights that was seriously misinformed and that seemed designed to inflame anti-gay prejudice. A few strong words from the gay writer might have struck at the editor's conscience, might have helped him to understand just how wrong, and how hurtful, that article was. Yet the writer remained silent, and continued on friendly terms with the editor. Who, I could not help wondering, was the more guilty party: the gay writer or the editor?

This book is intended to be a meditation, not a manifesto—though I suspect it will be something of both. In any event, my aim is to address the questions at hand with reason, not rancor. On the part of many "professional gays," there has been too much invective and too little effort to explain and clarify; on the part of anti-gay bigots, there has been too little effort to understand, to see beyond prejudice and stereotype, to walk in the other party's shoes. On both sides there have been too many threats and condemnations, too many voices indulging in angry and divisive rhetoric that has served only to perpetuate an atmosphere of confrontation. For the issue of sexual orientation seems to bring out the very worst in many otherwise civilized people. Ordinarily kind and compassionate heterosexuals are confronted with homosexuals and turn startlingly malicious. Ordinarily polite and intelligent gay men come together to "act up" and reveal a dismaying capacity for counterproductive foolishness.

Indeed, the rhetorical battlefield has sometimes appeared to be occupied almost exclusively by extremist demagogues—by far-right fundamentalist superpatriots without an ounce of Christian charity or respect for American liberties, and by radical gay activists who respond to anti-gay attacks by issuing wholesale condemnations of capitalism and Christianity. At one end of the spectrum, encouraging the idea that homosexuality represents a threat to marriage, the family, democratic values, and Christian faith, are people like the Reverend Walter Alexander of Reno's First Baptist Church, who has said that "we should do what the Bible says and cut their [homosexuals'] throats"; at the other end, a handful of radical gay activists who believe that marriage, the family, democratic values, and Christian faith are, by definition, a threat to *them*, and who consequently, in a perverse manifestation of their own fear and hate, enjoy fueling the notion that homosexuality in turn represents a threat to mainstream institutions and precepts. "Both sides agree that there is no middle ground," wrote Chris Bull in a 1992 article in *The Advocate*, a gay magazine. Bull quoted Steve Sheldon of the anti-gay Traditional Values Coalition: "It's a holy war that can have only one winner." This impression is fortified by the policies of issues-oriented talk shows, which tend to favor heated confrontations between inflexible radicals over productive dialogue between reasonable moderates. Discussing the national debate over the military's ban on gays, the host of a Southern California radio phone-in program explained to a reporter that "we lean toward more combative people for the sake of the show."

More than with any other issue of comparable importance, the loudest voices on both sides rely in their arguments not upon common sense, reason, and democratic principle but upon the exploitation of negative emotions, chiefly fear and anger. Radical gay activists trade on the antagonism of many homosexuals toward the parents who rejected them, toward the bigots who insult them on the street, and toward the men of power who treat them as second-class citizens; professional gay-bashers, for their part, trade on the ill-informed fears and suspicions that haunt the minds of millions of otherwise decent heterosexuals. In a strange way, these two fellowships—the radical gay activists and the professional gay-bashers—may be seen as integral components of a closed system, each needing the other for its own existence.

There are in fact people on both sides whose self-images, as well as their careers, depend on preserving the antagonistic status quo—heterosexuals who (in many cases because of their own sexual insecurity) have a psychological need to denounce homosexuals loudly and insolently and at every opportunity, and homosexuals who (in many cases because of the self-doubt often fostered by prejudice) have a psychological need to proclaim their homosexuality, also loudly and insolently and at every opportunity. The excesses of one side fuel the rhetoric of the other. Rather than concentrate on correcting the grotesque public image of gay life and on working to enable gays to live responsibly under the protection of the law, many radical gay activists perpetuate at every turn the widespread view of homosexuals as freaks, outlaws, sex addicts, and sexual exhibitionists. Anti-gay propagandists, in turn, make use of videotapes of the fringe element on display at Gay Pride Day marches to support their argument that homosexuality poses a threat to America. Radical gay activists, in turn, assert the need for extreme action by pointing to the threat represented by gay-bashers. And so on, in an endless angry circle.

In pointing out the existence of this circle, to be sure, I do not mean to draw a moral equation between homophobia and the response to it by certain gays. Nor, in criticizing various aspects of gay activism and of that marginal but obtrusive phenomenon that I shall refer to in these pages as the gay subculture, do I mean for an instant to equate the manners and methods of even the most shrill and obnoxious gay activist with the malicious and menacing lies of the most soft-spoken and gentle-seeming anti-gay propagandist. If I am tough on the gay subculture and on some gay activists, it is not because I consider myself morally superior to or in some essential way different from those whom I am criticizing, but precisely because I *identify* with them; for however much I may differ from them in other particulars, I share with them the knowledge of what it is like to live as a homosexual in a society that considers homosexuals contemptible and unworthy of equal rights under the law. To live day after day with such knowledge imposes remarkable stresses that can generate a variety of reactions, ranging from the gay protester who screams at the top of his voice, "We're here! We're queer!" to the mild-mannered husband and father who keeps his homosexuality forever a secret.

Like most homosexuals, I can empathize deeply with both the livid protester and the closeted husband, for I have known both the impulse to rage and the urge to retreat. Most gays have. But I also know that to succumb to either of these temptations under the pressure of society's opprobrium, however great, is neither wise nor responsible. Such capitulation is not in my own interest; it is not in the interest of homosexuals in general; and it is not in the interest of society at large. If I sometimes seem impatient with some gays, then, for having responded to prejudice in fractious or foolish ways, let it be understood that my impatience is the impatience of identification and that my motivating concern is not only my welfare but theirs. Let no reader of this book forget for a moment, moreover, that the aspects of the gay subculture and of gay activism that come in for criticism in these pages are *not* intrinsic aspects of homosexuality but are invariably the manifestations of institutionalized prejudice. In criticizing some aspects of the gay subculture and gay activism, in short, I am not attacking homosexuals or homosexuality; rather, I am deploring the effects of that prejudice on a segment of the gay population.

If on the other hand I appear to be extremely patient with certain homophobes, it is because I've come to realize that many of those whose attitudes toward homosexuality seem to me and other homosexuals to be extremely vicious and hurtful don't themselves realize how vicious and hurtful they are. On the contrary, they consider themselves to be decent, respectable, and sensitive, and in fact many of them *are,* so long as they're not dealing with people whom they know to be homosexual. I think that the attitudes of most of these people toward homosexuality spring from ignorance and fear and thoughtlessness and sheer habit, and that one stands a better chance of getting through to such people— of helping them, that is, to see the injustice and insensitivity of prejudices that they have taken for granted all their lives—if one addresses their best side rather than their worst and speaks to them calmly, sensibly, and politely.

Yet, as I say, it should not be forgotten that the angry circle I have described begins with anti-gay prejudice, to which the ire of some gay activists is a thoroughly understandable response. In some circumstances, as I know very well, anger is not easy to avoid. Reading the paper or watching television or simply going about my daily business, I often find myself growing angry over the way homosexuality is thought about, talked about, and argued about. I grow angry at slick Sunday-morning televangelists who condemn me as a sinner; angry at militant gays on talk shows who deliberately antagonize heterosexual Americans by equating homosexuality with radicalism or promiscuity; angry at professional anti-gay agitators who draw the same equations; angry at secretly gay married men for using their wives and children as smoke screens; angry at ordinary middle-class people of the kind I grew up around in Queens, New York, for their horror of homosexuality; and even angry, sometimes, and unfairly, at well-meaning folks who, without any malicious intent, say things that wound. Day by day I am tempted to explode in anger, and day by day I fight the temptation, because I know that—with the exception of a few twisted or malevolent or ruthlessly ambitious people, gay and straight, who have made careers out of willfully spreading disinformation and hate—everyone on every side is operating out of fear, or ignorance, or both.

Part of what makes this vicious circle so hard to break is the highly distorted view of homosexuality and the gay-rights struggle held by many heterosexuals. This distorted view, promulgated by hatemongers, has not been countered effectively by, and has in fact been strongly reinforced by, the actions and public statements of many radical gay activists. A key element in all this is the fact that the modern gay-rights movement burst into prominence as an element of the 1960s counterculture and continues to bear its marks. Let it be said—and never forgotten—that for all the vanity and imprudence that many of us associate with 1960s culture and politics, the decade's emancipatory atmosphere encouraged homosexuals to stand up for themselves as never before. Indeed, it is hard to imagine a large-scale gay-rights movement springing to life in less reckless times, for, before the movement began to change things, saying "I'm homosexual" in public *was* an almost insanely reckless thing to do. There is no question, then, but that the silent majority of gays owe a huge debt of gratitude to the drag queens who, by challenging the right of police to raid a Greenwich Village gay bar in 1969 and arrest people simply for being there, turned what had been a small-scale movement, begun in California in the 1950s, into a high-profile international crusade.

But the movement has suffered ever since from the counterculture's baleful influence. Instead of endeavoring to secure domestic-partnership legislation, the most visible gay activists of the 1970s and early '80s made almost a sacred cause out of the right of gay men to anonymous and promiscuous sex. Even during the AIDS crisis, some activists in New York, San Francisco, and Los Angeles have mounted the barricades to oppose attempts to close bathhouses, which they describe as centers of "gay culture," at the same time deriding committed homosexual relationships as bourgeois, conformist, reactionary.

Partly because they are hesitant, moreover, to do anything that would smack even remotely of the sort of repression that homosexuals suffer at the hands of the mainstream culture, the fringe elements of the gay population have failed in large part to set moral standards for themselves, with the result that every year, at the Gay Pride Day march in New York, anti-gay agitators are provided with yet another opportunity to photograph the North American Man-Boy Love Association banner for propaganda purposes. The fact that the NAMBLA contingent routinely consists of no more than a half-dozen of the two hundred thousand or so marchers by no means mitigates the offensiveness of allowing them in the parade in the first place.

Such extreme phenomena have helped to spread among heterosexuals an appalling, and profoundly distorted, image of homosexuality—and, indeed, to yoke the very idea of homosexuality, in the minds of many, with the most far-out images of the 1960s counterculture. Radical gay activists' advancement of the notion that homosexuals are a socially, culturally, and politically homogeneous group, furthermore, has made it harder for many heterosexuals to see gays as individuals, and in particular to make distinctions between the largely invisible millions of gays who lead more or less conventional lives and the conspicuous few who don't.

For these reasons, it is much more difficult than it might otherwise be to convince heterosexuals that nothing about homosexuality is intrinsically contrary to their values. Indeed, the fringe elements of the gay population have so skewed the popular image of homosexuality that most straight people tend to regard causes that are essentially conservative—such as gay marriage—as radical.

Until very recently, there were few fulfilling options for a man who discovered himself to be homosexual. He could pretend that he was heterosexual—perhaps even marry and have children—and either (a) spend his life tormented by suppressed feelings and by the knowledge that he was living a lie or (b) lead a clandestine second life, sneaking off to one-night stands with other men, married or unmarried, who also were leading clandestine second lives. There was a third possibility: falling in love with a man and making a home with him. Though laws and social conventions made this a difficult, even dangerous proposition, some managed to carry it off anyway. But they lived on tenterhooks; they were as secretive about their private lives as enemy spies; they risked losing everything—job, home, social position, even freedom—if someone who didn't like their homosexuality decided to make an issue of it and expose them.

Until recent decades, therefore, few homosexuals dared to lead such lives. This is the central irony of gay history: that laws and social conventions regarding homosexuality have long had the effect of discouraging monogamous relationships and of encouraging covert one-night stands. The Gay Liberation movement of the 1970s did much more to extend the opportunities for the practice of indiscriminate sex than it did to change the conditions that made committed gay relationships legally, socially, and professionally problematic. Indeed, far from helping to foster among young people who discovered themselves to be gay the self-knowledge, self-respect, and sexual self-discipline that would make possible meaningful, enduring relationships, the mentality cultivated by the Gay Liberation movement tended to induce such young people to throw self-discipline to the winds; self-knowledge, they were led to believe, mattered less than self-expression, self-respect less than self-indulgence.

As some homosexuals gradually became more candid about their homosexuality with friends and colleagues, however, levels of tolerance did rise gradually. A *New York Times*/CBS News poll taken in March 1993 showed that 36 percent of Americans consider homosexuality "an acceptable alternative life style," 46 percent support legalization of homosexual relations between consenting adults, and 78 percent support equal job opportunities for gays. Though these statistics suggest that homophobia remains the nation's most enduring form of prejudice, they are nonetheless encouraging: certainly tolerance is greater than it was a generation or two ago. Things *have* improved. People *are* more enlightened. Today, because of this tolerance and the legal safeguards that it has made possible in some jurisdictions, the possibilities for gay lives are somewhat less restricted. A gay man can still marry and live a lie. He can still lead a clandestine second life. But he also has the option of living, either alone or with a companion, as a more or less openly gay man.

If he does this, he will be said by some to be leading a "gay lifestyle." But this is a misleading term, for there is no one "gay lifestyle," any more than there is a single monolithic heterosexual lifestyle. There is in fact a spectrum of "gay lifestyles." Near one extreme one might imagine a gay man whose sense of identity is centered upon the fact of his sexual orientation, and whose tastes, opinions, and modes of behavior conform almost perfectly to every stereotype. Born into a more or less ordinary family in Wisconsin or Missouri or Georgia, he lives in a small walk-up apartment in a gay ghetto like Greenwich Village or West Hollywood or San Francisco's Castro district. He holds down a job that is marginal and at least vaguely artistic; he socializes almost exclusively with other homosexuals; he dines in gay restaurants, dances at gay clubs, and drinks at gay bars; and his reading matter consists largely of gay-oriented magazines and of novels by and about gays. His "life-style" (if you want to use that word) would probably be considered aggressively nonconformist by most Americans, his politics uncomfortably left-wing; his manner of dress would probably draw stares on the main street of the average American town or city. He is active in at least one AIDS-related organization—either a social-service group like Gay Men's Health Crisis or an activist group like Queer Nation, or both.

Toward the other end of the spectrum one might imagine a gay couple that most heterosexuals would not even recognize as gay. They live not in a predominantly gay community but in an ordinary neighborhood in a big or small city, suburb, or town. One may be a doctor and the other a business executive, or one a garbageman and the other a cop. They don't spend much time in gay bars or clubs, and they don't read gay newspapers and magazines; they dress conservatively, and have more straight friends than gay friends. Their politics would be described by most people as conservative or middle-of-the-road; both of them voted twice for Reagan and twice for Bush. (Despite Bill Clinton's unprecedented support of gay rights and the attacks on homosexuality by many leading Republicans, about one-fifth of American gays still pulled the levers in 1992 for Bush-Quayle.) They may send a check every year to Gay Men's Health Crisis or to a gay lobbying group like the Human Rights Campaign Fund, but they are not, in any real sense, politically active. In its essentials, their "lifestyle" is indistinguishable from that of most heterosexual couples in similar professional and economic circumstances.

For young gay men who have been rejected by their families and who feel estranged from (and perhaps even scared of or angry at) the mainstream culture, a gay ghetto like Greenwich Village—which is, in a way, a world within a world, with its own political and social and cultural norms—can feel like a godsend. It's a place where they can feel safe and loved, or at least not hated; for many, it's the first place where they can really feel at home. Living among other homosexuals can help dispel their fear and loneliness, and help them to avoid many of the insults, intentional or not, that homosexuals who live outside gay ghettos frequently experience.

For other homosexuals, however, living in a gay ghetto is not a desirable option. Like most adult heterosexuals, most adult homosexuals simply don't *want* such a life. They were raised in conventional middle-class homes in conventional middle-class neighborhoods, and they want to spend their lives in similar homes and neighborhoods, and they don't see why being gay should prevent them from doing so. Nor do they like the idea of inhabiting an exclusively, or even mostly, gay world: such a world feels artificial to them, feels like an escape from reality. They want to live in the *real* world, to have straight as well as gay friends. They recognize that they are widely despised and are in many respects considered second-class citizens under the law, but they don't want to be rebels. They may believe, too, that the only way to exercise a positive influence on heterosexuals' attitudes toward homosexuality is to live among them, not apart from them.

There is a broad cultural divide, and often considerable hostility, between gays who tend toward the two extremes of the spectrum. We might call them, at the risk of drastic oversimplification, "subculture-oriented gays" and "mainstream gays." Some subculture-oriented gays accuse mainstream gays of "acting straight," the assumption here being that it comes naturally to all gays to speak and walk and act in a certain way, and that if you do otherwise you are suppressing your natural self; some mainstream gays, for their part, shake their heads at the stereotypical gestures and mannerisms of some subculture-oriented gays, which they see as a pathetic manifestation of the gay subculture's lockstep mentality. Some subculture-oriented gays like to say that mainstream gays, by conforming to societal norms, are smothering their "gayness" and demonstrating self-hatred; some mainstream gays argue that, on the contrary, the stereotypical behavior and attire of many subculture-oriented gays represent the ultimate in self-hating conformity, and provide a quintessential example of the stifling of individual distinctions in favor of group values and conventions. Subculture-oriented gays often blame anti-gay prejudice on mainstream gays who refuse to put themselves on the line for gay rights and to make their sexual orientation known to their neighbors and co-workers; mainstream gays often blame anti-gay prejudice on subculture-oriented gays whose way of life only confirms heterosexuals' sense that homosexual men are a bunch of silly, effeminate, and irresponsible nonconformists. Politically, subculture-oriented gays specialize in confrontational activism; mainstream gays work within the system. Subculture-oriented gays ridicule mainstream gays as prisoners of the closet; mainstream gays retort that subculture-oriented gays are prisoners of the ghetto.

Let it be understood that the great majority of homosexuals fall between these two extremes and combine various aspects of both. There are radical gays who are fiercely devoted to their life partners, and publicly closeted right-wing politicians (like the late Roy Cohn) who are very promiscuous. It's safe to say, however, that the average gay man comes far closer, in most respects, to the mainstream end of the spectrum. For the great majority of gays, as an acquaintance of mine has remarked, the subculture is not something you live in—it's something you go to. Some may go to it several times a week, some less than once a year.

To say that the subculture is "something you go to" may be misleading, however, for the subculture is not a place—not a "gay ghetto" like Greenwich Village or West Hollywood. (It is possible to be a gay man in Greenwich Village without buying into the subculture at all.) Nor would I use the term as an exact synonym for the "gay community." No, when I speak of the gay subculture I am describing a way of thinking, a philosophy of being, a set of ideas about politics, high culture, pop culture, society, religion, manners, fashion, and above all sex—ideas inside of which a relatively small proportion of gay people spend their entire adult lives, inside of which many others spend a good deal of their adult lives, and with which virtually every gay man has some sort of relationship, whether of attraction or repulsion or (most often) some complex combination of the two. The subculture is a cocoon, a nest, inside of which its most fervent partisans seek to protect themselves from the larger world—their victimization by which is a central fact of their identity and the chief tenet of their common sensibility.

To be a subculture-oriented gay, then, is to center one's identity on one's homosexuality. Naturally, many people who do this soon discover considerable individual differences between themselves and other homosexuals. Instead of learning from this the limitations of descriptive labels, however, some—ever in search of a label that will fit them perfectly, explain every last thing about them, and incorporate all the elements of their identity on account of which they feel themselves to have been victimized—react by labeling themselves still further, descending from the category of "gay" into some even more confining subcategory that they share with an even smaller, more tightly embraced group of brothers and/or sisters. So it is that a contributor's note to a recent article in a gay magazine identified its author as "co-founder of . . . a queer people of color media production company." Similarly, an announcement of a New York poetry reading explained that the participants had all been published in an anthology of "lesbian, gay & bisexual Asian/Pacific American Writers." Such Balkanization may seem a harmless means of self-affirmation, but in practice it is more often not only personally but (for an artist) creatively constricting. The narrower the subcategory, the more likely it is to demand not only allegiance to one's fellow members but suspicion of nonmembers. Ultimately, then, such Balkanization of identity can have grievous consequences. It was this kind of label-consciousness, after all, that caused the Chicago chapter of the direct-action group ACT UP to separate in 1992 into two factions—one for HIV-positive members and one for HIV-negative members.

Granted, even gays who reject the dictates of the subculture can feel a certain sense of fellowship in the company of other homosexuals. This sense of fellowship is founded partly on a shared awareness that most heterosexuals (even if not strictly prejudiced) view homosexuality as bizarre or at least in some way distancing, and partly on the fact that many homosexuals, having been rejected by their parents, want desperately to see the gay community as a perfectly accepting and non-judgmental substitute family. Even homosexuals who are profoundly wary of the subculture and cynical about the idea of the gay community as a family can be swayed occasionally into a feeling of kinship by the subculture's more appealing aspects—such as the dance that used to take place on the night of every Gay Pride Day on New York's Christopher Street pier. (In 1993, the dance was relocated from the pier to the nearby waterfront.) Yet it is excessive to speak, as some do, about gay "brotherhood." Certainly too many naïve young gay people, wholeheartedly crediting the subculture rhetoric about the brotherhood of all gay people, have suffered terribly because they were too quick to trust a stranger who happened to be gay. It is often claimed that gay bars, where members of upper-class WASP families mingle with Puerto Rican janitors, are the perfect democracy. But mingling in a pickup bar is hardly a good example of the sort of mutual respect that democracy seeks to encourage, and one-night stands do not erase socioeconomic barriers.

The fact is that things work essentially the same way in gay bars as they do in straight bars: the beautiful and the moneyed tend to get what they want, and God help the rest.

Homosexuality does not, by its nature, carry with it certain habits, tastes, mannerisms, politics, or sexual mores. Just as carbon chemically reacts with other elements to produce a wide variety of compounds, none of which looks or feels like carbon, so homosexuality interacts with other factors to produce a wide variety of individuals. Its presence always makes a difference, but so do other things. Homosexuality itself doesn't circumscribe, it contributes; it doesn't commit all gay individuals to a single path in life, it merely exerts an influence on the distinctive course traveled by each individual.

The gay subculture—which I shall discuss at some length in the third section of this book—does not see things this way. It disdains the notion of individual identity and takes a reductive, narrowly deterministic view of homosexuality. It believes that there are correct and incorrect ways of being gay. For the subculture, homosexuality is not simply a fact of sexual orientation but also an act of sexual emancipation, political rebellion, social experimentation, and cultural self-assertion. If the subculture has increasingly embraced the word "queer" in recent years, it is because the word is better than "homosexual" or "gay" at suggesting the subculture's notion of homosexuality as something that makes one essentially different, eternally the Other. The subculture is stubborn in its insistence that it knows what homosexuality is: homosexuality is what it sees when it looks in the mirror. For this reason, the subculture can be intolerant. It welcomes you, but on its own terms; it accepts you, but exacts a price. As gay visibility has grown steadily over the past couple of decades, the subculture, with its narrow sense of what it means to be gay, has played a key role in defining homosexuality for the general public. Subculture-oriented gays visit schools to talk to young people about "gay life," by which they mean gay life as it is understood by the subculture. They develop university-level Gay Studies programs in which the subculture's view of homosexuality is presented to students, gay and straight, as the definitive truth about the subject. Subculture-oriented gays form political action groups that tell politicians what gay voters want.

And they do other things:

• Some make media curiosities of themselves, all the while telling America that they are what being gay is about. In the past couple of years, with the rising prominence of homosexuality and gay rights as political issues, self-styled gay spokespeople have turned up more and more frequently, in increasingly conspicuous venues. At the 1992 Democratic convention, for example, a drag queen who identified himself as Queer Nation presidential candidate Joan Jett Blakk was quoted as saying: "I heard the delegates voting for 'other' and I just knew they meant me. I was clearly the most 'other' Ms. Thang on the convention floor." To read this quotation from Blakk was to wonder why such a person, who presents himself as a representative of the gay population, insists on playing the fool, the absurd outsider; the whole idea of gay politics, after all, should be to *stop* heterosexuals from thinking of gays as the most "other" thing around.

Dismaying in much the same way was a network-news "town meeting" with Ross Perot at which the standout, in the otherwise polite and neatly dressed audience, was a shrill, effeminate man who, when called upon, jumped to his feet, announced that he was gay—in order, it was clear, to invoke the authority of his victimhood—and proceeded to attack Perot, whom he called a "pint-sized tyrant," for reportedly firing a gay employee. One did not have to be a Perot supporter to find the man's combative tone inappropriate and his use of the term "pint-sized" unnecessary (not to mention surprising, under the circumstances, for its lack of political correctness). It was hardly a major incident, but to at least one TV viewer that night it seemed depressingly typical of gay image-making in our time.

• Some engage in counterproductive acts of public protest. Watching the 1992 Republican convention on TV, I was of course disturbed by the flagrant homophobia of Pat Buchanan, and by the scores of clean-cut, wholesome-looking teenage boys, members of the Republican Youth Coalition, who waved signs that read "Family Rights Forever, Gay Rights Never." But what made me want to weep was the news that ACT UP members were outside the Astrodome burning an American flag. *Fools!* I thought. What they should have been doing was standing out there looking every bit as clean-cut and wholesome as those Republican Youth Coalition members. They should have been *waving* American flags, not burning them.

The flag-burning episode wasn't the only thing in Houston that made me wince. In the course of its convention coverage, C-SPAN took viewers inside the "Voice '92 Action Center," where a gay and lesbian lobbying organization had set up temporary shop. The camera zoomed in on a young man talking on a telephone. On his T-shirt, in big letters, were the words "JUICY FRUIT." Above his head, a wall poster read:

I'm your worst fear
I'm a fed-up queer.
Queer Nation—Houston

It was an incongruous picture. Why try to lobby people on the one hand while putting up posters that seek to frighten them? Why wear a T-shirt that trivializes your identity and reinforces stereotypes while seeking to be taken seriously as a responsible citizen and a representative of an oppressed group? In a similar vein, there was the chant heard at a gay march in Manhattan in September 1992:

Stop the violence
stop the hate
queers bash back!

How, one could not help wondering, was bashing back consistent with stopping violence?

• Some create entertainment that seems designed to reinforce stereotypes. In an April 1993 review of Funny Gay Males, a comedy trio, *New York Times* critic Stephen Holden described an act in which one performer caricatured Joan Rivers and imagined Bette Davis in *The Wizard of Oz,* another characterized his high-school drama club as "a head-start program for homosexuals," and the third compared himself to Barbra Streisand and demonstrated "How to Be a Sissy in Gym Class." Commented Holden: "They don't offer a vision of gay life that begins to transcend those stereotypes." Two months later, Holden wrote about "Homo Alone: Lost in Colorado," a set of skits that, according to Holden, traded "on stereotypical images of gay men as limp-wristed sissies and lesbians as stomping macho soldiers. If such skits were performed by heterosexuals on 'Saturday Night Live,' there would almost surely be a storm of protest over the insensitive, irresponsible perpetuation of such stereotypes."

• And some produce television shows like *Out,* a British series about homosexual life and gay issues that demonstrated, among other things, that the subculture mentality is far from an exclusively stateside phenomenon. Indeed, the program, which appeared on PBS in 1992, provides a stellar example of the subculture's inflexibly pro-left and anti-Western politics, which motivates subculture leaders to proclaim "solidarity" with Third World societies whose homophobia far outstrips that of North America and Western Europe.

A typical episode of *Out* began with a segment entitled "Khush" (an Urdu word meaning both "ecstatic pleasure" and "gay") about the life of Indian homosexuals. The segment's point was that gay Indians have a rough time both in their homeland and in Britain; but in neither case, apparently, was this the fault of Indian society and culture. If there is intense homophobia in India, we were told, it is because the British raj imposed on the country a distinctively Western antagonism to matters erotic; likewise, if Indians residing in London pressure their gay children to marry, it is because English racism makes it necessary for Third World immigrant communities to "place a great premium on marriage."

The segment was laden with politically correct attacks on men, whites, Westerners, and heterosexuals; one interviewee after another condemned Western classism, imperialism, racism, and homophobia. An Indian woman who had returned home from the West said: "It's really wonderful to not be among white people anymore. I wish India didn't have so many men." She and others who voiced similar sentiments were viewed sympathetically by the program—indeed, they were seen as attractive and charming. The segment had a staggering philosophical purity: no one offered a dissenting view, and no one explained why, if Indian anti-gay prejudice is indeed the fault of the West, law and society are in fact much tougher on homosexuality in India than in any First World country. Nobody mentioned that in India homosexual acts are legally punishable by life imprisonment. "Homosexuality in any form," reports the *Spartacus* guide (an annual handbook for gay travelers), "is seldom tolerated in Indian society." But it would be politically incorrect for a subculture-oriented TV program to admit that a given Third World society is far more prejudiced against homosexuality than is a given First World society.

If the apparent purpose of "Khush" was to suggest that Western Europe is more homophobic than Asia, the point of "Tintenhaus," an *Out* segment about the effect of German unification on a houseful of *Schwul-*

Radikal (gay radical) squatters in East Berlin, was to suggest that democratic societies are more homophobic than were the Communist societies of the former Eastern bloc. The segment consistently equated homosexuality with radicalism; the squatters declared themselves to be "anti-patriarchal" and "against the dominant male image." Though they lauded the workers' state, none of them actually held a job. Instead, they spent their time drinking and smoking. Neighbors who told interviewers that they resented the squatters' rent-free presence were patently meant to come across as fascist. In the end the West Berlin police, newly in control of East Berlin, drove the squatters out. "When they came in," one of the squatters said, "we started singing the 'Internationale.'" As the segment ended, viewers heard a few bars of the "Internationale" played on an electric piano. The music was pretty, delicate, plaintive, the filmmakers' aim plainly being to equate Communist sympathies with childlike innocence and homosexuality with both. *Out* was a British show, but its politics were typical of the American gay-subculture mentality and plainly owed a great deal to the past two decades of American gay-subculture rhetoric.

Socially, politically, and culturally, the majority of homosexuals identify no more with the Joan Jett Blakks, the Houston flag burners, and the Berlin squatters than does the average heterosexual. Yet when you mention homosexuality to most heterosexuals, it's subculture phenomena such as these that they think of. This is because the subculture-oriented gay is far more conspicuous than his mainstream counterpart. Walking home from work, you may pass three dozen gay men in suits and ties, but the only passerby whom you'll register as gay will be the fellow in the short haircut, skin-tight black jeans, and JUICY FRUIT T-shirt. To say this is not to put down gay people who look different: it was, after all, drag queens who fought the first battle of the modern gay-rights wars, and it was promiscuous, subculture-oriented gays who, in the early 1980s, were the first victims of AIDS and the first to agitate for drug testing, government funding for AIDS research, and faster approval of effective AIDS treatments by the Food and Drug Administration. Throughout these struggles, in fact, subculture-oriented gays like the fellow in the JUICY FRUIT T-shirt have taken the lead while mainstream gays, for the most part, kept safely hidden. Yet while some subculture-oriented gays have manifested extraordinary courage and selflessness, others have demonstrated a lamentable capacity for foolishness, a counterproductive belligerence, and a frightening tendency toward authoritarianism. To look at and listen to some of the subculture-oriented gays who have presented themselves as spokespeople for the homosexual population, alas, is to be disturbed at the thought of their influence on the views of homosexuality held both by heterosexuals and by the countless young people who every day discover their own homosexuality.

Indeed, a young man who discovers himself to be homosexual nowadays faces two distinct challenges that he must overcome if he wishes to grow into an emotionally healthy and intellectually independent person. One challenge is the predominantly heterosexual mainstream society, with its prejudices, stereotypes, and imperatives. Growing up in a society that teaches the awfulness of homosexuality, young gay men may take a long time to recognize their sexual orientation fully and, when they do, may then struggle for a long time to fight it off. Some, as a matter of fact, manage to fight it off for a lifetime: they marry and have children and spend their lives hoping that their families don't notice when they stare longingly at other men in the street.

This challenge to gay men is a formidable one. But equally imposing, for many, is the other challenge: that of the gay subculture, which has its own prejudices, stereotypes, and imperatives. For gay men in whose lives the gay subculture does not figure importantly, one of the major frustrations of being homosexual is being made to feel by its devotees that one must think and dress and act a certain way, that one must have certain artistic interests and political views and a certain sense of humor, and that, if one does not, one is a traitor to one's kind.

When some subculture-oriented gays find out that you're homosexual, for example, they may automatically assume that you're promiscuous, or that at the very least your life revolves around sex more than it does for the typical heterosexual; if they discover that you have a companion, it may not occur to them to look upon the relationship any more respectfully or seriously than would Pat Buchanan. From the minute you timidly pick up your first copy of a gay newspaper or magazine, you find yourself being encouraged to look down upon the place you come from, to resent your parents, and to mock the faith in which you were raised. In particular, you're expected to subscribe to the laundry list of leftist politics, on the theory that the left is more tolerant of gays than is the right. In fact, the situation is far more complicated than that: for twentieth-century socialist thinking, at its purest, considers homosexuality decadent and exerts a strong pressure to conform. In the Western hemisphere in recent decades, homosexuals have suffered the most persecution not in the United States or Canada, nor even in the right-wing dictatorships of Latin America, but in Castro's Cuba.

I have been asked: how can a homosexual man call himself a conservative? Well, for my part I don't call myself anything. Labels, political and otherwise, have often seemed to me to create divisions where there need be none, to magnify minor divisions into great ones, and to bind people to extreme positions that they might in other circumstances find anathema. Often, discord based on political labels springs not from genuine differences of ideology but from semantic disputes. Many homosexuals, of course, say that homophobes see only one's homosexuality, and that one should consequently embrace the "gay" label with fierce pride and make homosexuality the burning core of one's identity. But it seems to me that to do such a thing for such a reason is to capitulate to the oppressor's limited view of oneself, and therefore to allow the oppressor a kind of victory.

None of us, to be sure, can entirely escape labeling. I *am* a homosexual. I *am*, in many ways, a conservative. Of course, many of these things are relative: in the Manhattan literary crowd I often feel quite the reactionary; five miles away, in the central Queens neighborhood where I grew up, I feel quite the radical. It all depends on context. A friend of mine once complained that my views on various issues didn't add up neatly into an ideologically orthodox position. The fact that they added up *for me*, that in my mind they had a philosophical consistency that meant far more to me than ideological conformity, seemed to be lost on her. She wanted to be able to label me, to put me on a shelf. This is what most people want, because focusing on labels makes life easier. Label yourself and you'll always know what to think, even without thinking; label others and you'll always know who are your enemies and who are your friends.

Yet we are living in a time when political labels, anyway, seem increasingly meaningless. Right? Left? What we call the "right" is, in the 1990s, an uneasy and increasingly fractious alliance of social reactionaries who believe above all in legislating their own version of morality—anti-gay rights, anti-abortion, and so forth—and libertarians whose chief political doctrine is that this kind of morality should not be legislated. What we call the "left," meanwhile, is an alliance of liberals who believe in tolerance and freedom from prejudice and leftist demagogues who are prejudiced against whites and males and who are intolerant of all those who aren't politically correct. Gays can be found in all four of these groups—even the first. If the liberals and libertarians share a regard for the rights of the individual, the far-right social reactionaries, who increasingly control the Republican Party and state and local politics in the Pacific Northwest and South, and the far-left political-correctness crowd, who increasingly control the humanities and social science departments of America's universities and local politics in places like New York City, have a great deal in common as well. They oppose high culture, tolerance, free speech, freedom of worship, and individual rights.

The far right, presuming to speak for the interests of God, divides everyone into two neat classes—the saved and the damned—and is quick to label as immoral anyone who does not share its views on such issues as abortion and sexual orientation. The far left, meanwhile, divides positions on all possible issues into two classes—politically correct and politically incorrect—and is quick to label as racist, sexist, elitist, or homophobic anyone who does not toe the party line. Because I happen to be gay, the far right expects me to keep my personal life a deep, dark secret, while the far left expects me to buy into its entire political platform or risk being designated a "self-hating homosexual." Both groups share, moreover, an abiding devotion to the gay-subculture stereotype. Both would be more comfortable with me, in short, if I talked, walked, dressed, and thought in accordance with that stereotype. That would make it easier for the far right to condemn me and easier for the far left to embrace me. The far right wants me to climb back into the closet; the far left wants to force me into another closet.

Fortunately, the extremes aren't the only options open to me. Yet many a young man who has privately accepted his own homosexuality may not realize that this is the case, and may not recognize how wide a range of options he has—not just as a political and sexual being but as a *human* being. He may well labor under the misapprehension that the subculture-oriented gay male is the only kind of gay male there is. The subculture may so strongly repulse and alienate him that he ends up doing something psychologically unhealthy, such as marrying a woman to whom he is not attracted or, like many gay Catholics, entering the priesthood even though he has no calling. Or, standing at the edge of a subculture that may look to him very much like a sociocultural cesspool, he may shrug his shoulders, hold his nose, and plunge in, thinking that he has no alternative but to throw aside the manners and morals, the hopes and ambitions, the romantic ideals and the ideas about commitment on which he was raised, and to behave utterly unlike the person that he knows himself to be.

For such a young man will almost certainly be in a very vulnerable position: he will probably feel cut off to some degree from his family and friends, as well as from many of the rules and assumptions by which he has lived, and will feel a profound need for a new way of understanding himself and his relationship to the world. Since not everyone has the imagination, insight, and independence of mind to fill an order like this on his own, many a gay young man will fall prey easily to the subculture mentality, with its off-the-rack set of values and ideas. So it is that such a young man, after emerging from the closet, may well find himself climbing into what is arguably an even smaller closet; rather than growing beyond his awareness of his sexuality—growing into *himself* as an individual—he may grow into a subculture clone.

And he may stay in that closet for life. Chances are, however, that after a period of years, he will grow disillusioned by the subculture and try to put some distance between himself and its prescriptions. But that may be easier said than done. For meanwhile he may have burned bridges to family and friends; he may have discarded valuable educational or career opportunities that cannot be recovered; he may have degraded himself in ways that he can never forget and for which he can never forgive himself; and he may have become infected with the AIDS virus. For such a young man, then, the subculture may not be a permanent sanctuary but may, in a variety of ways, be permanently debilitating.

Some young gay men, however, do manage to defy the subculture's reductive notions of what it means to be homosexual. Though different from one another in many respects, they share the perception that homosexuality should not be defined by a set of approved cultural, political, and social attitudes, that it shouldn't be monolithic, and that it shouldn't be a second closet. They recognize that in developing into an adult, it is best to grow into someone who will be as comfortable in the company of heterosexuals as in the company of homosexuals, who is honest and untroubled about his sexual orientation but knows that it is only one aspect of the totality of his being, and who understands that discovering oneself to be gay is only a part of discovering oneself. And they recognize, too, that while reactionary bigots represent a decided threat to them as homosexuals, the unwritten canons of the gay subculture may pose no little danger to them as individuals.

And it is these canons, as I've said, that inform the views of most of the gay people who speak to these matters on the television talk shows and newspaper op-ed pages. Even as these gay people talk about promoting inclusiveness, they assume an exclusionary and antagonistic posture. They tie gay rights to other issues to which it has no natural relation. They equate homosexuality with the gay subculture—an entirely different phenomenon. They equate the struggle for gay rights with the issue of sexual freedom—again, these are two different subjects. They suggest an essential connection between homosexuality and radical politics: there is no such essential connection. They act as if a gay person faces a simple black-and-white choice: either to be a meek, frightened closet case or to be a strident radical who makes the average heterosexual feel all the more threatened and unsympathetic. They think that their enemy is conscious oppression and that their salvation lies in the amassing of power, when in fact their enemy is ignorance and their salvation lies in increased understanding.

America is not the gulag that some gay activists believe it to be. One can very well understand, of course, why they might have such a notion: many were severely wounded in childhood by authority figures—parents, clergy, teachers—who rejected them for being gay. In recent years, moreover, as Randy Shilts has documented, more than a few U.S. servicemen and women have been jailed for being homosexual. But even such horrible violations of individual rights should not blind us to the fact that America is basically a tolerant nation in which a misunderstood and persecuted minority's best chance lies not in sowing antagonism but in attempting to sow understanding. Indeed, the challenge facing all Americans, straight and gay, is to move beyond the malice and misunderstanding that have created the present social and cultural impasse and, for everyone's sake, to bring the public image of homosexuality into closer alignment with the reality of the majority of gay lives. Mainstream gays, who like most homosexuals know what it means to be puzzled by and to struggle to fathom their own sexuality, must help heterosexuals to recognize gays as people whose sexual orientation is as natural an occurrence as their own and to understand that the homosexual population manifests the same range of ambitions, beliefs, and "lifestyles" as the heterosexual population. Most important, young gay people must be helped to realize that homosexuality is not bizarre, extreme, or monolithic. Homosexuals must also help heterosexuals to recognize that, without ever realizing it, many of them expect from homosexuals, as the price of their tolerance, a degree of reticence about our personal lives that, if they tried to carry it off for a week, would make them feel as if they were in prison. And everyone needs to understand that if anti-gay prejudice is responsible for the existence and endurance of an adversary gay subculture, that subculture's insistence upon homosexuality as by definition adversarial has made it harder for many heterosexuals of good will to distinguish between those things that are intrinsic aspects of homosexuality and those that are merely characteristic of certain subculture-oriented gays—and, consequently, has made it harder for them to recognize the common humanity, common backgrounds, and common values that they share with most homosexuals.

In his book *Coming Out Conservative,* Marvin Liebman, a founder of New York's Conservative Party, remembers the day that Ronald Reagan confided in him, then a closeted gay man, about Ron Junior's plans to become a ballet dancer. "Now, I don't care what the kid does so long as it's legal and makes him happy," Reagan told Liebman, "but . . . aren't dancers . . . aren't dancers sort of . . . funny?" Liebman writes: "He meant homosexual, of course, but couldn't say it. What do you tell a troubled father when he fears his son is gay and can't ask, can't even bring himself to say the word, when you yourself are in the closet?" Liebman consoled Reagan by telling him that a lot of male ballet dancers are notorious ladies' men. But afterward he felt (rightly) a sense of disappointment in himself for having passed up an opportunity to confront Reagan's fears and stereotypes head-on. "I had failed to tell him," Liebman laments, "that many of us were 'funny' and that there would be nothing degrading about it if 'unfunny' people, like him, did not make it so."

The composer Ned Rorem has said much the same thing: "Homosexuality in and of itself is not an interesting subject, except insofar as it's a problem, and it's only made a problem by heterosexuals who make it one."

Indeed. In and of itself, homosexuality is morally neutral and without interest. Most people in our time, however, have been brought up to think otherwise. They have been brought up on the notion that it is a deadly serious matter. They may not be able to explain very clearly why it is a deadly serious matter; they may not have spent so much as ten seconds of their lives thinking about why it should be considered a deadly serious matter; and they may not even agree on what kind of deadly serious matter it is—an ethical offense? a psychological aberration? a violation of the social order? a transgression against God's law?—but they concur that it is, most assuredly, a deadly serious matter. It is "wrong." Or "sick." Or "evil." It is, at the very least, a *problem*. And because it is considered a problem, it has been, in countless lives, the occasion of extraordinary human drama and moral struggle. Because it is considered a problem, countless teenage boys lie awake every night in beds across America, baffled and grieved by their own differentness, cursing themselves as traitors to their families, feeling as if they are carrying within them the equivalent of a cancer, wishing that they were dead. Because it is considered a problem, countless nice young men have been thrown out of the house by their parents or have run away from their small hometowns to big cities, where many of them have become alcoholics, drug addicts, prostitutes, suicides. Because it is considered a problem, countless grown men have disobeyed their hearts by marrying and fathering children, have gone on to spend their adult lives playing a part in front of their families, and have hated themselves all the while for harboring within their breasts a simple, morally neutral, and intrinsically uninteresting truth that seems to them the most horrible secret in the world.

Because it is considered a problem, furthermore, millions of gay men have succumbed to the understandable temptation to proclaim an untruth diametrically opposite to the vicious untruth trumpeted by those members of the mainstream culture who repudiate them. To the cry of "homosexuality is evil," they reply "gay is good." But it is neither good nor evil. It simply *is*. And it will not go away.

Because it is considered a problem, some gay men live meticulously compartmentalized lives, keeping their homosexuality a secret from their co-workers and families, and other gay men huddle together in gay ghettos and live, obedient as Marines, in utter conformity with the unwritten rules of the gay subculture. Because it is considered a problem, those gays retreat into the comfort of such concepts as "gay identity" and "gay brotherhood"—when in fact, aside from their sexual orientation, the only thing that all gay men have in common is that they all know what it is like to have their sexuality regarded as a problem by others.

Yet the truth is that homosexuality is not a problem and should not be seen as one. If the widespread recognition of this truth sometimes seems nonetheless to be a pipe dream, it is because the genuine principles to which both homophobes and gay-subculture extremists cling so fervently are overlaid with a great deal of misunderstanding and ignorance on the part of the former and resentment and belligerence on the part of the latter. In the wake of Communism's fall in Europe and elsewhere, and at the outset of a new era of promise for global peace and democracy, it seems to me that the United States should be taking a position of moral leadership on the issue of homosexuality as well as on all others. Yet we're surprisingly behind some of the other democratic powers on this one. In Denmark, the Netherlands, and Norway, homosexuals are accorded full equal rights as citizens, including domestic-partnership laws that allow members of same-sex couples to call each other family; by contrast, while a handful of American municipalities provide for some kind of domestic-partnership registration, full domestic-partnership rights for gays and lesbians are a long way from being granted by the U.S. Congress or state legislatures. Likewise, though the former Soviet republics of Ukraine and Latvia abolished their antisodomy laws in 1992, an effort to overturn a similar law in the District of Columbia failed in December of the same year, and such laws still remain in effect in many American states. What's more, though all the NATO countries (except Britain) allow homosexuals into their armed forces, and though Canada's 1992 revocation of its military ban caused little or no controversy, Bill Clinton's announcement after the 1992 presidential election that he planned to reverse the Pentagon's policy on gays initiated a firestorm of angry debate.

It seems to me that what we need to do in the United States is to realize that the essential questions relating to homosexuality and gay rights are not illuminated but obscured and distorted by the rhetoric of both the implacable homophobes and the most radical gay activists. What we need to do is to realize that those essential questions, if properly understood and stripped of age-old preconceptions, are not innately unresolvable. In order for things to be set right, heterosexuals must be willing to listen and learn. And the general guiding philosophy of the gay populace should be one not of confrontation but of connection, not of agitation but of education, not of revolution but of reform. Our aim should be not to use our "power" to change laws but to use our humanity to change hearts and minds. If the heterosexual majority ever comes to accept homosexuality, it will do so because it has seen homosexuals in suits and ties, not nipple clamps and bike pants; it will do so because it has seen homosexuals showing respect for civilization, not attempting to subvert it.

Only a few years ago the subject of homosexuality rarely appeared in the mainstream press. Now every day brings a new headline—sometimes, in a big daily newspaper like the *New York Times* or the *Washington Post,* half a dozen or more, often on the front page. Never in history have the words "homosexual" and "gay" appeared in so many *New York Times* headlines as they did during the week after Bill Clinton's announcement of his intention to lift the military ban. An NBC News special in January 1993 predicted that as the 1960s had been the decade of black civil rights and the '70s the decade of the woman, so the century's last decade would, in the United States anyway, be the "Gay '90s." There is certainly no question but that homosexuality is now a more conspicuous topic of public debate in America than it has been at any place and time in human history. Never has it been so widely and openly discussed; never has it been so vociferously attacked and vehemently defended. Never has it seemed more certain that the issue of homosexuality is at—or fast approaching—a crossroads, a turning point, a moment of truth.

Of all those who have contributed to the movement for gay rights, perhaps no one, ironically enough, has done more than Pat Buchanan. With his speech at the 1992 Republican convention, he sent shock waves through what I have called the "silent majority" of homosexuals—those millions of people who live quiet, low-key lives in places like Boise and Nashville and Omaha (and even in parts of New York City and San Francisco), people who may never have set foot in a Gay Community Center, may never have gone near a Gay Pride Day march, may never have given a thought to gay-related issues when casting their presidential ballots. Buchanan, I would wager, made the vast majority of those "silent" gays angry—not only at him and his supporters but at themselves as well. They'd been good little boys and girls; they'd kept a low profile; they'd endured uncomplainingly the inequities, inconveniences, insults, and indignities to which gays are regularly subjected. They'd been good Americans; many of them had also been good Republicans, good neighbors, good soldiers, and, yes, good Christians or Muslims or Jews. But now here was Pat Buchanan on the Republican convention podium attacking homosexuals and denouncing the Democratic conclave a month earlier as an exhibition of "cross-dressing." And in the ensuing days, Dan Quayle, George Bush, and other convention speakers fell into line, saying nothing in direct repudiation of Buchanan's remarks and saying many things that could only be taken as agreement with them. "Americans try to raise their children to understand right and wrong," Quayle proclaimed, "only to be told that every so-called 'life-style alternative' is morally equivalent." Television viewers around the world were treated to the spectacle of the President and Vice President of the United States passing moral judgment on homosexuality and pronouncing ill-informed convictions about its etiology while party delegates roared their approval. The longtime gay conservative leader Marvin Liebman lamented that the GOP had "fallen into evil hands." Passing a reporter, the veteran GOP political consultant Roger Stone gestured toward some Republican Youth Coalition marchers and said under his breath: "Hitler Youth."

The immediate consequence of the anti-gay oratory at the Republican convention was strong gay backing for the candidacy of Bill Clinton. "Support crystallized overnight with Pat Buchanan's speech," said gay activist David Mixner, a Clinton friend and adviser. "It created a voting bloc and tripled the money." With Buchanan, said William Waybourn of a gay lobbying group called the Victory Fund, "the last remnants of complacency fell. . . . That was the wake-up call to our community." Gregory King of the Human Rights Campaign Fund agreed: "This is the election of our lives."

The history of the modern, high-profile gay-rights movement breaks into three pretty well-defined phases. The first, roughly congruent with the 1970s, is generally thought of as having begun with the much-mythologized Stonewall riots in 1969. Those riots ushered in a period of greater gay visibility and the expansion of gay rights. As Southern blacks had once flooded into Northern cities in search of greater freedom and opportunity, now gays from rural and small-town America poured into New York, San Francisco, and Los Angeles, where they felt they could live more openly. Under pressure from gay groups, a number of jurisdictions around the country passed gay-rights ordinances during this period. The '70s saw the production of a number of movies (such as *Dog Day Afternoon,* in 1975) with homosexual protagonists, the appearance on the hit TV sitcom *Soap* of an explicitly gay recurring character played by Billy Crystal, and a TV movie, *That Certain Summer* (1972), that sensitively examined a boy's discovery of his father's homosexuality. The rise of musical groups like the Village People made it clear that in some parts of some cities, homosexuality was not only acceptable but chic. In 1972, a San Franciscan named Jim Foster delivered the first gay-rights speech ever heard at a major-party national convention. In 1975, the Eisenhower-era ban on gay employees in the civil service was lifted, the American Psychological Association removed homosexuality from its list of medical disorders, and an ousted air force sergeant named Leonard Matlovich appeared on a *Time* cover above the words "I AM A HOMOSEXUAL." And in 1976, Armistead Maupin's "Tales of the City" column, in which gay people's lives were treated as matter-of-factly as straight people's, began to appear in the *San Francisco Chronicle*. For all this, however, homosexuals remained marginal in American society. It was because some urban gays took full advantage of their greater sexual freedom during this decade that the gay subculture was the first segment of the American population to fall victim to the AIDS epidemic.

The tide of change began to turn in the late 1970s with the rise of the religious right and the emergence of Anita Bryant's "Save Our Children" crusade, which sought to preserve misguided stereotypes and misbegotten prejudices and to keep gays in the closet. Instead of seeing the gay-rights movement as a civil-rights crusade along the lines of the struggle for black equality in the 1960s, the religious right portrayed it as a manifestation of social and moral decline, along with the rise in crime and drug use. Bryant's 1977 defeat of a gay-rights bill in Miami ushered in an era of struggle and controversy during which gay-rights advances slowed and (in some cases) were reversed. (If such European countries as Denmark and the Netherlands have strong gay-rights laws that date back to the 1970s—and that would not have been enacted when they were if not for the example of the Stonewall riots—it is because there were not powerful anti-gay religious groups in those countries to prevent the passage of such measures.) During this second phase, which was roughly congruent with the 1980s, the advent of AIDS compelled many gay activists to shift their emphasis from backstairs lobbying for civil rights to more publicly visible, and often clamorous,

AIDS activism. Though civil-rights gains were stalled—a state of affairs symbolized by the Supreme Court's notorious 1986 decision upholding Georgia's sodomy law—AIDS brought famous homosexuals out of the closet and homosexuality into the headlines as never before, and compelled heterosexual Americans to have opinions about something most of them had previously preferred not to think about. Results, as I have said, were mixed: more tolerance in some quarters, more gay-bashing in others.

The third phase began in the early 1990s with the resurgence of civil-rights struggles on a host of fronts. If the '70s saw the beginning of monumental changes in gay lives, the '90s seemed likely to transform the way in which many heterosexuals view those lives. In the '90s, both pro-gay and anti-gay forces are louder and more visible than ever. Homosexuals are coming out of the closet in record numbers. The 1992 presidential election was the first in which gay rights was a major issue. That year's Democratic convention was the first major-party national conclave at which the presidential candidate declared his support for gay rights; the Republican convention was the first at which homosexuality was explicitly vilified from the podium. (After President Bush's acceptance speech, ironically, the band broke into "The Best of Times" from *La Cage aux Folles,* the first Broadway musical about two openly gay lovers.)

The early 1990s saw scattered advances in gay rights. In 1992, New Jersey, Vermont, and California became the fifth, sixth, and seventh states to ban anti-gay discrimination. Stanford University, the University of Chicago, and such corporations as Levi Strauss and MCA extended health-insurance and other benefits to gay and lesbian domestic partners. Massachusetts granted spousal bereavement leave to gay and lesbian state employees living in domestic partnerships; the province of Ontario extended pension benefits to government employees' surviving gay and lesbian partners. And Canada and Australia, with little fanfare, lifted their bans on gays in the military. But 1992 also saw the first specifically anti-gay local legislation in the U.S. (in Springfield, Oregon) and the first statewide referenda (in Oregon and Colorado) on amendments outlawing gay-rights legislation. These referenda had mixed results: the Oregon resolution failed, the one in Colorado passed. The Colorado voters' decision resulted in calls by gay-rights proponents for a boycott of the state and plans by gay-rights opponents for similar ballot measures in other states.

One telling event has followed hard upon another. In March 1992, demonstrators outside the Academy Awards ceremony denounced what they saw as Hollywood's tendency either to ignore gays or to portray them offensively (as in the film *Basic Instinct*). In May, the *Detroit News* became the first major metropolitan daily newspaper to run a regular column on gay and lesbian issues. A soap opera, *One Life to Live,* featured a story line (which was handled with admirable intelligence and sensitivity) about a teenage boy's announcement of his homosexuality and its repercussions within his family and community. Expelled from the Boy Scouts for being gay, James Dale, a New Jersey Eagle Scout with thirty merit badges, and Chuck Merino, a San Diego police officer who had served as a Scout leader, both sued for reinstatement; in defense of Dale's expulsion, a Boy Scouts of America spokesman named Blake Louis issued a statement declaring, "We don't think a homosexual presents a role model that's consistent with the expectations of mainstream American families." The 1992 National Book Award for nonfiction went to Paul Monette's gay coming-of-age memoir, *Becoming a Man,* while the year's most highly praised dramatic work proved to be Tony Kushner's seven-hour *Angels in America,* a highly ambitious pair of plays about homosexuality and AIDS that opened in Los Angeles in November and the first half of which, produced in New York in 1993, won several Tony awards.

In late 1992, the *New York Times* reported that mainstream publishers were issuing more gay novels than ever, and one of those publishers, Chelsea House, announced that it would be issuing "a series of books on gay and lesbian topics for teen-agers." Gay Studies scholar Martin Duberman, the series editor, was planning at least forty books, thirty of which would be biographies of figures ranging from Walt Whitman to Liberace, from Gertrude Stein to Elton John, from Noël Coward to the black radical poet Audre Lorde. The first two books would be a biography of James Baldwin by Randall Kenan and a study of "gay and lesbian culture" by Donna Minkowitz, the radical lesbian columnist for *The Village Voice.* In March 1993, a teenage character in a comic strip called "For Better or Worse" came out to his friends; the refusal of several newspapers to run the strip made headlines. April saw the largest gay-rights demonstration ever, the March on Washington. In May Hawaii's Supreme Court held that the prohibition of homosexual marriage violates gays' right to equal protection under the state constitution, and Boris Yeltsin announced that a month earlier he had signed a decree repealing Russia's brutal anti-gay laws. (An editor of a Russian gay magazine noted that "Russian law is now more liberal than in Britain and in some parts of the United States.") In June the American Medical Association voted to ban bias against gay doctors, and residents of four counties and two towns in Oregon approved initiatives prohibiting laws that would protect gays from discrimination. Lon Mabon, chairman of the anti-gay Oregon Citizens Alliance, said, "We're in a full-scale cultural war now, and we've just picked up a lot of momentum." Mabon claimed to have distributed about six thousand copies of a videotape, *The Gay Agenda*, that included excerpts from the 1987 March on Washington. (Meanwhile the Reverend Jerry Falwell was on TV promoting his own videotape of excerpts from the 1993 march.) On June 23, a group of Roman Catholics took over the altar during the evening Mass, which had been designated as a remembrance of gay men and lesbians, at Saint Paul the Apostle Church in New York City and shouted anti-gay slurs at parishioners; one of the protesters, who wrested a microphone away from the celebrant and injured him in the process, was later charged with assault. (If a few years earlier gay activists' disruption of a Mass at Saint Patrick's Cathedral made the front pages of newspapers around the world, the incident at Saint Paul the Apostle's wasn't even reported in most of the local press.) In July, Governor William F. Weld of Massachusetts announced the first statewide program to prevent gay teenage suicide and anti-gay violence and harassment in the schools; a scientific study purportedly demonstrating a correlation between homosexuality and a certain pattern of genetic markers added to the growing body of evidence that sexual orientation is hereditary; and the Colorado Supreme Court, ruling that "fundamental rights may not be submitted to a vote," struck down the anti-gay measure that had been passed the previous November.

As never before, institutions from the church to the military wrestled with the issue of homosexuality and generated mixed messages of increasing acceptance and continued intolerance. On June 10, 1992, the Associated Press reported that the Southern Baptist Conference, by "an overwhelming show of hands," had broken a long tradition of respect for congregational autonomy by expelling two North Carolina congregations—one in Raleigh for blessing a homosexual union, and one in Chapel Hill for licensing a homosexual to preach—and had initiated "a precedent-setting change in bylaws" mandating "the ouster of any church that 'acts to affirm, approve or endorse homosexual behavior.' " These two churches' actions, according to the conference, were "contrary to the teachings of the Bible on human sexuality and the sanctity of the family and are offensive to Southern Baptists."

A month later, newspapers reported that a Vatican office, the Congregation for the Doctrine of the Faith, had issued a directive urging "Roman Catholic bishops in the United States to scrutinize laws intended to protect homosexuals and to oppose them if they promote public acceptance of homosexual conduct." The directive stated that "there are areas in which it is not unjust discrimination to take sexual orientation into account." According to a liberal American archbishop, the Vatican was worried that U.S. "domestic partnership" laws would put gay relationships on an equal footing with traditional marriages. In an advertisement designed for the *National Catholic Reporter,* two bishops joined over 1,500 other Roman Catholics to publicly protest the Vatican document, which, they said, was based on "several misconceptions regarding homosexuality. . . . There is an irrational fear that lesbians or gay people influence the sexual orientation of children or youth with whom they live or work. There are erroneous beliefs that lesbian and gay persons are erotically attracted to every person of their own gender and that they cannot control their sexual impulses in same-sex environments." (Interestingly, the report of the advertisement appeared in the same week that the Vatican acknowledged the correctness of Galileo's heliocentric view of the solar system and admitted that the Inquisition was wrong to force him to recant in 1633—a timely reminder that the Church's slowness to discard old, discredited notions, and its tendency to view those notions as doctrinal issues, are not confined to matters of sexuality.)

During the 1992 presidential campaign, aware that most of the electorate differed from them on abortion, fundamentalists made homosexuality their banner issue. According to the *New York Times,* attendees of a religious-right gathering in Dallas at which President Bush delivered an address were "warned that the Democrats would let militant homosexuals take over the armed forces." The Reverend Donald Wildmon, president of the American Family Association, in Tupelo, Mississippi, said that "if Bill Clinton goes to the White House, he'll take his friends the homosexuals, the abortionists and the pornographers." And a "religious lecturer" named Gene Antonio condemned the Democratic convention as "a sea of homosexuals and lesbians [sic] and this is the White House we will be facing in a few months if we do not put in a lot of shoe leather."

Yet the leader of at least one major Christian denomination was sending out a different message. In a sermon delivered at the 1992 national convention of Integrity, the gay Episcopal organization, the Most Reverend Edmond L. Browning, the presiding bishop of the Episcopal Church, said:

> Is it possible to know the pain of what you have known and still find it within yourself to remain in the body where so much of that pain has occurred? Can you be the reconcilers Christ calls all of us to be without either denying the reality of your pain on the one hand or denying the possibility of its coming to an end on the other, without either minimizing what you have felt or allowing it to overcome you? How can we struggle together in love, when so many of the models of struggle which we have are models of hate?
>
> We need a model for the struggle other than the ones the world presents us. What do we see when we look around us? We see the model of warfare: I will have more soldiers and more money and better strategy than you have, and I will defeat you. I will have the best defense of my position and I will convert you and everyone else to it. I will win and you will lose. To the victor go the spoils. But that is not the model for our struggle. We did not learn this way of war from the One who died for us on the cross of injustice and reached down from his agony to touch the ones who nailed him there with a loving word of forgiveness.

Bishop Browning said: "It may sound patronizing, but you're contributing to the health and well-being of the whole church. You've got to hang in."

Meanwhile, the issue of gays in the military hit the front pages. In June 1992 came reports of a congressional study indicating that "the ban on homosexuals in the armed forces costs the Pentagon at least $27 million a year and perpetuates a policy unsupported by science and sociology." In August, it was reported that the chaplain of the Marine Corps, a Southern Baptist minister named Captain Larry H. Ellis, had distributed a position paper by his deputy chaplain, Commander Gene

Gomulka, saying that homosexuals in the armed forces pose a "physical and psychological" threat. "Legislators and military leaders," contended Gomulka, a Roman Catholic priest, "have a legitimate role to play in checking the spread of homosexual behavior, especially among young people whose minds and characters are in formative stages, thus preventing physical and/or psychological harm that could injure many innocent people." He further argued that "the military services, with its predominantly young male population, would pose a major challenge to gay men who might wish to arrest their behavior. On the other hand, would the military not be an attractive occupation for homosexuals who see no reason to restrict that same behavior?"

During the period between President-elect Clinton's election and inauguration, the first major news story about the incoming administration concerned his announcement that he planned to rescind the ban on gays in the military. Military leaders expressed their displeasure with the decision, and a new poll showed that national support for gays in the military had dropped to below 50 percent for the first time in over a decade. When USA Today's Sunday magazine did a cover story on the ban, focusing on the ejection of former Naval Academy cadet Joseph Steffan, respondents in an unscientific survey came out two-to-one for the ban; the editors reported that "the 13,719 mailed votes represented by far the most cards and letters on a single topic ever received by USA Weekend."

But it wasn't until after Clinton's inauguration that the controversy reached fever pitch. For a week, the issue dominated newspaper headlines and radio call-in programs. The Joint Chiefs of Staff came out strongly against Clinton's plan, members of Congress threatened legislative action, and the religious right went into high gear. The temporary compromise hammered out between the President and his congressional adversaries pleased nobody. Among the sensational events occasioned by the controversy was Sixth Army Soldier of the Year José Zuniga's public revelation of his own homosexuality. The Senate Armed Forces Committee's hearings on the subject also made for some dramatic moments, such as the outing by Colonel Fred Peck, the U.S. Army spokesman in Somalia, of his son Scott, whose articulate and respectful disagreement with his father on the issue brought him considerable attention in the succeeding weeks. Colonel Peck's support for the ban was based entirely on his recognition of anti-gay prejudice in the ranks; he said that if his son were an army officer, "I would be very fearful his life would be in jeopardy from his own troops." Scott Peck's rejoinder: "I have a little more faith in members of the military."

Engineered by Senator Sam Nunn, who strongly opposed lifting the ban, the hearings were notable for their lack of balance. Complained Linda K. Kowalcky in a letter to the *New York Times:* "the committee allowed the hearing to degenerate into a pep rally for supporters of the ban. . . . The questions posed by most committee members were designed to evoke emotional responses, more concerned with what they believed were the moral dimensions of homosexuality than with eliciting information or reflection. Unsupported statements of a medical, psychological or sociological nature were offered by witnesses untrained in those areas and were left to stand as fact." In the most notorious episode, Nunn led a C-SPAN camera operator and a group of pro-ban senators on a tour of two Navy ships, pointing out for the camera the closeness of the bunks and shower stalls and asking groups of sailors how they felt about the idea of "open homosexuals" in the armed forces. It was a disgraceful spectacle. When had the American legislature ever based a civil-rights policy decision on the prejudices and insecurities of twenty-year-olds? Given, moreover, that suspicions about a sailor's sexual orientation might well lead to an aggressive investigation of his private life and, ultimately, to discharge or even imprisonment, how could one expect any of these young men to draw suspicion to himself by speaking up against the ban? The amazing thing was that several of the senators' interviewees were nevertheless courageous enough to voice opposition to it.

Yet anti-ban forces failed to mount a strong, cogent campaign. Randy Shilts's book *Conduct Unbecoming: Gays and Lesbians in the U.S. Military,* published in May 1993, provided powerful testimony against the ban simply by delineating its devastating consequences in the lives of many first-rate servicemen and women. One after another of these people's stories demonstrated that it was the military's recurrent anti-gay probes and purges, not the presence of homosexuals in the ranks, that were destructive of good order and discipline. Yet the book seemed to have appeared too late to make a difference. Part of the problem, too, may have been that the anti-militarism of many gay activists diminished their eagerness to fight for the rights of gays in uniform. In any event, it seemed clear by the end of May that the Senate would not approve of lifting the ban entirely and that President Clinton was unwilling to expend much more of his dwindling political capital on the issue.

Instead, both the Senate and the White House seemed ready to support a compromise proposed by Sam Nunn. This compromise, which went by the name of "don't ask, don't tell," would essentially write into law the institution of the closet: while heterosexuals would continue to enjoy their right to lead private lives and to discuss those lives freely, gays would be allowed to remain in the armed forces only so long as they didn't mention their homosexuality to anyone or have relationships on or off base. As former Air Force Staff Sergeant Thomas Paniccia told the Senate, the Nunn compromise would force "people like me to live a lie." And as David Morgan wrote to the *New York Times,* "If we needed further evidence that even proponents of the ban on homosexuals in the military don't believe their own arguments, their latest suggestion for a 'compromise' is surely that," for, after years of suggestions that gays were a security risk because they might be blackmailed, the "don't ask, don't tell" policy was "a blueprint for blackmail."

It was also thoroughly undemocratic. Trying to sell a panel of gay servicepeople on the "don't ask, don't tell" option, Senator John Warner of Virginia told them, "We all have to give up something. . . . Give up a little something." Yet the "little something" that gays in the military would be required to give up by the Nunn compromise was something that it would never occur to military authorities to compel heterosexual personnel to relinquish. Specifically, the compromise would require that gays be celibate, that they forgo romantic relationships and domestic partnerships throughout their military careers, and that they never say anything that would communicate their sexual orientation to their associates. And why would all this be demanded of them? Simply because their homosexuality made some of their heterosexual colleagues uncomfortable.

Yet the Nunn compromise, inequitable though it was, seemed to be consistent with the wishes of the American public. A *Wall Street Journal*/NBC News poll in April 1993 found that while 47 percent of Americans opposed allowing gays in the military and 43 percent supported it, most respondents said they could accept gays in the military "as long as they didn't openly declare their orientation." It all confirmed that, as Randy Shilts wrote, the anti-gay policy is "not a statement about homosexuals but about heterosexuals."

When in July President Clinton unveiled the plan that his administration had worked out in consultation with the Joint Chiefs, his essential capitulation to their antagonism toward homosexuality was reflected in the fact that he announced it before an audience of military people; not a single gay activist or openly gay serviceperson was invited. The new policy, a slight improvement on the Nunn proposal that was dubbed "don't ask, don't tell, don't pursue" (the last part meaning that anti-gay witch hunts would supposedly be discouraged), drew fire from prominent homosexuals for its preservation of inequities between gays and straights. Randy Shilts complained that gays in the military "will be forced to take a pledge of chastity, which is something heterosexuals don't have to do"; Miriam Ben-Shalom, a former Army staff sergeant dismissed for being a lesbian, argued that gay servicepeople would also be compelled "to, in essence, lie, to deny who they are." And a *New Republic* editorial, while recognizing the policy as "a real advance for civil rights . . . a relatively solid foundation for security for most gay soldiers," pronounced it "morally and intellectually contemptible," noting that "implicit lies, deceptions, concealments, euphemisms and half-truths are often more psychologically destructive and morally corrupting than explicit ones. This is something the president still does not understand; that too many heterosexual Americans do not see; that General Colin Powell and Senator Nunn cannot even conceive. And the most demeaning assumption about the new provisions is that they single out the deepest moment of emotional intimacy—the private sexual act—as that which is most repugnant. Its assumption about the dignity and humanity of gay people, in and out of the military, in public and in private, is sickening."

In New York City, two additional gay-related issues commanded front-page headlines. The Ancient Order of Hibernians, an Irish organization that had been allowed to bar a gay group, the Irish Lesbian and Gay Organization, from its 1992 Saint Patrick's Day parade on Fifth Avenue, was told by a judge in November 1992 that its next parade would have to include the ILGO. The Hibernians refused, and Mayor David Dinkins's subsequent decision to grant the 1993 parade permit to another Irish organization that promised to include the ILGO provoked outrage on the part of John Cardinal O'Connor and other Irish Catholics. Maintaining that the parade was a religious event and that its organizers were therefore entitled to bar any group on doctrinal grounds, O'Connor threatened to lead a boycott of any parade that included the ILGO.

Eventually another judge determined that the Hibernians had the right to bar the ILGO from their parade. And so the celebration went on as usual, with the Hibernians in charge and the gay group excluded.

Meanwhile, angry parents and school board members assailed the inclusion of homosexuals in a new curriculum designed to teach tolerance to public elementary-school students. The defense of this so-called Rainbow Curriculum by the Board of Education chancellor Joseph Fernandez was the major factor in the board's decision, in early 1993, not to renew his contract.

Given the choice, few homosexuals would have chosen to wage the struggle for gay rights on these two particular battlefields. Both the parade and the Rainbow Curriculum issues were muddied by legal complexities, moral ambiguities, and widespread confusion about the facts; both provided homophobes with a first-rate opportunity to sensationalize and misinform, to draw fallacious equations between gay rights and other matters, to make homosexuality look like a threat to order and tradition and the family, and to foster anger and suspicion rather than enlightenment and understanding.

For me, at least, the parade issue involved a host of yes-buts. First of all, I can't say I'm unequivocally enthusiastic about organizations like the ILGO: instead of furthering the integration of openly gay individuals into mainstream society, such groups often tend to reinforce the idea of gays as a separate set of people, segregated from everyone else by their sexual orientation. To be sure, given the particularly harsh treatment of gays in Ireland (where, ironically, an ILGO contingent marched without incident in Dublin's 1993 Saint Patrick's Day Parade), one can understand why Irish gays would feel a special need to band together. In any event, since some Irish gays have indeed chosen to form such an organization, I think the fair thing would have been for the Hibernians to treat the ILGO's application for inclusion in the parade as they would have treated an application from any other Irish-related group. Certainly O'Connor's claim that the parade was a religious event didn't hold water. As the Reverend John Andrew, rector of Saint Thomas Church (Episcopal), pointed out in a letter to the *New York Times*, the anti-English slogans that are brandished annually by some marchers aren't exactly consistent with Roman Catholic creeds. Yet the Hibernians refused the ILGO's application, and it's my view that they had a right to: it's their parade. Dinkins's attempt to force their hand made me uncomfortable—for in a democracy any organization, however reprehensible its views, should have a right to make its own decisions about who is allowed to participate in its public activities.

As for the Rainbow Curriculum controversy, public debate centered on a few paragraphs in a document of several hundred pages and on three children's books—*Heather Has Two Mommies, Daddy's Roommate,* and *Gloria Goes to Gay Pride*—that appeared not in the required curriculum but on a supplementary list of hundreds of children's books about a variety of subjects. The curriculum's purpose was to promote tolerance from the first grade onward; the disputed pages focused on tolerance of homosexuality. For gays, the main point of those pages was unarguable: children should be taught to respect their elders, even if they happen to be homosexual; children of gay parents should not be made to feel like freaks. As it turned out, a large majority of New York City parents, according to a survey, agreed on this score. Yet one powerfully placed woman did not: Mary Cummins, head of the school board in District 24 in Queens. Cummins and the propagandists who joined her crusade engaged in a vast disinformation campaign, suggesting to parents that *Heather* and the other books would be required reading and that grade-school lessons in tolerance of homosexuality would include graphic descriptions of gay sex. According to a *New York Times* article, Cummins "repeatedly insist[ed] that 'Children of the Rainbow' discusses sodomy when in fact no references to sex appear." "The level of misinformation was such," wrote one reporter about a parents' meeting on the subject, "that xerox copies of gay porn were passed off as illustrations from the new first grade text books." Cummins's campaign was supported by such influential figures as the neoconservative writer Midge Decter, the main purpose of whose *Commentary* essay "Homosexuality and the Schools" was apparently to discredit the Rainbow Curriculum's lessons in tolerance of homosexuality by linking those lessons to repulsively explicit sex-education proposals that have no actual connection to the curriculum and by implying the possibility of gay recruitment of young children.

In point of fact there was much to dislike in the Rainbow Curriculum: it didn't just promote tolerance, it promoted a multicultural mindset. Instead of encouraging children to judge one another as individuals, it sought to reinforce their awareness of differences, to think of one another as belonging to this or that group. The curriculum's gay-related material, moreover, had been prepared under the influence of subculture-oriented gays and tended to define homosexuality in strict sub-culture terms. Yet these valid arguments were lost amid the homophobic rant of the curriculum's most vocal opponents.

To many heterosexuals, these and other gay-related news stories rep-resented the further escalation of a phenomenon that had baffled and vexed them increasingly for over a decade. Yes, there had always been homosexuals. But they'd kept a low profile. Why were there so many of them now? Where were they all coming from? What were they all complaining about? And why were they suddenly out, it seemed, to change the rules, topple the existing order, crash the gates of the nation's most cherished institutions? In an April 1993 column, William Rasp-berry said that the recent March on Washington had not answered any questions for him but only left him "with more questions": "Am I the only one still not sure what the demonstrators want America to do?" And a Jacksonville, North Carolina, man named Bob Esenwein spoke for many when, at a March 1993 town meeting on the gays-in-the-military issue, he said: "We despise gays and all these people usurping the country." *Usurping:* to many heterosexuals, that's what gays are doing to America.

By contrast, for most homosexuals—even for those who felt that the ILGO and the Rainbow Curriculum supporters were misguided in im-portant ways, and that these and other controversies had obscured the real issues—such news stories had another meaning: They underscored the degree to which many heterosexuals, after two decades of the gay-rights movement, still didn't get it. Those heterosexuals didn't under-stand that the great majority of homosexuals had no desire to destroy national institutions, but wanted only to be a part of them—as homo-sexuals had always, covertly, been—without pretending to be something they weren't. More fundamentally, many heterosexuals didn't under-stand what homosexuality *was.* This lack of understanding wasn't a matter of intelligence or educational background or good will. The play-wright and activist Larry Kramer has noted how a presumably well-educated official of the AIDS office at the Centers for Disease Control once asked him, "Why don't you people just get married? . . . If you guys had been married to women, this [AIDS] never would have happened." Likewise, Joseph Steffan recalls how a sympathetic friend at the Naval Academy asked, "Can't you just wake up one morning and decide that

you're going to be straight—decide that you're going to like girls from
now on?" (To which Steffan replied, "That would be just as easy as your
waking up tomorrow and deciding that from now on you were only going
to be attracted to men." Steffan's comment: "He got the point, but I
found it remarkable that he had never viewed my sexuality in the same
way that he viewed his own. He had only envisioned it as a deviation
from some universal norm.") Steffan was also told by a Navy commander
that

> if I was willing that evening to accept Jesus as my personal savior and
> renounce my homosexuality, he would personally call the commandant
> and inform him that I had been converted and recommend that the
> proceedings against me be dropped.
>
> I could hardly believe what he was saying; rather, I couldn't believe
> that someone I knew and respected, an otherwise intelligent, thought-
> ful, and compassionate person, could be so ignorant, and so capable of
> the cruelty that flows from it. . . . Of everything I experienced at An-
> napolis, there was nothing more depressing or disturbing than realizing
> how many good, intelligent people simply have no concept of what
> homosexuality really is.

That many intelligent, sophisticated people do indeed misunderstand
homosexuality was reflected in the antagonistic response to a cover story
on "Gays at Law" in a 1992 issue of *California Lawyer* magazine. Correspondents facetiously suggested follow-up articles on lawyers who
were guilty of child molestation or bestiality. "Who cares about some
sodomizing legal faggots?" wrote one attorney. (The author of the article,
Jane Goldman, opined that the Republican convention had "helped our
correspondents frame their gripes. . . . Lord knows it legitimized homophobia.") Then there's what happened to me recently during a private
conversation with a distinguished educator. I had assumed that this
man, a Harvard-trained philosopher, knew about my homosexuality, but
during our talk it became clear that he didn't. One moment he was
praising me excessively; then, maligning a mutual acquaintance who
happened to be gay, he suddenly launched into a tirade in which he
described homosexuals in terms directly antithetical to those he had
just applied to me. If I was "solid," they were "sick"; if I was a man of
honor, they were unscrupulous; if I was selflessly devoted to the highest
principles of art and knowledge, they had only one purpose: to seduce
young boys. The absolute contradiction between his notion of me and

his notion of the group to which he was unaware I belonged would almost have been funny if it had not been chillingly representative of the views of many smart, well-educated people.

For all their intelligence and education, such people—as I shall make clear in the following section—misunderstand homosexuality on every level. They misunderstand it as a psychological phenomenon, as a moral issue, as a social construct. When they look at it, they see things that aren't there and don't see things that are. They magnify its inconsequential aspects and pay little attention to its vital features. To a gay person reading the previously quoted remarks about homosexuality by the Marine chaplain and the Boy Scout spokesman, it might well seem that they were speaking a language different from his own, or discussing some condition he himself had never experienced or observed, so wide was the gulf between the way he viewed himself and the way many others saw him.

Consider, for example, the Boy Scout spokesman's remark that a homosexual is not "a role model that's consistent with the expectations of mainstream American families." Many heterosexuals would agree readily with this statement. But to any gay person, the obvious point was that James Dale, the expelled Eagle Scout, had himself grown up, as do most homosexuals, in a "mainstream American" family. Certainly when Dale realized he was gay, he *knew* it wasn't consistent with his parents' expectations—or, for that matter, with his own. But what could he do? Lie? Why not? Thousands of Scouts do hide their homosexuality in order to keep their uniforms—and tens of thousands more are gay but don't know it yet. (I was one such Scout myself.) But Dale didn't want to lie. In his Boy Scout oath he'd vowed to be trustworthy. So he told the truth—the most difficult truth he would ever have to tell—and instead of being honored for his courage and rectitude, and recognized on this account as a superb role model for gay and straight boys alike, he was ejected.

The choice facing that Boy Scout was the same choice that faces countless seminarians and ministers, cadets and soldiers, nuclear physicists and sales clerks, men and women and boys and girls in all walks of life who discover themselves to be gay: lie and be safe, or tell the truth and face the consequences. For generations of homosexuals to whom the truth would mean certain ruin, the choice was to lie. For increasing numbers of homosexuals today, when the consequences of honesty are somewhat less severe, the choice is to tell the truth. This is, indeed, the real question at the heart of the current conflict over homosexuality: not whether gays should be allowed to be gay—for one has no choice in that matter—but whether gays should be allowed to be honest. Should gays live openly or in the closet? Time and again, fervent opponents of gay rights make it clear that what they desire is a return to the closet—a return to a time when it was necessary to lie about one's sexual orientation and when the prevalent ideas about homosexuality were nothing but lies.

Yet more and more people—gay and straight alike—realize that the perpetuation of the closet is harmful not only to homosexuals but to society at large. It harms the woman who marries a secretly gay man and one day, perhaps after twenty years of marriage, finds him in bed with another man. It harms the children of such unions. It harms straight Americans, male and female, adult and child, who learn to hate and fear where there is no reason to hate and fear. It harms parents who turn out to have a gay child, and, as a result, experience years of needless anguish and guilt. And most of all it harms the young people who, discovering themselves to be gay, are benefited more than anything else by understanding parents and by an acquaintance with responsible, emotionally balanced gay adults with whom they can identify.

It is perhaps appropriate here to say something about tolerance and acceptance. The two words are not exact synonyms. Tolerance is more a political concept, acceptance more a moral concept. One can tolerate without accepting; acceptance lies beyond tolerance as knowledge lies beyond curiosity. To tolerate homosexuality is to acknowledge the right of others to have homosexual relations even though one disapproves of them; to accept homosexuality is not to disapprove but rather to recognize that it and heterosexuality are, morally speaking, analogous to lefthandedness and righthandedness, and that disapproval of homosexuality—as distinguished from disapproval of certain aspects of the gay subculture, or of the "lifestyle" choices of certain gay individuals—is not a morally legitimate option.

Traditionally, tolerance has been viewed as a democratic virtue. In a democracy, we are taught to tolerate personal habits that offend us, to tolerate religious beliefs that we do not share, and to tolerate the seemingly odd tastes and customs of people whose backgrounds differ dramatically from our own. One element of this tolerance is an at least formal acknowledgment that under the democratic system we are all equals. But as homosexuality has become an increasingly prominent issue, it has become increasingly clear that this acknowledgment doesn't necessarily apply to homosexuals. Indeed, where homosexuality is concerned, tolerance often means "I'll leave you alone, but keep your mouth shut about being gay; though I reserve the right to spread lies about homosexuality and to condemn you publicly for being gay, I will consider it offensive for you to even so much as raise the subject." Tolerance of homosexuality, as opposed to acceptance, is bound up with sheer ignorance; it requires that gays lead a life of dishonesty. The bottom line is that the closer one is to a homosexual, the less sense mere tolerance makes. Simply to tolerate the sexuality of one's own child is to fail in one's love; it is to establish a distance, a separation, where none is necessary.

A tolerant society is one that allows gays to have their own subculture—their own little table, as it were, in the corner of the dining room; an accepting society is one that welcomes gays at the big table, with the rest of the family. People who tolerate homosexuality concede the necessity of protecting gays from eviction or job termination on account of their sexual orientation; people who accept homosexuality are willing, in addition, to support such causes as domestic partnership, which involve acknowledging committed gay couples.

The irony of all this is that a tolerant society, by agreeing not to interfere with the operation of such institutions as gay bars and bathhouses, makes it vastly easier and less stressful for homosexuals to lead promiscuous sex lives but, by refusing to grant committed gay couples legal rights comparable to those granted married heterosexual couples, doesn't effect a similar improvement for gays who want to live in monogamous relationships. In a society where homosexuality and the gay subculture are viewed as synonymous both by many heterosexuals and by subculture-oriented gays, widespread acceptance of homosexuality is virtually impossible to achieve, both because misinformed heterosexuals have a grotesquely distorted image of what they are being asked to accept and because the subculture-oriented gay man is a rebel whose understanding of himself is predicated on a powerful sense of identification with the subculture and an equally powerful sense of antagonism toward the manners and mores of the mainstream culture. To such a person, acceptance would mean assimilation, and the plain fact is that he doesn't *want* to be assimilated. He enjoys his exclusion. He feels comfortable at his little table.

Or at least he thinks he does. But does he? What is it, after all, that ties him to his little table—that drove him, in other words, into a marginal existence? Ultimately, it's prejudice. Liberated from that prejudice, would he still want to sit at his little table? Perhaps, and perhaps not. Certainly most homosexuals don't want to be relegated to that little table. We grew up at the big table; we're at home there. We want to stay there (and want every gay person to feel that he has a real opportunity to join us there) and we don't want to have to lie about ourselves in order to do so.

2

"Don't you think homosexuality is wrong?"

My job as a movie reviewer ended, in June 1990, the same way it had begun four years earlier: with a telephone conversation between myself and an editor of the conservative magazine the *American Spectator* whom I shall call Jozef. It was I who placed that final call. Several days earlier I'd sent a review by modem from my New York apartment to the magazine's offices in suburban Virginia, but I hadn't heard yet from Jozef, who usually called to thank me, to chat for a few minutes (if he wasn't too busy), and, sometimes, to raise a question or two about factual details or to ask for a minor change in wording. That day in June, I phoned Jozef merely to make sure that the review had reached him and that there were no problems with it.

It was an enjoyable job, reviewing movies for the *American Spectator,* and I never did find out what had made Jozef offer it to me. Our professional affiliation had begun in 1985, when I'd sent him a short unsolicited piece about writing, which he'd accepted enthusiastically. A few months later he ran a brief essay of mine on Manhattan yuppies. Some time afterward, he invited me to review a Pauline Kael book; soon after running that review he asked me to become the magazine's movie critic. In the intervening four years we'd worked together very amiably. I'd neither told him I was gay nor said anything to suggest I wasn't. Nor had I ever met (or talked or corresponded with) the magazine's editor-in-chief or publisher, although I'd seen them across the room at *American Spectator* functions in Washington and New York—two small, natty, ambitious men.

Jozef was different. A second-generation Polish American in his thirties, he was a perfect second-rung editor: modest, loyal, hardworking, and friendly with his writers. He encouraged me to do whatever I wanted to with my *American Spectator* space. For my August 1990 piece, about which I was phoning him on that day in June, he'd suggested that I review some Broadway plays, as I had a couple of years earlier. So I'd dutifully taken in a cross section of Great White Way offerings: a musical (*Les Misérables*), a whodunit (*Accomplice*), a comedy (*Some Americans Abroad*), and a romantic fantasy (*Prelude to a Kiss*). I was happy with the piece, which didn't strike me as being particularly different from my other reviews, and I had no reason to believe that my editors would find anything wrong with it.

The moment Jozef picked up the telephone, however, I knew something was wrong. He sounded unlike himself: remote, grumpy. When I asked about the review, he was blunt. "We can't run it," he said, "unless you cut the part about *Prelude to a Kiss*."

A chill went through me. "Why?" I asked.

"Because," he said, "we can't have any mention of AIDS or homosexuals in the magazine."

The instant's silence lasted an eternity. I knew, of course, what he meant: they couldn't have any mention of AIDS or homosexuals *that wasn't homophobic*. For it wasn't as if the editors of the *American Spectator* shied away from the subjects of AIDS and homosexuality; on the contrary, a regular feature called "The Continuing Crisis," in which the editor offered a scornful roundup of the month's news events, often included homophobic sneers: "In San Francisco Mr. Donald C. Knutson, 59, a co-founder of the National Gay Rights Advocates, died of Rock Hudson's Disease, as did the fashion designer Halston." "The Bar Association of San Francisco voted unanimously to support a change in state law backing homosexual marriage by changing the definition of marriage from a contract between a 'man and a woman' to one between 'two people.' The move delighted homosexuals, though it might not go over equally well with animal rights militants and domestic pet lovers." Sometimes the editor got so weird on the subject that it seemed he was working out a deep-seated problem:

As a matter of pride, if not terminological exactitude, the homosexual community should have a fresh designation, unsullied by the past and emblematic of some genuine characteristic of homosexual life. Homosexuals need not endure slur terms but should be given an attractive appellation that pleases them and represents them as they are. I think we can all agree that the word squash is such a word. Cephalic indices and empirical observations of homosexuals at public demonstrations and on Halloween night in San Francisco have established that many homosexuals develop heads shaped very much like squash (*Curubita maxima*). Youthful, nicely-muscled homosexuals often have heads shaped like the well-known butternut squash, best served plain or with butter. Homosexuals less favored by nature frequently have heads reminiscent of the squat acorn squash, which is even tastier than the butternut, particularly when braised in brown sugar. . . . Let us henceforth speak of our homosexuals as squashes. Let the universities hold their Squash Rights Week. And let us accord proper respect to the Squash Community.

The *American Spectator* had run a piece by Michael Fumento, entitled "The Myth of Heterosexual AIDS," that combined a sensible argument against AIDS hysteria with blatant homophobia: AIDS, Fumento argued, wasn't really spreading into the heterosexual population as extensively as the media claimed it was, so why spend scads of money on research? Then there was P. J. O'Rourke's piece "Manhattan Swish," occasioned by the enactment of a New York City law guaranteeing homosexuals freedom from housing discrimination. The piece is a consummate example of the *American Spectator*'s approach to gay issues. Proudly adducing the heterosexual escapades of his youth, O'Rourke begins by saying that "it has been my personal experience that whatever the Catholic Church says about sex—it's wrong." Yet this doesn't mean that the gay-rights law is a good idea. On the contrary,

> a man who does an abnormal, distasteful, and, as it were, queer thing like make love to another man deserves all the ordinary protection of the law. But does he deserve *extra*ordinary protection? . . . To set sodomy up as a "right" opens the door to all kinds of other silly "rights" such as the right to be hired as a salesman for Brooks Brothers when you insist on wearing brown shirts with a blue suit.

Besides, O'Rourke continues,

> The rights of inverts are debatable. A school board may feel it has good reason not to want a lesbian girl's gym teacher. A hospital may not want a promiscuous gay surgeon swinging a scalpel in its pa-

tients. . . . Some people believe (and the First Amendment allows them to do so) that homosexuality is a horrid transgression of God's plan. Do these people have to live and work with a man whose activities they detest? . . . Their prejudice is, no doubt, as foolish as any other prejudice, but there is a difference. A black man is not free to be white, but a sodomist is free not to sodomize.

Finally, O'Rourke introduces the conceit that he is an alcoholic, and proceeds to make a tongue-in-cheek plea for the "rights" of himself and his fellow alcoholics: "We're made this way. . . . I'm a victim of prejudice. That's what I am. Spare me a buck for a little shot and a chaser?"

One would have to be either stupid or dishonest to compare a homosexual's wish to be protected from being evicted or fired simply for being gay to a drunk's demand for a free drink or a man's expectation that he has a right to be hired by an upscale clothing store. But then O'Rourke's reasoning is both mendacious and inconsistent throughout the piece. For instance, many surgeons—some of them straight, some of them gay—are sexually promiscuous; by speaking of a "promiscuous gay" surgeon, O'Rourke deliberately confuses the issues of promiscuity and sexual orientation. He argues that prejudices in the workplace and in housing should be respected, but then, recognizing that this might not sit well with blacks, qualifies his argument by saying that there's a difference between blacks and gays: blacks cannot become whites but "a sodomist is free not to sodomize."

There are several illogical and offensive things happening here. First, O'Rourke is essentially suggesting that prejudice should be legally permissible against categories of people who can switch to another category, but not against people who can't. But since people can convert from one religion to another, this would seem to imply that it should be legally acceptable to bar people from employment or housing on the basis of religion. Second, by saying that "a sodomist is free not to sodomize," O'Rourke obscures a fact more germane to the issue: namely, that a homosexual man can no more stop being homosexual than a black can cease being black. Yes, he can stop having sex, or can even marry a woman and father a dozen children; but his attraction to men will not disappear. Third, by referring to "sodomists" when he plainly means "homosexuals," O'Rourke is equating the two terms; this is an erroneous equation, because many homosexuals are not sodomists (assuming that by "sodomy" O'Rourke means anal intercourse) and many heterosexuals are. Performing acts of sodomy does not make one gay, and not performing them does not make one straight. Like many heterosexuals, O'Rourke, when writing about homosexuality, fixates not on sexual attraction but on certain activities that are associated in the public mind with the idea of homosexuality. Yet homosexuality is not a matter of what one does—some homosexual men never perform an act of "sodomy" in their entire life—but of which sex one is attracted to.

Even more loathsome than O'Rourke's piece was an *American Spectator* article entitled "AIDS: A British View," in which a British journalist named Christopher Monckton advocated universal AIDS-virus tests and a quarantine on those testing positive. The article was so outrageous that the then assistant managing editor, Andrew Ferguson, denounced it in the letters column of the very same issue. So did I, in a letter that ran two months later:

> Yes, AIDS is a horror. Before this epidemic is over, its effects may bring the Holocaust to mind. But to impose lifelong quarantine upon everyone that has been exposed to the virus, as Christopher Monckton proposes ("AIDS: A British View," *TAS*, January 1987), would be to allow AIDS not only to rob countless Americans of their lives but also to rob us all of our fundamental liberties—thus perfecting the resemblance to the Holocaust. Granted, Monckton acknowledges that (at present anyway) his proposal is too extreme to be acceptable to most Americans; but he is plainly more dismayed than cheered by this fact.
>
> Ever since the time of Patrick Henry, Americans have claimed to prize liberty as dearly as life. I'm afraid that in the coming years the spread of AIDS will sorely test this claim. But we must stand firm. We must, as Andrew Ferguson implies, maintain our dedication to "limited government, prudence, and individual responsibility." And we must hold before ourselves the words of Benjamin Franklin: "Those who would give up essential liberty to purchase a little temporary safety, deserve neither liberty nor safety."

If I continued my association with the *American Spectator* despite its publication of such articles as Monckton's, it was because I felt that as long as I was allowed to write what I wanted, I could hardly complain that other writers were granted the same privilege. What's more, I felt that as an *American Spectator* writer I had a singular opportunity to nudge its readers some small distance from their knee-jerk philistinism toward a more reflective, tolerant variety of Toryism—a variety that, among other things, didn't look upon homosexuality as something to be automatically condemned or ridiculed.

This is not to say that I made a point of celebrating movies with homosexual characters, but simply that when they did appear, I accepted the gay content matter-of-factly and appraised them critically as I would any film. At the outset, this approach seemed completely acceptable to my editors. One of the first movies I reviewed was *My Beautiful Laundrette,* and though I praised it highly and explicitly outlined its story of an affair between a young Pakistani man and a Cockney street tough, there wasn't so much as a murmur of protest from Jozef (or, for that matter, from any of my readers). The same went for my piece on *Prick Up Your Ears,* which depicted the tawdry and violent liaison between the British playwright Joe Orton and his lover Kenneth Halliwell. There *was* some trouble, however, about the Merchant Ivory film *Maurice.* I didn't like the movie, which was based on E. M. Forster's silly novel about the idyllic romance between two young men at Cambridge, one of whom eventually marries and becomes a politician and the other of whom, after a period of confusion and self-loathing, finds love and lives happily (and improbably) ever after with his ex-lover's gamekeeper. After reading my review of that film, Jozef phoned and explained to me, in an embarrassed, apologetic tone, that his boss wanted me to add a sentence expressly condemning the characters' homosexuality. I said I would do nothing of the kind. He tried to debate the issue: "Don't you think homosexuality is wrong?"

In response, I launched into a furious jeremiad against homophobia. Jozef, apparently taken aback, insisted that his boss was not bigoted— that he had gay friends, never made fag jokes, and didn't treat homosexuals any differently from the way he treated anyone else. That the man was constantly waxing homophobic in "The Continuing Crisis" didn't seem to faze Jozef; nor, evidently, did he see any contradiction between his boss's supposed tolerance and his insistence that I add that sentence condemning homosexuality. It was not until I threatened to quit over the matter that Jozef backed off and agreed to run the piece as written. "I guess we conservatives have a lot of growing up to do on this particular issue," he finally acknowledged, to my amazement, and apologized for having made such a request in the first place. When I hung up I was shaken, but impressed by the strength of character that had enabled Jozef to admit his error.

My *Maurice* review ran as written in the January 1988 issue. Since then there had been no further friction between me and the *American Spectator* editors. In the spring of 1990 I attended the magazine's anniversary dinner at the Willard Hotel in Washington, at which President and Mrs. Bush were the guests of honor; in May, at Jozef's suggestion, the magazine treated me to a week in Cannes, where I covered the film festival.

It was there that I saw the film *Longtime Companion*. The picture had its failings—the lighting and cinematography were of TV-movie quality, the story contained elements of soap opera, and the ending was absurd—but it moved me deeply nonetheless, because I'd never before seen the everyday life of middle-class gay male couples portrayed so convincingly on screen. What's more, the couples in the movie were youngish Manhattanites like me and my lover; they walked the same streets we did, shared the same body of cultural references. If most movies about gay men depicted them strictly according to stereotype— shallow, neurotic, sex-obsessed, self-hating—here finally was a movie that, however imperfectly, held up a mirror to a version of "gay life" that was familiar to me. The characters were portrayed neither as saints nor as sensualists but as ordinary people who led generally responsible lives, held down more or less respectable jobs, and lived with partners to whom they were as committed as most heterosexual spouses.

I didn't include *Longtime Companion* in my Cannes piece, because I felt my response had been too subjective to make a fair review possible at that point. A month later, however, when I saw the play *Prelude to a Kiss* by the same writer-director team, I decided to incorporate in my paragraph on that play a reference to the movie, which by then I'd seen again and from which, I felt, I'd achieved the requisite critical distance. The portion of the review that dealt with *Prelude* and *Companion*, and that Jozef insisted I delete, struck me as supremely innocuous. It read as follows:

Like the film "Longtime Companion," the play "Prelude to a Kiss," which is now playing at the Helen Hayes Theater, was written by Craig Lucas and directed by Norman René. Though superficially different, the two works share a similarity of method and purpose: in each of them, Lucas sets up a romantic situation of a sort that most audience members are likely to think of as idiosyncratic, if not outrageous, and sets about trying to persuade the audience to recognize its common humanity with the characters, to identify with them in their affections, and to sympathize with them in their plight. Both works are skillfully and sensitively written, and both, despite the unusualness of their material, are extremely conventional in dramatic terms. In the affecting realistic drama "Longtime Companion," the protagonists are four gay male couples facing AIDS; in the charming romantic fantasy "Prelude to a Kiss," they are a young man named Peter (Timothy Hutton) and his bride, Rita (Mary-Louise Parker), who finds her mind and personality trapped in the body of an old man (Barnard Hughes). Lucas handles the story with wit and compassion, and manages to keep things light even as he steers his story through weird, dark territory. One problem with the play, however, is that, thanks to such recent movies as "Big," "Vice Versa," and "18 Again," its plot gimmick feels very stale; another problem is that Hutton—who, for no good reason, bares his painfully scrawny upper body at least twice—seems as slender of talent as he is of physique: he has no wit, no moral weight, no presence whatsoever. (And he's the Oscar winner in the cast.) That the play comes off in spite of this liability can be credited largely to the winsome, vivacious Miss Parker, who almost singlehandedly infuses the proceedings with urgency, movement, credibility, life. Along with Bruce Davison, she is the best thing in "Longtime Companion," and she shines in "Prelude to a Kiss."

That was it. How, I wondered, could *anyone* find this paragraph offensive?

"You've got to be kidding," I said to Jozef. "That paragraph is completely innocuous."

"We can't print it," Jozef said. "We have a conservative readership. There are a lot of gay conservatives in Washington, but they keep it to themselves because they understand that other conservatives don't want to hear about it. We'll print the rest of the piece but we can't print that part."

"But it's completely innocuous," I repeated. I mentioned the line about "common humanity." He reiterated: no AIDS or homosexuality. He was firm—much firmer, certainly, than he'd been during the *Maurice* episode. This time, I gathered, he'd been given explicit orders: the "no AIDS or homosexuality" stipulation had, it was clear, been drummed into him. If in the case of *Maurice* he had sounded apologetic, this time he sounded rankled, as if he resented me for putting him in this position, for making him feel like a worm. He even sounded (could it be?) a bit spooked, as if he'd put up a fight on my behalf and been put in his place—perhaps even been threatened with loss of his job. (Jozef was a family man, with a wife and two young children to support.)

"Well," I said, "in that case, I think we should call it a day."

"Just like that?" he said.

"Yes."

I felt oddly at peace. Why wasn't I angrier? Partly, I suppose, because I was in shock: it hadn't occurred to me for a moment that my exceedingly tame review would bother anybody. And partly because I was feeling, among other things, relief: I'd been increasingly uncomfortable as an *American Spectator* writer in the last couple of years, and now the magazine had presented me with a clear-cut situation, one in which there was plainly no alternative but to resign and withdraw the entire review. The thought even crossed my mind that I should be grateful to Jozef for making my position so unambiguous, my decision so easy.

Neither of us hung up. "I can't believe this is it," he said, a hint of wonder in his voice.

"Neither can I," I said.

"I've got to hand it to you," he said. "You're being very gentlemanly about this. If I were in your shoes I'd be a lot angrier."

"Thank you," I said.

There was a lull. He told me he'd enjoyed working with me and had always thought of me as a friend. I told him I'd felt the same way. Then we hung up.

I reflected on the affair a great deal in the months that followed. Had I been wrong to write for so reactionary a publication? If so, then how did one figure out where to draw the line? Should I refuse to write for *The Nation* because its editors frequently appeared to be apologists for Communism, or for *The World & I* because it was owned by the Reverend Sun Myung Moon's Unification Church? The fact was that most "serious" magazines had distinct political leanings and questionable financial connections; and there were none—*The New Criterion* had come far closer than any—whose editors' convictions lined up point for point with mine on the things that mattered most to me.

I wondered: had the *American Spectator* editors grown more homophobic since the days of *My Beautiful Laundrette*? Or had the influence of certain financial backers had something to do with the apparent change of policy? Or was something else going on? The editors had given me no trouble about my candid reviews of *My Beautiful Laundrette* and *Prick Up Your Ears*, both of which made homosexual life look pretty grubby and marginal. Could it be that the *American Spectator* didn't mind running pieces that confirmed the negative stereotypes of homosexuality and that their problem with my brief reference to *Longtime Companion* had less to do with the film's attention to homosexuality and AIDS than with its positive image of homosexual life?

There was another question. Was I wrong not to have told my editors at the outset that I was homosexual? No, I decided; that was none of their business. What was wrong was to lie about it, and that I had never done—not explicitly, anyway. I had determined from the start that if asked about my sexual orientation, I would answer honestly. But no one had ever asked.

I thought a lot about Jozef, who had always seemed to me an eminently decent person. Yet he had been willing to say something that struck me as abominable: that "we can't have any mention of AIDS or homosexuals in the magazine." Would he have been willing, at his boss's direction, to say, "We can't have any mention of Jews in the magazine"? In America in 1990, perhaps not. But what about Germany in 1933? Or Poland in 1940? What if Jozef had been an editor in Nazi-occupied Warsaw with a wife and two small boys to worry about? Even to experience something as inconsequential, in the scheme of things, as the circumstances under which I resigned from the *American Spectator* was to gain some insight into the terrifying ability of good people, under pressure, to brutalize their colleagues, friends, and loved ones. During that brief final conversation with Jozef, I had a glimpse of how adept good people can be at closing their minds to unpleasant thoughts, at hiding from themselves their own barbarism, and at pretending to themselves that, far from being unfair, they are upholding a moral principle.

What was in Jozef's mind, after all, when he told me that his boss was not prejudiced against homosexuals? Did he actually believe it, despite all the homophobic things his boss had written? I think he did. And what had been in his mind when he asked me to add a sentence to the *Maurice* review condemning homosexuality? I truly believe that he had managed to explain it to himself as just another editorial request. If I had complied, that would have been that; everyone would have been happy, and Jozef would not have suffered over it. To be sure, when I challenged him and forced him to think about the request and to consult his moral faculties, he was quick to recognize that he had been wrong and to apologize. Yet as a result of the *Maurice* experience, he was ready for me when the *Prelude to a Kiss* incident came along. When I phoned, he had already steeled himself against my attempts to address his conscience, had closed off that part of his mind.

Homophobia. In a world of prejudice, there is no other prejudice quite like it. Mainstream writers, politicians, and cultural leaders who hate Jews or blacks or Asians but who have long since accepted the unwritten rules that forbid public expression of those prejudices still denounce gays with impunity. For such people, gays are the Other in a way that Jews or blacks or Asians are not. After all, they can look at Jewish or black or Asian family life and see something that, in its chief components—husband, wife, children, workplace, school, house of worship— is essentially a variation on their own lives; yet when they look at gays— or, rather, at the image of gays that has been fostered both by the mainstream culture and by the gay subculture—they see creatures whose lives seem to be different from theirs in every possible way.

Peter J. Gomes, an American Baptist minister and professor of Christian morals at Harvard University, has described homophobia as "the last respectable prejudice of the century." Certainly there is no other prejudice in which people feel more morally justified; no other prejudice that reaches so high into the ranks of the intelligent, the powerful, the otherwise quite virtuous; no other prejudice, therefore, more deep-seated and polarizing. There is, one would wager, no other prejudice that takes more irrational forms. One sees Christians hatefully reviling homosexual love in the name of Christ, whose supreme commandment was to "love one another." And one sees defenders of "the family" citing gay rights as the greatest threat to "family values"—as if homosexuals didn't have families by whom they longed to be accepted, as if anything that deserved the name of "family values" didn't include the idea of parents responding humanely to the news of their child's homosexuality, as if it somehow served the cause of "the family" to heap abuse on the idea of same-sex couples (the obvious alternative to which, of course, is gay promiscuity).

. . .

There is no other prejudice whose practitioners play numbers games. From the appearance of the Kinsey Reports in 1948 and 1953 until very recently, it was a truism that about 10 percent of Americans are homosexual. This would make the gay population roughly equal to that of blacks and Hispanics and four times that of Jews. Some gays thought the percentage was even higher; others would have placed it closer to six or seven. Homophobes made a point of disputing these numbers, as if they found unbelievable or intolerable, or both, the very idea that so many Americans were gay, and as if it were somehow more permissible to abuse a smaller minority than a larger one. These homophobes argued that gays make up only 3 or 4 percent of the population, or even as little as 1 or 2. They based these figures on surveys in which people are asked if they have ever had "homosexual intercourse." One problem with using the results of such surveys to determine the percentage of gays in the population is that many gays have never had "homosexual intercourse," if by that term one means anal penetration; another problem, of course, is that a large percentage of gays are so deeply closeted that they would never respond truthfully to such a survey.

One of the most recent of these surveys, conducted by the Alan Guttmacher Institute, caused a media frenzy when its results were released in April 1993. Newspapers and network news programs gave the story prominent coverage; public-affairs talk shows made it the topic of the day. Why? Because according to the survey, which consisted of face-to-face interviews with over three thousand men in their twenties and thirties, gays constitute only 1 percent of the population—the lowest figure ever to be reported by a major survey.

For many reactionaries, this number represented terrific news. "Finally, the truth has surfaced," said the Reverend Lou Sheldon, chairman of the Traditional Values Coalition. "We've been vindicated!" said Bob Grant, a right-wing New York radio host. Activists, both gay and anti-gay, suggested that the results could deal a devastating blow to the cause of civil rights for gay men and lesbians. How many politicians, after all, care about the welfare of 1 percent of the population?

But most gays who gave the results any thought were, to say the least, highly skeptical. For one thing, the survey didn't really say that gays represent only 1 percent of the population. It said that 1 percent of respondents reported their sexual behavior to be "exclusively homosexual." This was, then, a study not of orientation but of behavior. It didn't count celibate gays—who, in the age of AIDS, make up a large proportion of the gay population. It didn't count men who don't yet realize they're gay. It didn't count married gays and other closet cases. Nor did it count those gays (probably a majority) who, though certain of their own homosexuality, have at various times, in various circumstances, and for various reasons slept with women. Does the fact that they've slept with women mean they're not gay? No. It *does* mean that a lot of them would be unlikely to characterize their sexual histories as "exclusively homosexual" (odd phrase!) in a direct personal encounter with a researcher.

Which brings us to the matter of the survey sample. When most heterosexuals think of gays, they picture young men brashly proclaiming their homosexuality at ACT UP rallies and Gay Pride Day marches. But the typical gay man is in fact very discreet about his private life. Most of the gays I know don't even talk to some of their closest friends about bedroom matters; I can't imagine nine out of ten of them agreeing to participate in a sex survey, especially one that, like the Guttmacher study, involved "face-to-face" discussion with a stranger. (In a telephone survey by Louis Harris and Associates, the results of which were released only a week after the results of the Guttmacher Institute poll, 4.4 percent of American men said that they'd had homosexual sex in the previous five years.)

The respondent pool for sex surveys is almost certainly skewed, then, in favor of people who are inclined to boast about their sex lives and against those who have something they prefer to hide. And who in this society feels more compelled to hide the truth about his sex life than the average homosexual?

This is the sad irony at the heart of the whole question of how many homosexuals there are: because of homophobia, most gays don't feel free to be honest about themselves. Not at work, not with their friends and families—and not in a sex survey. As a result of their secretiveness, the results of such surveys are dramatically distorted. And the homophobes, whose bigotry is ultimately responsible for those distorted results, rejoice in them. The 1 percent figure, in short, is not a measure of the number of homosexuals; it is a measure of the degree of fear—the degree of closetedness—that still exists among us.

Let's assume, for the sake of argument, that gays do constitute 1 percent of the population. What would that say about the extraordinary number of gays who have made important contributions in the field of art and culture? Many who have assumed that gays constitute 10 percent of the population, after all, have long thought it remarkable that both the quintessential American poet, Walt Whitman, and the greatest American novelist, Henry James, should have been homosexual (though since James was probably a lifelong celibate and Whitman celibate most if not all his life, neither would have counted as gay in the Guttmacher study) and that, in this century and country alone, such major cultural figures as Samuel Barber, Aaron Copland, Virgil Thomson, Ned Rorem, Philip Johnson, James Merrill, Edmund White, Tennessee Williams, and Edward Albee should all happen to be gay. But if gays were only 1 percent, the gay contribution to civilization would be so lopsided as to suggest that there exists an extraordinary correlation between homosexuality and creative intelligence—so much so that parents, far from worrying that their children might be gay, should perhaps *want* them to be. (Somehow, though, one can't quite imagine Lou Sheldon or Bob Grant taking this line of argument.)

In any event, I submit that homosexuals have a far better sense of these things than homophobes do. The typical homophobe would be astonished to realize how many homosexuals he deals with in the course of a day. Unless they fit his stereotype, he won't recognize them as gay, and they certainly aren't going to announce their sexuality to him in the course of ringing up his groceries, cutting his hair, or repairing his car. Homosexuals, by contrast, recognize other homosexuals everywhere they go. My own experience, not only in New York City but in cities and towns around the United States and elsewhere, suggests to me that the 10-percent figure is about right. On a 1992 segment of *60 Minutes* a gay FBI agent estimated that one out of ten G-men is gay, and said that he'd known gay agents in all the field offices at which he'd worked. In a *New York Times* interview, Petty Officer Keith Meinhold, who was expelled by the Navy and reinstated by a judge in the landmark 1992–93 case, told a reporter that, paging through his Naval Academy yearbook, he could go from picture to picture pointing out gays: "1, 2, 3, 4, 5, 6, 7, 8, 9, gay." Of the thirty boys who lived on my thoroughly typical dormitory hall when I was a college freshman—the closest I've ever come to being part of a random sample—at least three were gay.

• • •

There is no other prejudice, moreover, whose adherents routinely deny that it is a prejudice. "Homophobia," someone wrote a few years back in the *American Spectator,* "is a word for which there is no referent." Now there's a thought to comfort a gay teenager when he's getting beaten up in the schoolyard!

We've all heard the argument: gays are not a "minority group" like Jews or blacks—or at least not a "legitimate" or "authentic" group. (Curiously, however, some who take this line routinely refer to gays as a "special-interest group.") Refusing to implement a curriculum that would teach tolerance of gay men and lesbians, Mary Cummins, the community school board president in Queens, New York, who initiated the Rainbow Curriculum protests, said: "I will not demean our legitimate minorities, such as blacks, Hispanics and Asians, by lumping them together with homosexuals in that curriculum." "Demean"? "Legitimate"? It's bizarre. Turn on the local news and you'll see the same people who relegate gays to a despised category by waving signs about "fags" and "homos" suddenly denying the very existence of that category. As long as the category is an object of mockery, apparently, people like Mary Cummins accept its existence; it is only when people in that category ask to be considered worthy of respect that a Mary Cummins refuses to acknowledge it as a category.

To pause in the midst of gay-bashing to insist that gays aren't a real group is, in effect, to say that in some sense gays aren't real people. Because that's what we're talking about here: not about some abstract moral precept or philosophical idea, or about this or that kind of sexual activity, or about whether it should be considered reasonable for certain members of the species to consider themselves connected to others on the basis of a particular shared attribute, but about *people*—individuals who are being discriminated against precisely because of a particular shared attribute. To quote Chuck Merino, the San Diego police officer who was dismissed from his position as a Boy Scout leader for being gay, "A lot of my concerns are for my rights and if that turns out to be gay rights, so be it."

In a way, of course, it's true that gays aren't a minority group in the same way as Jews or blacks. A Jew, as a rule, is brought up by Jews, grows up surrounded by Jewish relatives, is raised on Jewish culture. As he grows older, he gradually meets more gentiles and finds a place in the larger community while maintaining his Jewish family and cultural connections. A gay person, by contrast, typically grows up among heterosexuals. It is only after he discovers himself to be gay that he may make gay friends and discover the gay subculture, all the while reassessing his relationship to the mainstream culture of which he has considered himself a part. As with Jewishness or blackness, a gay person's homosexuality is almost invariably a key component of his identity, but the extent to which he feels himself to be a member of his "minority group" varies widely from individual to individual. Since most gays do not have gay parents or grow up with an exposure to gay culture, the deepest bond with other gays, for many a gay person, is the shared experience of homophobia. To walk into a gay bar, in other words, is to realize that everyone else in the place, whether black or white, young or old, rich or poor, fat or thin, has suffered in some way for being gay—has lost a job or apartment, has been physically assaulted by strangers or schoolmates, has been rejected by a parent or friend.

Gays exist as a group, then, largely because there is anti-gay prejudice. If gay relationships were taken for granted by everyone and accorded the same legal and moral status as heterosexual marriages, and if gay children were educated to be as comfortable with their sexuality as straight children and given courtship rituals comparable to those of straight children, much of what we think of as the "gay subculture" would disappear. Individual gays would still gravitate to each other because of sexual or romantic attraction, but there would be nothing to bind homosexuals together en masse in gay bars or restaurants, gay churches or synagogues, or Gay Studies programs. It is precisely because anti-gay prejudice does exist that some gays, in the interest of self-protection, plunge into the gay subculture, cling to their sexual identity, and (in some cases) accordingly become preoccupied with sex.

A word for which there is no referent? No heterosexual has any business making such a judgment, any more than a white person can say that there is no such thing as racism directed at blacks. The fact is that for the average gay person, sexual orientation is at least as important an element of individual identity as race or ethnicity or gender. When people call one a "faggot," one feels just as Jews feel when they are branded "kikes," or blacks "niggers," or Hispanics "spicks": one feels as if one is being attacked not for something that one has done but for a morally neutral attribute over which one has no control.

Not a real minority group? One could play that game with any group. What, after all, makes someone a Jew? Does he have to be religiously observant? What if his father wasn't Jewish? What if he has converted to—or from—another faith? The Old Testament lists numerous reasons—from incest to castration—why someone should no longer be considered a Jew. Should these reasons be taken into consideration? Different Jews would have different answers. And what constitutes an African-American? What if one is only half black? A quarter? A sixteenth? Where to draw the line? And what about Hispanics? Listen to the Mexican-American writer Richard Rodriguez: " 'Hispanic' is not a racial or a cultural or a geographic or a linguistic or an economic description. 'Hispanic' is a bureaucratic integer—a complete political fiction." The more one thinks about such matters, the more one thinks that homosexuality is among the purest of minority groups; at least the criteria for inclusion are clear.

My point here is not to question the legitimacy of any other group but to underscore the absurdity of the very concept of minority group legitimacy. One of the unfortunate facts of our time is that people are encouraged more and more to identify themselves in terms of categories—black or white, male or female, gay or straight. This is not a congenial trend, because an excessive focus on such categories tends to blind people both to their individual qualities and to the human concerns and characteristics that they share with others; at its most extreme, such thinking can lead to the commission of unspeakable atrocities—slavery, holocausts—which are seen as justified because the victims all belong to a specific despised group. History, indeed, teaches us that it is not the democrats but the bigots who, time and again, place special emphasis on the lines that separate people into groups. The aim of every truly democratic society should thus be to lessen the importance of these boundaries—to recognize that it is unfair to be prejudiced either for or against individuals simply because they happen to belong to a certain group. My point throughout this book, accordingly, is not that homosexuals deserve preferential treatment of any kind because they belong to a victim group, but rather that gay individuals do not deserve to have their lives, careers, and committed relationships treated differently from those of heterosexuals simply because they are gay.

• • •

Of all prejudices, homophobia is the only one whose spread has been fostered by a widespread belief that good Christian values require it. At the same time, deep-seated though it may be, it is the prejudice that can be most dramatically challenged by a personal exposure to the object of prejudice. Since gays *do* come from everywhere, from every kind of family in every corner of the world, most heterosexuals have their first close encounter with homosexuality when they discover that a friend or relative or co-worker—someone whom they already know and trust and care about, whom they might never have suspected of being "different," and whom they would not in a million years think of as the Other—is in fact gay. A white racist can't suddenly discover that his teenage child is black, but countless homophobic parents have suddenly discovered their teenage children to be gay. In such situations, something's got to give. Either the loved one is rejected, turned out of the house, the very mention of his name prohibited, or—as occurs, fortunately, in most cases—the hated Other instantly ceases to be an Other and the misconceptions on which bigotry is founded begin to crumble. Every time I see a congregation full of fundamentalists on TV applauding an anti-gay sermon, I think that sooner or later some of these people will be told by their sons or daughters: "I'm gay." Of this there's no doubt; it will happen. And their assumptions will be jolted. Their sense of gays as something entirely Other will be shaken. In order to maintain this notion of gays as the Other, some of these people will reject their children, perhaps even tell them, "You're dead to me. I have no child." More, after a period of adjustment, will come to understand and accept.

The ultimate enemy of anti-gay prejudice, then, is the truth—the truth that gays, who to many heterosexuals seem the most alien of Others, are in fact not by nature an Other at all. Rather, they are made into an Other by ill-informed prejudice—and are then despised for being that imagined Other. The reason for all these headlines about gays in the military, gays in the Boy Scouts, gays in the public-school curricula, and so forth is that, in the 1990s, gays are at last demanding in huge numbers that they be recognized as *not* being some exotic Other, unsuited to participate in established institutions. They want to lead open, ordinary middle-class lives, not lives in the closet or on the bohemian fringe. Yet people who claim to stand for the values that underlie those ordinary lives continue to do everything they can to prevent gays from leading such lives.

If levels of homophobia remain high, it is largely because there are still many heterosexuals who don't know (or who think they don't know) any gay people. To alter this state of affairs is by far the most important factor in eliminating anti-gay prejudice. And it has, fortunately, already begun to come to pass. As more gays have become more honest about their homosexuality, more heterosexual friends, relatives, and co-workers have rethought ill-informed prejudices. "Individual contact," Joseph Steffan writes, "is the most powerful weapon we have in the battle against homophobia, indeed, against all forms of prejudice. It is a battle that can only be won from the ground up. Simply knowing someone who is gay or lesbian . . . is the best way to overcome hatred." This is why both the gay subculture and the closet are, practically speaking, allies of homophobia. The subculture keeps gays largely segregated from the straight majority; the closet keeps their sexual orientation a secret. (Knowing someone who is gay or lesbian doesn't make a difference, after all, unless one knows that the person *is* gay or lesbian.)

Closeted homosexuals are right to criticize those subculture-oriented gays who through reckless political actions, fatuous public antics, or irresponsible stunts have helped to perpetuate offensive images of homosexuality. By the same token, though, if these closeted homosexuals make such criticisms, they have a responsibility to place themselves on the line, to help rectify those images, and to lend what they may see as their superior intelligence, self-control, and rationality to the cause. For such homosexuals simply to shrug nervously and say "It's best not to talk about these things" is scandalous; in these eight brief words is summed up the whole long, sad history of homosexuals' failure to win respect and vanquish stereotypes.

Most people who condemn homosexuals are not wicked. More often, they're uninformed. Not unintelligent—on the contrary, as I have said, they are often very intelligent—but uninformed. They may not be aware that they know any homosexuals, and consequently the word may conjure up for them a variety of strange, disturbing, but unrepresentative images. Or they may be insecure about their own sexual orientation, and thus may be rendered especially uncomfortable by any exposure to people who are openly gay. Or they may believe that to accord homosexuals full civil rights would be to attack the institution of marriage and invite social breakdown—an argument that is valid only if you assume that most husbands and fathers are suppressing powerful homosexual urges and that in a society where homosexuality did not pose so many difficulties they would be living with other men.

The opposition of many people to gay rights is built on a thorough misunderstanding of what homosexuality is and what gay rights would mean for society at large. During the 1992 election campaign, *USA Today* reported that Sandy Sumner, a young woman who campaigned door-to-door for Oregon's anti-gay measure, was convinced that "radical groups like Queer Nation represent most homosexuals, and that they want to take over schools and government." In the fall of 1992, the *New York Times* quoted a Brooklyn mother's complaint that New York City's proposed tolerance curriculum would teach her children that "if any man touches me and I'm a little boy, it's O.K., or if any woman touches me and I'm a little girl, it's O.K."

Where do people acquire such inaccurate ideas about what homosexuals want and about what the gay-rights movement seeks to accomplish? Often from propagandists like the Reverend Lou Sheldon, who said in September 1992 that the newly enacted California law banning anti-gay job discrimination would "protect sex with animals and the rape of children as forms of political expression." Certainly from Rush Limbaugh, who has said, among many other things, that allowing gays into the armed forces would lead to the founding of Queer Nation chapters on military bases. And also from people like *Washington Times* columnist Samuel Francis, who described gay Eagle Scout James Dale's attempt to rejoin the Scouts as part of a "culture war" on the part of homosexuals. "For some reason," Francis wrote, homosexuals "would like to go camping out in the woods along with the packs of adolescent boys who compose the Scouts, and for some other reason the Scouts just don't want them. I think I know the reasons in both cases, but I'll leave them to your imagination." In another column, Francis wrote:

> A "society" that makes no distinction between sex within marriage and sex outside it, that does not distinguish morally and socially between continence and debauchery, normality and perversion, love and lust, is not really a society but merely the chaos of a perpetual orgy.
>   It is . . . to just such an orgy that the proponents of normalized and

unrestricted homosexuality invite America. Maybe most Americans have reached the point at which they are ready to immerse themselves in the illusion that a perpetual orgy pretending to be a society really doesn't hurt anybody.

How many of Sheldon's followers, one wondered, would note his absurd equation of rape with consensual homosexual sex? How many of Limbaugh's viewers would understand that gays who go into the armed forces and gays who join Queer Nation are two very different kinds of people? And how many readers of Francis's remarks about the need to make distinctions would recognize that it was Francis who—by implicitly equating heterosexuality with love and continence and equating homosexuality with lust and orgies—was guilty of a refusal to make distinctions? For sexual orientation is one issue, sexual irresponsibility another; homosexuals are innately no less capable of falling in love and being faithful, and innately no more inclined to lewdness and promiscuity, than heterosexuals. Sheldon, Limbaugh, and Francis are not the only commentators who seek deliberately to equate homosexuality, in the public mind, with rape, radicalism, and raunchiness.

Many heterosexuals gripe that they're sick of hearing so much about homosexuality. In a twist on the famous line in which Lord Alfred Douglas described homosexuality as "the Love that dare not speak its name," some have complained in recent years that homosexuality has turned into "the love that won't shut up." During a recent talk-show confrontation about the subject, for example, a heterosexual man argued that for gays to talk about homosexuality constituted "straight-bashing." "After all," he said, "*I* don't go around talking about being straight!" Such a man simply doesn't realize how wrong he is, and how unfair. As Joseph Steffan has noted, "the public expression of heterosexuality is such an integral and basic part of our everyday lives that it goes unrecognized." The proper response to the man who complained of "straight-bashing" is that he "talks about" being straight all the time without realizing it. He does so every time he mentions his wife, every time he tells a joke about marriage, every time he banters playfully with a waitress or female secretary. Indeed, from the homosexual point of view, "the love that won't shut up" is heterosexuality; and the major reason why anti-gay prejudice endures, I think, is that homosexuality,

despite all the discussion of it that has taken place on certain issues-
oriented TV and radio shows, maintains an extremely low profile in both
popular culture and everyday life.

Though the average American married couple may, in other words,
hear a good deal of talk about homosexuality in an abstract and general
sense, openly homosexual individuals are not an everyday part of their
life. They are not accustomed to meeting gay couples at church or the
P.T.A. It is likely that at least one of the couple's not-too-distant relatives
is gay, but that relative's homosexuality is likely to be as long absent
from the realm of family conversation as the relative himself has been
absent from family gatherings. Nor is the couple used to seeing gays
as characters on TV sitcoms or dramas (unless tolerance of homosexuality is itself the theme of a specific episode). Indeed, gays continue
to be depicted so rarely in mainstream movies and TV series that when
one such character does appear on *Melrose Place* or *Roseanne,* gay
periodicals treat it as a major event. While heterosexual celebrities talk
freely with Jay Leno or David Letterman about their romances or marriages, moreover, the overwhelming majority of homosexuals in public
life keep their sexual identity entirely under wraps.

If you're straight and you can't quite understand what I'm talking
about, take a look sometime at a rerun of the old *Andy Griffith* show.
If you're white, try to imagine what it's like being a black person watching the same show. Think of it: a North Carolina town with no blacks
whatsoever. None. Where are they? White viewers (especially non-
Southerners) might not even notice the omission. But to a black person,
at first sight, it must be stunning. What, many a black viewer must have
wondered when he or she first saw the series, is this program saying
about me? Well, that's what it's like being a gay man and watching
virtually every TV drama and comedy. The assumption is always that
every man is attracted only to women, that every teenage boy lusts after
teenage girls.

Homosexuality is, of course, a staple of shows like *Donahue* and
Oprah—and gays owe much to the vigorous and articulate support of
Phil Donahue, in particular, for gay rights. Yet while the conspicuous-
ness of gays on programs like *Donahue* has in one respect been a very
good thing, it has in another respect not been a blessing for homosexuals
(or anyone), since a disproportionate number of the gays who appear
on such programs tend to be highly politicized or to be people who (like

many of these programs' heterosexual guests) want the world to know that they are sexually obsessed or promiscuous or kinky. Too often, the image of homosexuality communicated to the general public by such talk-show guests is sensational, counterproductive, and extremely misleading. For too many viewers of these shows, homosexuality comes off not as an integral part of everyday reality but as the stuff of scandal, an excuse for freak shows, arguments, pietistic moralizing, and titillating revelations. (To quote a recent promotional announcement: "Is your husband secretly gay? Next *Oprah*.") Such shows reinforce the idea of homosexuality as something to argue about and worry about, as opposed to something to think about and learn about: it becomes a hot political issue, something with two inflexible opposing sides, rather than a matter on which people might reach a common understanding if only long-standing misconceptions and baseless mistrust were eliminated.

Indeed, it often seems as if the producers of these shows have deliberately booked the most extreme people they could find on both sides of the issue—however small their constituencies and however discredited their arguments—and have thus, incidentally, helped to build lucrative public careers for irresponsible people. (One show, for example, featured a spokesman for the "Exodus Ex-Gay Ministries," which claimed to be able to turn homosexuals into heterosexuals—something that simply cannot be done.) The revealing fact is that when Donahue and Oprah cover themes other than homosexuality—for example, infidelity or family conflicts or health issues—openly gay individuals are rarely, and gay couples virtually never, included. The shows don't reflect the reality of homosexuals as people who have interests and problems like everyone else and whose lives are not entirely about being gay. Ultimately, in short, these series reinforce the notion that homosexuality is not a part of the social fabric but an isolating, alienating trait.

There are, to be sure, scattered exceptions to the rule of gay invisibility on TV and in the movies. There was, of course, *Longtime Companion*. The year 1993, moreover, saw the production of at least three potentially important projects: *Philadelphia,* which was touted as "the first big-budget Hollywood movie on homophobia"; *And the Band Played On,* an HBO miniseries adaptation of Randy Shilts's book about the AIDS crisis; and *Tales of the City,* the first TV miniseries to focus largely on gay life. (Like David Leavitt's gay novel *The Lost Language of Cranes,* which became a 1991 TV movie, *Tales of the City* scared off American pro-

ducers with its gay content and is being adapted for British television.)
Yet it remained to be seen what form these dramas would take and what
sort of impact they would have.

Surely most of the exceptions to the rule of gay invisibility on TV and
in the movies give gays little to cheer about. The occasional gay-themed
PBS program routinely looks at homosexuality through the single window of the subculture, and thereby serves only to reinforce mainstream
stereotypes and prejudices. On local news programs where the homosexuality of hero cops or firemen or celebrity interviewees is routinely
avoided, the subject of homosexuality tends to come up only in stories
about AIDS and gay-rights issues or when someone—a priest, day-care
worker, or scoutmaster—is accused of sexually abusing boys. (This practice of breaking the silence on homosexuality only to cover sex crimes
tends, of course, to obscure the fact that homosexuals are no more likely
than heterosexuals to sexually abuse children.)

As I've mentioned, prime-time shows like *Roseanne* and *Melrose Place*
have included gay characters—but these aren't *major* characters, portrayed fully enough so that viewers can feel involved in their lives; rather,
they are invariably peripheral, placed in the background in self-con-
scious gestures of tolerance and diversity on the part of the producers.
Yes, *One Life to Live* offered that admirable story line about a gay teenager's coming out—but it didn't dare to give the clean-cut, wholesome-
looking young man an actual boyfriend. For a while it seemed that every
other episode of *The Golden Girls* was about some friend or relative of
one of the girls who turned out to be gay—an obvious attempt on the
part of the show's producers to teach their audience a lesson in acceptance. But the episodes in question invariably treated homosexuality as
an issue, and reinforced the idea that gay people never do anything
except have sex and talk about being gay. Watching such programs, one
could understand why some people say they get sick of hearing about
homosexuality. And one could not help reflecting that the first sign of
real change will be when TV series have regular homosexual characters
(not marginal ones) who have actual romantic relationships, who talk
about something other than homosexuality, and whose family and work
lives are treated in the same way as those of straight characters.

The most striking fact about anti-gay prejudice in America is not that
it has endured for so long; it is that Americans who disapprove of homo-

sexuality have refused to face the deep contradictions inherent in their attitudes. But of course doing so would involve *thinking* about those attitudes, and homosexuality is something that many people simply don't want to think about.

For many, these attitudes seem to come terribly easily. Most people who engage in anti-gay rhetoric, while claiming to speak from profound religious or moral conviction, haven't put much serious thought into their censures. The widely held view of homosexuality as "wrong" is not unlike antebellum Southern whites' notion that slavery was morally defensible: both attitudes are long-established, socially entrenched, taken for granted. One would think that any Christian halfway sincere in his religious beliefs—which demand of him that, above all else, he love and not hate—would be anguished at the thought of having to condemn millions of people for their sexual orientation. One would think that such a person might examine the relevant scripture in order to see if there was some basis for acceptance instead of condemnation; one would think he might read a book like John Boswell's *Christianity, Social Tolerance, and Homosexuality* in order to understand how it is that many good, intelligent people, straight and gay alike, sincerely see no contradiction between homosexual life and Christian belief. But such serious reflection and soul searching on the topic of homosexuality appear to take place far less often than they should. On the contrary, when it comes to discussions of the moral dimension of homosexuality, illogic, closed-mindedness, and the reiteration of age-old formulas are the order of the day.

What underlies most of this prejudice? Opponents of homosexuality use different words. They contend variously that they find it "evil," "wrong," "sick." "Evil" is a religious person's verdict; "wrong" is a secular person's verdict; "sick" is the verdict of a person with pretensions to psychological expertise. Each verdict is the result of someone reaching for the nearest available term to label, and to damn, something that confuses him or makes him uncomfortable.

What can someone mean when he says that "homosexuality is wrong"? That to be born homosexual makes one automatically a malefactor? Or could it be that the crime lies in accepting one's sexuality and in trying to lead a loving and committed life with another human being? Or does the crime not begin until your hands touch? Your lips? Your genitalia? Moreover, if homosexuality is wrong, who is wronged by it—the homosexual person? Society in general? Young people who are in danger of being "recruited"? Do these questions sound frivolous? They're not. What's frivolous is to state unequivocally that homosexuality is "wrong" without asking oneself such questions and figuring out exactly what one means.

And what of the argument that homosexuality is not wrong but "sick"—a psychological disorder? This popular view is expressed by one D. L. Forston, M.D., of Gary, Indiana, who in a letter to *The New Republic* argues that "the depression, mental illness and substance abuse associated with the lifestyle cannot be fully accounted for by reaction to societal isolation and hostility. In short, homosexuality is a personality disorder at best and a mental illness at worst." "Cannot be fully accounted for"? How can Dr. Forston possibly know this? He obviously has no idea what most homosexuals have to go through day by day in the way of inadvertent reminders that they are considered evil, depraved, emotionally disturbed, or just plain anomalous. Dr. Forston's views notwithstanding, it has for many years seemed remarkable to me that, given these daily assaults, there aren't *more* gay alcoholics and depressives and so on.

Of course, if one considers homosexuality a personality disorder or mental illness, then every homosexual is by definition an emotional cripple, however sane and stable he may be in comparison to the average heterosexual. But to make such a blanket diagnosis is preposterous. Medical science has always classified psychological phenomena as disorders, rather than as mere variations, on the basis of their consequences in the real world. In other words, a given psychological phenomenon cannot be objectively classified as a disorder unless it gives rise, of itself, to some sort of maladjustment. A generation and more ago, in a time when one could not even go to a gay bar without fear of arrest, homosexuals suffered severe neuroses—or even psychoses—at a rate higher than they do now and manifested higher rates of alcoholism, drug addiction, and suicide. They suffered these problems not because they were gay but because they had been raised to think that homosexuality was an abomination, because they had to live with the knowledge that virtually everyone around them considered them morally corrupt, and because the fear of ostracism, denunciation, and imprisonment forced them to keep their sexual orientation a secret. Only the most uncommon individuals could live with perfect sanity and serenity under such circumstances; most could not. So it was that psychiatrists designated homosexuality as a psychological disorder.

The almost universal opprobrium with which homosexuals once lived has not entirely dissipated. Yet homosexuals are now permitted to live more openly and with less fear of persecution, and are accordingly more productive and more emotionally balanced than ever before. It is clear that self-respecting homosexuals who live openly among accepting people have no more problems or different problems than anyone else; in an accepting society, they can lead lives that are, in every respect but sexual orientation, indistinguishable from the lives of heterosexuals. This is not true of schizophrenics, psychotics, and other people classified as suffering from psychological disorders. Such people suffer real problems of adjustment that are caused entirely by their psychological disorders and that could not be avoided by any modifications in social attitudes or behavior. Given this simple practical fact, to label homosexuality a "sickness" or a "psychological disorder" is simply name calling—an attempt to pigeonhole and patronize something that the pigeonholer may well find threatening for reasons having to do with his own psychological problems. Certainly if homosexuality were a psychological disorder, it would have to be considered a unique one: for the "sufferers" who experience the greatest emotional health are those who confidently reject the idea that it is a psychological disorder, while the greatest psychological damage is suffered by those homosexuals who have allowed themselves to be persuaded that they're suffering from a sickness.

Some people compare homosexuality to various addictions. Commenting on the gay-tolerance lessons in New York City's proposed Rainbow Curriculum, a local school board member told a TV news reporter: "We have a number of children in the school system whose parents are crack addicts. Are we supposed to tell them that that's OK? It might make them feel better but I don't think it's prudent." Similarly, in response to a *New York Times* editorial favoring tolerance of homosexuality, David Blankenhorn, the president of the Institute for American Values, wrote:

> You remind us that tolerance is an important social value. Yes, but you also imply that tolerance is a synonym for approval. As a nonsmoker, I tolerate smoking. But I do not approve of it. Even less do I believe

that the public school system should teach my child that smoking and nonsmoking are equally praiseworthy.

Tolerance is not the only important value in life. Other values, such as the value of a child receiving the love of both a mother and a father, are also important. You reduce the issue to a false polarization: accept all possible family forms as morally equivalent or incur the accusation of intolerance.

Is tolerance always our society's highest-order value? Is there any circumstance in which society might have a legitimate stake in promoting certain behaviors while discouraging other behaviors? Your reflections on tolerance come across as simplistic moralizing.

The addiction most often compared to homosexuality is alcoholism. In a letter to *Newsweek*, Peter B. Langmuir of New Haven, Connecticut, wrote that "describing homosexuality as an acceptable alternative lifestyle is like encouraging the alcoholic to return to the bottle." The same comparison appears in an article by George W. Barger, a canon at Trinity Cathedral in Omaha, who considers himself to be motivated by compassion and generosity toward gays. "Despite our best efforts," writes Canon Barger, whose essay represents a typical ecclesiastical approach to the subject, "we don't know much about the developmental sequence of either [alcoholism or homosexuality]. . . . The socio-biological roots of homosexuality are obscure. Shall we label it a simple moral perversity? Is it best understood as an alternative lifestyle for a rather small percentage of persons?" As with alcoholism, Canon Barger suggests that further study is in order and points to alcohol rehabilitation programs as a model for dealing with homosexuals. "Why wouldn't something similar be a step forward in the homosexuality debate? The non-judgmental framework, the willingness to accept the personhood of the other despite personal moral misgivings, surely commend themselves. On the other hand, it would be equally legitimate to raise questions about ordination of practicing homosexuals, or the blessing of same-sex relationships."

Though his intentions may be virtuous, Canon Barger's essay is essentially a political document; he is interested less in promoting understanding between human beings than in achieving compromise between factions. What moral difference, after all, do the "developmental sequence" and "socio-biological roots" of homosexuality make? Is Canon Barger suggesting that homosexuality is or may be morally offensive in some way, and that a fuller scientific accounting of its origin might either mitigate its immorality or help us to decide whether it is indeed immoral? This proposition itself seems highly dubious in moral terms. Would any neurological discovery make Saddam Hussein less evil?

And what is one to make of Canon Barger's mention of alcohol rehabilitation? To rehabilitate has two possible meanings in this context. It can mean "to restore to a former capacity"; but the word could not apply in this sense to homosexuals, for no true homosexual was ever anything other than homosexual. Or it can mean "to restore to a condition of health or useful and constructive activity"; but experience has shown that the most healthful, useful, and constructive thing for homosexuals to do, as far as their sexual orientation is concerned, is to be honest about it with themselves and others. As for the blessing of same-sex relationships, priests routinely bless all sorts of things other than heterosexual marriages—including houses, cars, pets, Saint Patrick's Day parades, and the work of clubs and committees. Why, then, should it be considered outrageous to bless a loving relationship between two Christians?

These four men—Langmuir, Blankenhorn, Barger, and the New York school board member—all have something in common. When they think of homosexual people, they think immediately of sexual behavior. That's what homosexuality is to them: a kind of behavior that is deviant, disturbing, undesirable. But homosexuality is not something you do; it's something you *are*. To compare it to substance abuse or addiction is to suggest that, just as alcoholics are better off without alcohol and smokers better off without cigarettes, homosexuals are better off without homosexual behavior. To imply such a thing is to denigrate the importance in life of devoted, loving relationships. This implication is especially astonishing coming from a clergyman like Canon Barger or from a man who claims, as David Blankenhorn does, to care intensely about children's psychological development. Can such people not understand how callous it is to equate a committed human relationship to something like crack addiction, chain smoking, or alcoholism?

If words like "sick" and "wrong" are often used to put homosexuals in their place, the words "homosexual" and "gay" themselves are often the principal stumbling block for some people. There are parents, after all, who can deal with the fact that their son will never marry, that he lives with another young man to whom he is very close, and even that the two of them share a car, a checking account, and a bed. What bothers the parents more than any of these things are the words "gay" and "homosexual"—powerful words that seem, for them, to turn the acceptable and familiar into the strange and stigmatized. Even some homosexuals don't feel comfortable with these words and prefer not to use them, saying that they "hate labels." Well, I hate labels too, but to reject a label is as unhealthy as to cling to it obsessively; both are ways of limiting oneself. The only reasonable thing to do is to accept the label, figure out its place in one's life, and put it there.

This is complex and, for many, uncomfortable psychological territory. F. Scott Fitzgerald once remarked in a letter that the "fairies" had ruined everything for relations between men—the idea apparently being that he could enjoy an intimate friendship with another man, perhaps even involving homosexual sex, if only there weren't all these sissies around, and all these words like "fairies," to make him feel that doing such a thing was over the line. Such thinking is observed frequently in the lives of men who fall in love with other men and enjoy sexual relations with them but simply can't call the attachment by its proper name. Recalling his youth, the narrator of Edmund White's novel *A Boy's Own Story* says, "What I wanted was to be loved by men and to love them back but not to be a homosexual." In a recent issue of *The Village Voice*, several personal advertisements under the category "Men Seeking Men" specified: "No gays." It was remarkable: though each of the men who placed these ads recognized his own intense need for an intimate physical relationship with another man, none could bring himself to acknowledge that these desires made him and his prospective partner gay. In this connection one thinks of the longtime FBI chief J. Edgar Hoover and his best friend, housemate, and second-in-command, Clyde Tolson, who, whatever did or did not take place between them in the bedroom, were patently a homosexual couple. It's conceivable that Hoover and Tolson were thoroughly sincere in their vilification of homosexuals, who of course, when discovered in the ranks of the FBI, were drummed out unmercifully; it may simply be that they put a different name to what they were—and to what they were to each other.

Then there's the late entertainer Liberace, whose fans tended to be middle-aged middle-American middlebrows—the sort of people whom one might expect to be homophobic in large numbers. Liberace was the most obviously gay celebrity of his time, yet even when he was dying of AIDS he didn't dare to acknowledge either his homosexuality or the nature of his illness for fear that he'd lose a lot of fans. And he probably would have. What he recognized is that certain fans don't mind a celebrity's homosexuality; they just don't want him to acknowledge it. Why? Because if he doesn't acknowledge it, they don't have to think about it; they don't have to confront the fact that someone they admire is gay. The story of Liberace's life and death is a pathetic illustration of the fact that, in an age when there seems to be an insatiable public appetite for the details of heterosexual celebrities' love lives, there exists between many a gay celebrity and his fans an unwritten contract that demands, as the price for fame, his absolute silence on the subject of his sexual orientation.

Time and again, in fact, it seems as if homosexuals are punished not for being gay but for telling the truth about it. There must be hundreds of thousands of gay Boy Scouts, gay servicemen and women, and gay clerics, but the ones whom the system has tended to penalize are the handful who have the most integrity—the ones who answer truthfully when asked if they're gay. Instead of being held up to their peers as models of probity and courage, they're ousted.

It's a grotesque paradox: certain people who happen to have been born gay want to be foursquare pillars of our society—Scouts, soldiers, clergymen. But they can't, unless they lie about their homosexuality. Those who most vigorously reject their right to fill those roles are people who distribute, as anti-gay propaganda, the most outrageous videotapes they can find of homosexuals publicly disporting themselves in drag, say, or in leather jockstraps. These propagandists want heterosexuals to think that all gays behave in such a fashion. The best argument against them would be to show videotapes of actual gay soldiers and gay Scouts. But thanks to those propagandists' efforts, that's not possible. Gays who are a part of these institutions are obliged to lie low. So it is that while those gays whom the average American would find the most outrageous are also the most visible, those whom he might identify with and find admirable are, for the most part, forced from view.

"What gays do in the privacy of their bedrooms is their own business," people say. "I just don't like when they flaunt it." The problem with this kind of thinking—which was codified recently in the so-called "don't ask, don't tell" compromise on gays in the military—is that no real relationship, gay or straight, exists only in the privacy of a bedroom. If it does, it isn't a relationship; it's just sex. Public conduct that, if exhibited by heterosexuals, would be considered inoffensive, if not downright charming—for example, kissing hello or goodbye, hand holding, walking down a sidewalk too close together—is, in the case of homosexuals, often denounced as "flaunting." What heterosexuals don't realize when they view homosexuality as a matter of the "privacy of the bedroom" and balk at any public display of homosexual affection or public acknowledgment of gay relationships is that, in taking such views, they only help to discourage committed gay relationships and to encourage homosexuals to lead personal lives consisting of one-night stands.

The prevalence of this "go ahead and be gay, I just don't want to see it or hear about it" attitude can hardly be overstated. Indeed, when people criticize homosexuality as "wrong" or "sick" or "abnormal," in most cases it would be closer to the psychological truth of the situation to say simply that the very sight of an openly gay couple on the street makes those people uncomfortable. There are two possible reasons why a person might feel such discomfort. One is utter incomprehension: he can't understand how other human beings could have such feelings, could experience such attractions; the idea is so foreign to him that he finds it frightening, threatening, repulsive. The other is identification: he has experienced homosexual attraction himself and fears that he may be gay, and it is *this* idea that he finds frightening, threatening, repulsive. The truth, of course, is that most straight men have been attracted at some time in their lives to other males (just as most gay men are occasionally attracted to women), but so incapable are some men of acknowledging such facts to themselves that they feel uneasy at the mere mention of homosexuality and, out of fear of the sensual element of any intense human attachment, may even shrink from close friendships with other men.

Whatever the reason for a given person's discomfort with homosexuality, however, it is in many cases the discomfort itself that comes first, and the carefully worked-out rationalization for prejudice that follows. P. J. O'Rourke's aforementioned essay "Manhattan Swish" offers a good example of this process at work. The picture that emerges from

O'Rourke's essay is not that of a writer who is sincerely distressed by what he views as the immorality of homosexual behavior, but that of a writer with schoolyard prejudices and insecurities who is casting about for a plausible-sounding justification for them. That there are gay conservatives who are respected and befriended by fellow conservatives so long as they keep their sexuality close to the vest only goes to show that most conservatives don't *really* see homosexuality as evil. Rather, as my editor Jozef told me in that phone call years ago, it's something they don't care for, something they'd prefer not to think too much about, something they'd rather keep out of sight.

In a 1992 interview between ABC reporter Stone Phillips and then-President Bush, there was the following exchange, which followed a discussion of how the President would deal with a granddaughter who wanted an abortion:

Q. There are some who feel that the phrase "family values" is a kind of code and an indirect condemnation of people who choose different life styles, like homosexuals. Let me ask you this. If in a few years another of your grandchildren came to you, boy or girl, and said I'm gay, what would you say?
A. I'd love that child. I would put my arm around him and I would hope he wouldn't go out and try to convince people that this was the normal life style, that this was appropriate life style, that this was the way it ought to be. But I, I—you know, for me, I think the Bible teaches compassion and love. But I would say I hope you wouldn't become an advocate for a life style that in my view is not normal, and proposes marriages, same sex marriages is a, is a normal way of life. I'm don't— I'm not—I don't favor that.
Q. But would you be accepting—
A. But I would love that child.
Q. Would you be accepting?
A. Accepting in what sense?
Q. Accepting of the life style that they would go on to lead?
A. Well, as I say, I would love that, I would love that person. And there's a difference between approving every step of the way and loving and treating with compassion. And it's clear to me that the latter is what I'd want to do, and I wouldn't, I wouldn't—you know—condone necessarily of something that I felt—that I felt was, was not right.

First of all, the terms used by Stone Phillips are ill-chosen. He shouldn't have used the word "lifestyle" in referring to homosexuality (there is as wide a variety of "lifestyles" among homosexuals as among heterosexuals) or characterized homosexuality as something that people "choose" (since homosexuality is not a matter of choice). As for Bush's remarks, their inconsistency and confusion typify the way many sophisticated people view homosexuality—people, that is, who are too intelligent and sympathetic to denounce homosexuals unequivocally but who are too uptight (or too afraid, perhaps, of seeming unmanly or morally lax) not to disapprove. What sense, after all, does it make to say in the first part of a sentence that one would have "compassion" for a gay grandson, presumably because one understands that his homosexuality is something that he has come by naturally and can't change, and add in the next part of the sentence that one would tell him that one hoped he wouldn't go around "advocating" homosexuality, as if it were something that people could take up voluntarily and deliberately impart to others? What kind of grandfather, on being told by a grandson of his homosexuality, would say such a thing to him? President Bush says that such a "lifestyle" is not "the normal life style . . . the appropriate life style . . . the way it ought to be." What on earth is the usefulness of introducing the concept of normality into a discussion of a grandson's homosexuality, except as something with which to hurt the young man, to make him feel there's something wrong with him? This is most certainly the *last* thing one should do when dealing with a young person who has just begun coming to terms with his homosexuality. As for Bush's remark about homosexuality not being "appropriate," to discover one's homosexuality is, on the contrary, to recognize that appropriateness is an individual matter, that what is appropriate for other people is not necessarily appropriate for oneself, and that, in one's own case, living as a homosexual is precisely what *is* "appropriate." Perhaps being homosexual is not "the way it ought to be" as one's parents or friends may see it, but in one's heart one knows that it is "the way it ought to be" for oneself, and the brave and proper thing to do, under such circumstances, is to accept oneself honestly and to live and love with honor. Bush's remarks, which reflect the attitudes of millions of generally decent people, reflect a refusal, conscious or unconscious, to give serious moral thought to the subject of homosexuality, a refusal to attempt to see it for what it is and what it is not.

There are two general views on homosexuality that are internally consistent—only one of which is consistent with the facts. One is the view that homosexuality is an immoral choice that all ethical individuals must deplore and that can be spoken of reasonably as having "advocates" who corrupt youth by "recruiting" them. The other is the view that homosexuality is a morally neutral condition to which certain people are born and into which the notion of advocacy or recruitment simply does not enter. But Bush and millions of others insist on viewing homosexuality simultaneously as (1) something immoral that can be advocated and (2) a condition that comes naturally to some people and on account of which one should feel compassion.

What is this, by the way, about "compassion"? The word crops up often in discussions of homosexuality. Gays, according to the 1992 Vatican document on homosexuality, "do not choose their homosexual condition . . . for most of them, it is an ordeal. They should be treated with respect, compassion and sensitivity." Respect and sensitivity, yes. But most gays do not want "compassion," at least not in the sense of pity. To be gay is not, after all, to suffer from a disease or a disfigurement. If gays should be pitied for any reason, it is because they are forced to contend daily with prejudice and the adjustment problems that many suffer as a long-term consequence of homophobic upbringings. It is precisely that prejudice and those kinds of upbringings—for both of which, one might add, the current teachings of the Vatican are in no small way responsible—that can make homosexuality an "ordeal."

What kind of compassion is it, in any event, that leaves the object of compassion no means of living honorably with his situation other than that of leading a tortured, empty, loveless life? In the view of someone like George Bush, for a homosexual to be promiscuous is anathema; for a homosexual to set up house with someone else of the same sex is to mock the idea of marriage. Omit these options for a homosexual, and all that's left are (1) heterosexual marriage and (2) lifelong celibacy. As to the former, any intelligent, sensitive person who has ever seen such unions in real life knows that they are the *real* mockery of marriage. As to the latter, the Roman Catholic Church and many Protestant denominations insist upon lifelong celibacy for homosexuals, but gay Christians simply cannot conceive of a God who would bless them with the ability to love and yet demand that they spend their lives alone.

In a time when the arguments for homosexuality as "wrong" or "sick" or "unnatural" sound increasingly antiquated and ignorant and pose a risk of turning tolerant-minded readers and viewers and voters against whoever is propounding them, there has developed in the conservative press and among some conservative politicians a veritable politico-literary genre consisting of attempts to establish new, reasonable-sounding justifications for an opposition to homosexuality and/or to gay rights. The arguments are generally characterized by an attempt to sound open-minded and in touch with the contemporary world, and often feature references to the author's "gay friends" and to his anguish over having to take such a position, which (we are meant to understand) he presumably feels forced into by moral, practical, and/or philosophical considerations. Yet these arguments invariably embody inane contradictions. Such an "enlightened" argument appears in "Straight Talk about Gays," a 1992 *Commentary* article by E.L. Pattullo, a retired Harvard psychology professor. Acknowledging that most people are by nature either heterosexual or homosexual, Pattullo posits the existence of adult "waverers" who might yet develop in either direction and who can be turned homosexual by "temptation." He opposes gay equal rights—or, as he puts it, defends the perpetuation of "legal and social distinctions between straights and gays"—by arguing that those "distinctions" serve to check waverers' temptations and to drive them firmly into the heterosexual camp, thus serving society's "interest both in reproducing itself and in strengthening the institution of the family" and parents' "interest in reducing the risk that their children will become homosexual." After all, he says, "in a wholly nondiscriminatory world, the advantages of heterosexuality would not be so obvious."

This argument is multiply flawed. First, to concede (as Pattullo does) that individuals who happen to be gay have done nothing thereby to deserve second-class status, and then to defend that status on any grounds whatsoever, is morally insupportable in a democratic society. Second, the only objective reason why heterosexuality should be considered preferable to homosexuality is that heterosexuals aren't the target of those oppressive "legal and social distinctions." Third, it is absurd to suggest that society's ability to "reproduc[e] itself" depends on coercing into marriage and parenthood people who, freed from legal and social constraints, would live in same-sex relationships. Fourth, while it may well have an environmental component, the great majority of psychiatrists agree that sexual orientation is certainly fixed by early childhood (if not by birth), long before Pattullo's "legal and social distinctions" could have the coercive effect he desires. Fifth, Pattullo's remarks on "temptation" defy logic. Sexual orientation is defined by urges, not actions; a man who is more tempted by homosexuality than heterosexuality *is* a homosexual. Even if a few people remained on the fence into adolescence or young adulthood, the present "legal and social distinctions" would not affect their ultimate orientation: such "distinctions" don't alter sexual urges, they only foster sexual neurosis.

Sixth, Pattullo defends his "waverer" category by pointing out that many adults have had sex with members of both sexes. This does not, however, mean that such people have "a capacity for becoming either straight or gay." What it means is that (a) in certain situations—military school, prison, long naval voyages—heterosexuals deprived of opposite-sex contact resort temporarily to same-sex intercourse; (b) in an atmosphere of oppressive "legal and social distinctions," many gays deny or seek to change their homosexuality by engaging in heterosexual relationships; and (c) a small minority of people are genuinely bisexual. They are not "waverers" in Pattullo's sense, because they are not potentially either straight or gay: they are and always will be attracted to both sexes in roughly equal measure, and would fare best psychologically in a society in which they could settle down with whomever they loved, male or female, without feeling socially or legally pressured in either direction.

What is most offensive about Pattullo's argument is not what he says but what he does not say. For there *is* a borderland between the straight-forwardly gay and the unequivocally straight with which we should be concerned but which Pattullo doesn't even take into account. Homosexuals often encounter inhabitants of this borderland. Any reasonably attractive gay man knows what it is like to be stared at with anxious longing by a dubious young daddy pushing a pram, or to drop into a gay bar after work and find himself the object of lewd, desperate overtures by a weepy, bibulous middle-aged husband. Are these men "waverers"? No; they're homosexuals who have been driven by "legal and social distinctions" into playing it straight. Is this a good thing, for them or anybody? No. They're living a lie, condemning themselves to remorse, frustration, and loneliness, and (in pathetic attempts to conform to legally and socially sanctioned notions of "the family") creating households that are perched on the edge of disaster.

Some keep up the act forever. Many eventually crack. Recently, after twenty years of marriage, a friend of mine with several children was told by her husband that he's gay, that he'd been struggling against this fact and keeping silent about it all his life, and that he could no longer endure the guilt and alienation. The only segment of society to profit from his prolonged suppression has been the psychology profession: the entire family is now in therapy.

It is in the lives of families like this, whose situation is far more common than most heterosexuals realize, that one can observe some of the effects of Pattullo's "legal and social distinctions." We can thank those "distinctions," too, for the extremely high suicide rate among gay teenagers and for the number of adolescent males from the South and Midwest who, rejected by their parents for being gay, nightly hawk their sexual services to married men down the block from my midtown Manhattan apartment.

It is irresponsible of Pattullo, then, in discussing the inequities visited upon homosexuals, to invoke the conjectural interests of the "institution of the family" while ignoring the circumstances of actual families. It is cruel of him to defend those inequities by making unrealistic claims about their containment of homosexuality while disregarding the profound, often deadly damage that those inequities cause in the lives of countless very real people. And it is outrageous of him to reinforce the myth that parents can reduce "the risk that their children will become homosexual." Above all, what parents must be helped to understand is that they *cannot* reduce this "risk." What they *can* reduce dramatically, however, by raising their children not to draw oppressive "distinctions" between straight and gay, is the risk that those children, if they do discover themselves to be gay, will despise the idea so much as to be incapable of facing it honestly and living with it responsibly.

Many homophobes routinely claim that homosexuals want "special privileges" and seek to engage in "social engineering." Yet Pattullo's defense of "legal and social distinctions" between gay and straight, the purpose of which is to cajole young people into being straight, makes it clear that it's not gay rights but institutionalized prejudice against gays that amounts to social engineering and that what he opposes is not "special privileges" of any kind but equal treatment. In his published comments on the many responses to his *Commentary* article, Pattullo reiterates his support for the institutionalization of *"straights' bias in*

favor of heterosexuality" (Pattullo's italics), his support for the place-
ment of "greater value on the straight life than on the gay one," and his
disapproval of the fact that "gay political leaders . . . now wish to use the
law to force public and private institutions to treat gays *exactly* as they
treat straights." Read that carefully: what Pattullo believes is that certain
individuals should be denied equal rights and that their lives should be
valued less on account of their sexual orientation.

In the last paragraph of his further comments, moreover, Pattullo's
distinction between admitted gays and those "who reject their gay in-
clinations" and whom "I have chosen to call waverers" makes it clear
that when he speaks of "waverers" he is speaking of homosexuals who
refuse to accept their homosexuality. To him, one gathers, a homosexual
is not *really* a homosexual until he acknowledges himself to be a homosexual; and instead of recognizing that a person's refusal to make such
an acknowledgment is essentially an act of fear, Pattullo characterizes
it as well-nigh heroic. Indeed, his comments suggest that he sees open
homosexuals not as people who have bravely faced up to the reality of
their lives and whose sense of morality compels them to be honest about
it, but as emotional weaklings who have succumbed to a temptation and
whose openness is vulgar and self-indulgent; by the same token, he
appears to view his "waverers" not as people who haven't worked up the
nerve to confront the truth about themselves but as heroes who have
valiantly struggled against a loathsome temptation. By imposing conventional moral postulates and outdated psychological concepts on the
subject of homosexuality, he makes it clear that he is essentially blind
to its real moral and psychological dimensions.

Pattullo concludes his comments by saying that "the spectacle of a
child growing up gay when he might have been straight is little short
of tragic." Tragic? The "tragedy" here, of course, exists entirely in Pattullo's mind, just as the "tragedy" of a racial intermarriage exists entirely
in the mind of the third-party observer who opposes miscegenation; the
actual lives and feelings of the parties involved don't influence the verdict. To Pattullo, in short, the important thing about the miserable,
profoundly neurotic closeted gay man with a wife and children is that
as far as the world is concerned he's *straight,* thank goodness; and the
important thing about the happy, well-adjusted openly gay man with a
loving, fulfilling relationship is that he's *gay,* poor thing. Tragic? The
real tragedy is that men who, but for the Pattullos of the world, might

have been happy, well-adjusted homosexuals grow instead into tormented, closeted husbands and fathers.

One of the exasperating ironies of the "enlightened" anti-gay arguments of conservatives like Pattullo is that during my years of occasional contact with conservative writers I have learned that there are enormous numbers of gay conservatives. Indeed, it sometimes seems to me that there are a lot more gay conservatives than gay liberals. Once, at a cocktail party for young conservative writers held at the New York headquarters of a right-wing think tank, I looked around the room and thought to myself: *This is the gayest crowd I've ever seen outside of a gay bar.* The truth is that conservative publications and foundations that oppose gay equal rights nonetheless publish and employ numerous individual homosexuals, many of whom they know very well to be gay. What I have heard and seen of these working relationships recalls to me the phrase that many a white Southerner used to employ in describing a subservient black man: he was "one of the good ones"—which is to say that he accepted his second-class status without complaint and was properly grateful to his superiors for treating him with civility.

More and more, the catch phrase of choice for "enlightened" conservative opposition to gay rights has become "I have gay friends," a line that recalls, of course, the remark made famous by bigots of a generation or two ago: "Some of my best friends are Jews." These are both offensive statements, and the logic of both seems to be that such friendships demonstrate the speaker's own broad-mindedness: "How could I be a bigot if I'm willing to have gay (or Jewish) friends?" A person who thinks this way should realize that as friendship works both ways, so does tolerance in friendship. If he thinks he's to be commended for being tolerant of his gay friends' homosexuality, he should realize that they are in fact being extraordinarily tolerant of his opposition to their rights. (This is, of course, assuming—and it's a big assumption—that his "gay friends" do in fact think of him as a friend.) Yet what kind of a straight friend is it who, ignoring his gay friends' tolerance in this regard, makes use of the very fact of his own tolerance to support an argument against their rights?

The conservative newspaper columnist Mona Charen offers a typical argument along these lines. Most conservatives, she suggests, "are content to be tolerant of homosexuality." Charen approvingly quotes a conservative professor who had appeared with her on a "sexual politics" panel at the 1993 *National Review* conference in Washington, D.C. "We all have gay friends whose friendship we treasure," the professor said. "And who wouldn't rather spend an evening with Noël Coward than Al Gore?" Yet Charen balks at "aggressive measures by homosexuals to go beyond tolerance to endorsement" and to institutionalize gay marriage. Responding to the argument that "marriage civilizes men," she says: "it is not marriage that civilizes men. It is women." In saying this, Charen denies the reality of millions of committed gay relationships. The empirical fact is that gay men who fall in love and make a home together *can* civilize each other; by contrast, if the same men followed society's dictates and married women in defiance of their own biological urges, they would almost certainly experience years of emotional torment and eventually cave in to their sexual needs.

Charen writes: "The whole weight of the homosexual claim to equal status with heterosexuals rests on one pillar—the belief that homosexuality is innate, unchosen and immutable. . . . This is an article of faith in gay and lesbian circles. . . . Yet the evidence for this key belief among homosexuals remains elusive." One wonders: if Charen really has gay friends, why doesn't she take their word for what they feel and sense so powerfully, and which she herself has no way of knowing about? If they say that they haven't chosen to be gay, and that their homosexuality is so essential and deeply rooted a part of their identity as to be unchangeable, what kind of friend is she to refuse to believe it? Charen goes on to iterate what she calls the "traditionalist" belief that "homosexuality should not be treated like race or gender in any case. Not because it is a sin . . . but because it is not a trait that is obvious to outsiders. Forbidding discrimination against gays is like forbidding discrimination against mystery readers. How does an employer know?" This is absurd: what does the obviousness of a trait have to do with the logic of protecting people from prejudice? (Is a person's religion or national origin always obvious?) Besides, mystery readers can be pretty easy to identify: they read mysteries on their lunch hours. Some gays can be easily identified, too, either by their stereotypical mannerisms or by the fact that they have same-sex life partners—though, of course, the bottom line with a person like Charen is that she doesn't want gays to have loving homes and open, committed relationships; on the contrary, she'd apparently prefer to see them living alone, doing whatever ugly things they must with strangers, and keeping quiet about it when consorting with decent people. *Then* she'd be happy to honor them with a seat at her dinner table, where they could provide amusing dinnertime chitchat à la Noël Coward or Truman Capote.

What is so outrageous about people like Charen is that they can say one minute that they have "gay friends" and then declare quite blithely the next minute that those "friends" should not be given "equal status" under the law. How can an intelligent woman not see how brutal it is to say such things about one's supposed "friends," and that, indeed, no true "friendship" exists when one party insists on the other's social and legal inferiority? Perhaps a person like Charen doesn't realize how many times her "gay friends" have listened silently to her unconscious slights and casual cruelties, not protesting because, for a homosexual, every friendship with a straight person that founders on the shoals of prejudice only pushes one further toward subculture marginalization. For Charen, obviously, to "treasure" a person's friendship is not the same as to care about that person's welfare. On the whole, one has even less respect for someone like her than for the kind of rabid anti-gay bigot who would never accept a homosexual as a friend: at least the latter is consistent.

Charen concludes her column as follows: "Conservatives neither hate nor despise homosexuals. But they do believe that society's preference for the traditional family is justified." This declaration of "preference for the traditional family" makes for good conservative-sounding rhetoric, of course; but what does it mean, really, in practical terms? It can mean only one of two things: either (1) it is preferable for gays to marry members of the opposite sex instead of living with each other, or (2) it is somehow in the interest of traditional families that gay men be encouraged to lead lonely, promiscuous lives rather than be permitted to marry each other and thereby form "nontraditional families." Charen's rhetoric obscures, in other words, that the *real* choice faced by society is not between traditional families and gay families, but between, on the one hand, the relative stability and monogamy of gay couples and, on the other, the relative volatility of the solitary gay or the secretly gay husband or wife.

What is particularly disheartening about many "enlightened" opponents of gay rights is that if an argument they have advanced fails to stand up to scrutiny, they don't rethink their opposition; instead, they invent another argument. The more this happens, the more shamefully clear it becomes that there are in fact no reasonable grounds for their discomfort with homosexuality and their disapproval of gay rights. It is as if these people consider it their obligation as ideological conservatives to oppose homosexuality and gay rights; to do otherwise, in their minds, would apparently be to cave in to liberalism, the left, the political-correctness crowd. Indeed, the term "political correctness" comes up with great frequency in arguments against gay rights. "Neither respectability nor political correctness," said John Cardinal O'Connor in his sermon on Saint Patrick's Day 1993, apropos of the Irish gay organization's attempt to win the right to march in that day's parade, "is worth one comma in the Apostles' Creed." But this equation of acceptance of homosexuality with political correctness is utterly erroneous. Accepting homosexuality is not a political act, because homosexuality itself is not a political act. Commentators like Charen see everything having to do with homosexuality through a political prism. She characterizes the replacement of the term "sexual preference" by "sexual orientation," for example, as a political ploy designed to eradicate the idea of homosexuality as something that is chosen. But the fact is that homosexuality is not a matter of preference; it doesn't *feel* like a preference. Many gays will tell you that being gay is such a hassle that they'd prefer to be straight. How, then, can homosexuality be called *their* "sexual preference"?

A rhetorical nicety familiar to readers of "enlightened" conservatives was employed by William Kristol, former chief of staff to Vice President Dan Quayle, in a *New York Times* interview on June 27, 1993. Said Kristol: "I do not think society can or should treat homosexuality the same as heterosexuality." Note well: not "treat homosexuals," but "treat homosexuality." But what might it mean to treat homosexuality in a certain way? In the real world, after all, it is not homosexuality that is treated unequally but homosexuals—human beings, Americans, people's parents, siblings, children, and friends. If commentators like Kristol prefer to speak in the abstract, and to pretend to be making relative value judgments about ideas rather than about groups of people, it is because if they were to say, in so many words, that "homosexuals should not be treated the same as heterosexuals," it would be a lot more obvious that what they are talking about is, quite simply, undemocratic.

Another spokesman for the "enlightened" conservative view is James Bowman, who in a June 1993 media column for *The New Criterion* makes a series of ill-informed comments about the March on Washington (which he apparently watched on television) and about homosexuality and the gay-rights movement generally. Bowman records that at the march

> a lesbian speaker, clearly expecting the answer she got, asked the crowd: if they could take a pill that would magically convert them all to heterosexuals, would they do it? And the crowd thundered back: No! But does such a building block in the edifice of gay solidarity make no one nervous? Would Martin Luther King have asked his Washington marchers if they would take a pill that would make them white? The very posing of the question implies an anxiety about the answer, a subliminal consciousness not only that heterosexuality is expected of them but that they expect it of themselves.

Bowman plainly doesn't realize that the speaker's question was not original with her; on the contrary, it's something that gays are always being asked by heterosexuals. Nor, in suggesting that gays have "a subliminal consciousness not only that heterosexuality is expected of them but that they expect it of themselves," does Bowman appear to understand that those expectations are a major, and thoroughly acknowledged, fact of gay life, and that in fact the speaker's whole point, in asking her question, was plainly to affirm and celebrate the fact that these people's presence in Washington demonstrated that they, at least, had triumphed over those expectations.

For many homosexuals, that triumph comes only after a long and difficult struggle—after years of denying who they are and of striving tormentedly to be straight. While some eventually acknowledge the futility of their exertions and accept themselves, others never come to terms with their homosexuality and go to their graves with a lie at the heart of their lives. Still others, raised on a loathing of homosexuality so intense as to seem insuperable, commit suicide in their teens. Instead of being sympathetic to this often tragic struggle, recognizing its profound moral dimension, and rejoicing in the victory of self-respect over self-hatred, Bowman is sarcastic and insulting. He may not know much about gay life, but he is an attentive student of bigotspeak, declaring, in a phrase borrowed from the religious-right playbook, that the marchers traveled to Washington not to demand equal rights but to agitate for "laws guaranteeing the rights of gays as a specially protected group."

Apparently incapable of imagining the sorts of personal and professional complications that many of the marchers risked in order to be in Washington on the appointed day, and thus incapable of recognizing the degree of mature responsibility and courage that they demonstrated, Bowman follows the familiar practice of likening homosexuals to children: he describes the marchers as "boys and girls" and compares them to "the teen rebel who wants to be bad just *because* it is bad" and to youngsters interviewed in a *New York Times* series on the urban underclass.

After several paragraphs of this sort of thing Bowman suggests that "the only aspect of the gay issue worthy of political consideration" is "its decorum." He offers by way of example an article about gay rights in the *New York Times* that, according to a subsequent correction, erroneously identified a certain White House aide as a lesbian. "Why a serious newspaper should be either identifying or misidentifying, as a matter of public record, the 'sexual orientation' of a White House adviser in the first place," writes Bowman, "remains murky. It suggests a blurring of the boundary between public and private which, if allowed its career unimpeded, must lead to the destruction of civil society." Yet if a person's sexual orientation is so private a matter that mention of it in a newspaper article about gay civil rights constitutes a breach of decorum, then the same should hold for gender. For if sexual orientation is strictly a matter of what one does (or desires to do) in bed, gender is, according to the same narrow logic, strictly a matter of what is in one's pants. In reality, of course, both gender and sexual orientation have to do with much more than private parts and bedroom business. The only difference between the two is that we are all used to discussing men and women as such without thinking automatically about their distinguishing genitalia; most heterosexuals, however, are not yet accustomed to references to an individual's sexual orientation and consequently, when told that so-and-so is gay, tend to conjure up indecorous bedroom images. This is not a good enough reason for requiring homosexuals to keep quiet about who they are and whom they love.

One comes across all sorts of exasperating perspectives on homosexuality. A professor of mine once said in my presence that "it's OK to be gay so long as you're ashamed of it." Describing homosexuality as "a bum rap," he recalled with great sympathy a deceased friend of his, a distinguished (and married) critic who, on many a night, after attending a Manhattan literary party or poetry reading and behaving like a perfect gentleman, would sneak off to the Hudson River docks and pick up sailors. The critic, a melancholy man and heavy drinker, never brought the two halves of his life together. My professor seemed to feel that this was the proper way for a decent, intelligent person to handle being homosexual: divide your life into two compartments, the respectable and the dissolute, and keep the gay sex confined to the latter. I've since met many people like my professor, who feel that being homosexual is by definition a sordid fate and that, while it's not wrong to be homosexual and to act on your homosexual impulses, it's wrong not to feel ashamed of it, wrong not to regard yourself as a tragic case and to conduct yourself accordingly.

The controversy over President Clinton's attempt to repeal the ban on gays in the military occasioned some remarkable examples of twisted reasoning on the part of the ban's supporters. For example, Sam Nunn, chairman of the Senate Armed Services Committee, suggested that heterosexual soldiers have a right not to have to associate with certain people: "We've got to consider not only the rights of homosexuals, but also the rights of those who are not homosexual and who give up a great deal of their privacy when they go in the military." President Bush's Secretary of Defense Dick Cheney concurred, arguing that if gays were permitted in the military, heterosexual soldiers would "lose the freedom of association" that they have in civilian life. Imagine: for the first time in history, a Secretary of Defense and a chairman of the Senate Armed Services Committee worrying about the "privacy" and "freedom of association" of people in the military! What makes this argument especially noteworthy is that other military officials defended the ban by taking precisely the opposite position on soldiers' "rights"—namely, by arguing that no one has a "right" to serve in the military, because the armed forces are not democratic but autocratic.

The issue of gays in the military occasioned another curious argumentative contradiction. The traditional reason given for the military ban was that gays posed a security risk: since they were closeted, they could be blackmailed. After Bill Clinton's election, however, military officers who supported the ban took precisely the opposite position. In an interview, Colonel Harry Summers said that closeted gay soldiers

posed no difficulty: "We've always had gays in the military." But if the
ban were repealed, there *would* be a problem—not because gay servicemen were closeted, but because after the ban was lifted they might
not be. "If people keep their sexual preferences private, as I think they
should do, there won't be a problem," Colonel Summers said. "If they
get confrontational and look for trouble, they'll get it." By "confrontational," Colonel Summers apparently meant "honest": if a homosexual
soldier acknowledges that he's gay and is beaten up by his platoon
buddies, in short, it'll be his fault for being "confrontational."

Some military people argued that repealing the ban on gays would
"lower morale." But this is an argument *for* repeal: that military people
think repeal would damage "morale" only testifies to the fact that fear
and ignorance are indeed at terribly high levels. There can hardly be a
better panacea for such fear and ignorance than day-to-day contact with
gays. Related to this argument is the contention that heterosexuals' very
discomfort over and contempt for homosexuality should disqualify
homosexuals from positions of authority in the military and elsewhere.
On a *Donahue* program, two young male audience members declared
bluntly that gays made them uncomfortable and insecure and that they
simply would not respect an officer whom they knew to be engaged in
sexual relations with another man. What this amounts to is the ultimate
absurdity: prejudice becomes its own excuse. Such young men can't
see that their attitude is the problem—and that it's *their* problem. Again,
far from supporting the argument for banning gays from the military,
the existence of such attitudes illustrates the necessity of fully incor-
porating open homosexuals into the fabric of American life.

Indeed, as the controversy over the military ban dragged on, it grew
increasingly clear that behind the long list of arguments in favor of the
ban lay one huge, looming fact that was unmentioned by Sam Nunn,
Strom Thurmond, the Joint Chiefs of Staff, or any of the other principals
in the debate: male sexual insecurity. If the ban was lifted, an airman
from Michigan confessed to a *New York Times* reporter, "I couldn't sleep
at night. I'd be worried that some homosexual is going to sneak over
and make a pass at me." In response to such concerns, the columnist
Andy Rooney noted pointedly: "It isn't like gay men go around har-
assing straight men the way some men harass women." Likewise, the
columnist Anthony Lewis noted: "If sexual conduct were the real concern of the critics, they would focus on the clear and present problem.

You don't have to be a genius to know what that is: assaults on *women* in the armed forces."

Servicemen interviewed about the ban returned again and again to a single preoccupation: communal showers. "We're all crammed together in the showers," said one airman, "and I don't want to worry that some gay guy is staring at me." One reporter after another discovered that servicemen who were trained to be cool under fire were unsettled by the thought of a homosexual glancing their way in a shower. On further questioning, many admitted that at some time, either in school or in the military, they must have showered with homosexuals; but that seemed to be all right, because they didn't know who the homosexuals were and when it was happening. What bothered them was the idea of *knowing.*

"What is this shower hang-up?" wondered the columnist Molly Ivins. Well, it's about sexual insecurity, of course. Many a young straight man feels his sense of his own masculinity to be threatened by situations in which he is naked and surrounded by other naked men. All that could make such a situation more uncomfortable for him is the idea that one of those other men might be sexually attracted to him—might want (as many a young straight man tends to think of it) to use him as a woman. As someone observed in a letter to the *New York Times,* "What these men fear most is that they will receive the treatment our society ordinarily reserves for women." The typical young gay man, by contrast, would be far less likely to feel such a sense of insecurity around other naked men, for he is far less likely than a young straight man to think of sex as a way of asserting manhood and power, or to base his sense of his own manhood on an illusion of sexual dominance over females or of sexual superiority to other men.

George Putnam, an ex-Marine and the host of a Los Angeles radio call-in show, echoed many soldiers in saying that repealing the ban "would give those who wish to flaunt their sexuality an opportunity to do so." Yet the military people who tend to support the ban most vehemently are precisely the kind of straight men who have no qualms about, and whose self-esteem is likely to depend strongly upon, flaunting their own sexuality. A fervent military supporter of the ban isn't apt to have been extremely upset by the sexual brutality exposed in the Tailhook scandal; rather, he is apt to be the kind of soldier who considers such aggressiveness toward women his prerogative as a male. Plainly, what such soldiers are worried about is not the flaunting of sexuality per se, but the flaunting of a kind of sexuality that they view as a threat to their *own* sexuality. As Richard Rodriguez noted in a *Los Angeles Times* op-ed, the more insecure type of heterosexual male, whether in the army or the corner bar or the United States Senate, "needed the idea of the sissy, the reminder of the sissy—all pink and flowery—to laugh at. He needed the sissy to stay in the pretty closet." The idea of openly gay servicemen disturbed such a heterosexual male, for "if the sissy is, after all, a warrior, then he is as brave and as 'male' as we always thought the heterosexual was"—and what does *that* do to the sort of man whose fragile confidence in his own masculinity hinges on an equation of masculinity with sexual predatoriness and on a belief in the heterosexual male's natural superiority to women and to gay men? As Randy Shilts writes in *Conduct Unbecoming: Gays and Lesbians in the U.S. Military,*

> The issue of women in the military was never about women; it was about men and their need to define their masculinity. That, more than the fighting and winning of wars, appeared to be the central mission of the armed forces, at least for many men. That was why they sought to limit the role not only of women in the military but of gays, as well. These exclusions were, in this sense, all part of the same package, a defense of traditional masculinity in a changing world.

Much of the support for the military's ban on gays, then, is founded not on legitimate considerations of either morals or morale, but on the prevalence among young military men of a macho sensibility that can endure only as long as certain false but gratifying assumptions about maleness and homosexuality are left undisturbed. The Joint Chiefs apparently regard this sensibility as a foundation of the armed forces' strength, but it is in fact a major structural weakness. Who, after all, is the better soldier: a psychologically insecure straight man who flips out at the thought of a gay man glancing at him in the shower or a gay man who is disciplined enough to have kept his homosexuality under wraps for years and who, despite the homophobia of many of his colleagues, has worked very well with them? As David Link has observed, most gay servicemen and women "have been fully able to do their work without revealing their attraction (if any) to other service members of the same sex. In most cases they have done this so successfully that no one suspects they are homosexual. Gays call this being in the closet, and everyone who is homosexual knows how to do it. It is a form of self-discipline that any military organization should find exemplary." And as Jane Hrubec wrote in a letter to the *New York Times,* "The more macho and homophobic a man is, the weaker and more insecure he is. Real men who happen to be straight are not threatened by homosexuality. Real men who happen to be gay should not have to feel threatened by heterosexuality." Perhaps, she suggested, "the shrieking homophobics . . . should be banned from the military, not gays." Or perhaps, far better, lifting the ban might be a first giant step toward helping the "shrieking homophobics" to overcome their misconceptions about gays and their insecurities about their own masculinity—and thus toward creating a military with a strength that is founded more on genuine self-confidence and less on bigotry and bluster.

One fact that is underscored by the widespread hostility toward gays in the armed forces is that many heterosexuals are so accustomed to homosexuals' second-class status that they regard it as a demand for "special rights" when gays ask to be freed from that status. They feel that a gay person, simply by refusing to lie when questioned about his personal life, is pushing his sexual practices "in their faces." If many soldiers assume that their "right" not to be seen in the shower transcends the right of a homosexual to serve in the military, so many civilians feel that their "right" not to have to be reminded that homosexuality exists outweighs the right of gays to live as openly as heterosexuals.

This attitude is reflected in a 1992 *Newsweek* letter by Robert B. Reilly of Burr Ridge, Illinois. "Though it may be a difficult concept for the liberal mind to grasp," writes Mr. Reilly, "there are people in this nation who are as morally offended by homosexuality as liberals are by racism and sexism. Shouldn't they be accorded the same right as liberals not to have a practice that offends them shoved in their faces? Or are people allowed to take offense only in the areas that liberals declare politically correct?" It's interesting: Mr. Reilly claims to be "morally" offended by homosexuality; yet his main concern is obviously not that this moral outrage exists, but that he is forced to be reminded of its existence. It's like saying, "I'm morally offended by murder, so if you're going to murder somebody, do it in the privacy of your own home and don't talk about it." The real reason for his objection to homosexuality, in short, is not that it is morally offensive but that it makes him uncomfortable.

Mr. Reilly feels that a "practice" is being shoved in his face. But are homosexuals having sex on his front lawn or outside his office window? One suspects not. No, what he means is that he doesn't even want to be reminded that homosexuals exist. But we do exist and have always existed. To say so is merely a statement of fact. Likewise, for individuals to say that they are gay is merely a statement of fact. If this makes Mr. Reilly uncomfortable, I'm sorry to hear it. But America is my country as much as it is his. Why should I lead my life in secret in order to save him from discomfort, when it wouldn't occur to me to ask such a thing of him? There is only one defense for this lopsided understanding of "rights": that things have been this way for generations.

When the prominent conservative Marvin Liebman came out in a 1990 letter to *National Review*, his supposed friend, the magazine's founder and editor-in-chief, William F. Buckley, Jr., offered a very curious response. "There is of course argument," he wrote, "on the question whether homosexuality is in all cases congenital." Well, yes, there's "argument" because bigots who know nothing about the subject refuse to accept the testimony of gays about their own lives and feelings. Buckley says: "Let us assume that this is so [i.e., that homosexuality is "congenital"], and then ask: Is it reasonable to expect the larger community to cease to think of the activity of homosexuals as unnatural, whatever its etiology?" What Buckley seems to be saying here is this: let's not accept homosexuality as a naturally occurring phenomenon, justified though such a position may be by the facts, because one simply can't imagine that people will accept it as so justified. But in fact people can come to understand and accept homosexuality, just as people once came to accept that the earth was round and not flat; it's all a matter of education. It is clear from this sentence of Buckley's about the reasonableness or unreasonableness of expectations that his concern here is not with what is true or false or right or wrong, but with what is politically achievable and advantageous.

But in Buckley's next paragraph this pragmatic matter of the larger community's ignorance about the naturalness of homosexuality somehow metamorphoses into a moral question: "Ought considerations of charity entirely swamp us, causing us to submerge convictions having to do with that which we deem to be normal, and healthy?" What a bizarre sentence! Suddenly the majority's misconception that homosexuality is not "natural" has been invested with the dignity of a "conviction." Also, Buckley speaks of "charity" rather than "equity," as if to suggest that the adoption of gay-rights measures and the legal recognition of gay relationships should be seen as a matter of munificence on the part of the straight population rather than as a matter of fair-minded extension to gays of rights already enjoyed by heterosexuals. And what is this implication that homosexuality is not "healthy"? The life of his friend Liebman, as related in his autobiography, testifies not to the unhealthiness of homosexuality but to the unhealthiness of lying to oneself and one's friends about one's sexual identity.

In his next paragraph, after a pro forma denunciation of gay-bashing, Buckley again raises the question of those "convictions," which he describes as being "rooted, in our opinion, in theological and moral truths." How can something which was two paragraphs earlier a misconception now be a conviction rooted in a truth? And why doesn't he examine the supposed theological and moral bases of those "convictions"? A paragraph later, just before reaffirming his friendship and brotherhood for Liebman, he says that those convictions "are more, much more, than mere accretions of bigotry." But if one recognizes that one's "convictions" don't square with the reality of a trusted friend's own personal testimony, how admirable are they? To refuse to examine the contradictions inherent in one's own attitudes—contradictions that one knows to be harmful to people who have done nothing to deserve harm—is an act not of moral conviction but of moral cowardice.

Liebman, whose curious attachment to Buckley and desperate desire to please him are evident throughout his autobiography, managed to convince himself that Buckley's response to his letter was something to applaud. On the contrary, it was a very good example of the sympathetic-but-disapproving posture of certain conservatives on the issue of homosexuality. These people say, in effect: I know that you were born this way, that homosexuality comes as naturally to you as heterosexuality does to me, that it would be wrong to ask you to marry a woman and that you can find happiness in intimacy only with another man, and that it's offensive for people to say ugly things about you because you're this way; but I feel obliged to view your sexuality as a moral offense anyway. Nothing personal.

Buckley—who in a 1993 column would refer to "the blight of homosexuality"—describes this as "a vexed and vexing subject." Yes, it is, for heterosexuals (mostly men) who are uncomfortable with it and who insist on finding moral or other "reasons" to hold it at arm's length even though there are gay people whom they call friends. At least the anti-gay crusaders who despise homosexuality *and* individual gays are consistent; those who condemn homosexuality while maintaining "friendships" with individual gays are simply hypocrites who refuse to face the inconsistency—and the brutality—of their attitudes.

Buckley is one of many people who, in disapproving of homosexuality, claim that they're standing up for moral principles—though the chances are that most of them have never given much serious thought to the question of why, exactly, homosexuality should be regarded as immoral. Some may have been raised as fundamentalists (the fundamentalist, of course, being a species that comes in Protestant, Catholic, Jewish, and Moslem varieties) and consequently consider the sinfulness of homosexuality to be a firm tenet of their faith.

Yet you don't have to be a fundamentalist to consider homosexuality contrary to the word of God. Even the children of non-fundamentalists tend to grow up with that notion. I know I did, though my parents have always had a very easygoing approach to doctrinal matters. My religious background is pretty strong, if eclectic. Both my paternal grandparents were Roman Catholics from Poland; my maternal grandfather was a Methodist evangelical singer in South Carolina; and my maternal grandmother was a devout Southern Baptist. None of them fit the stereotypes that may come to mind when you hear these descriptive phrases. My Polish Catholic grandmother, whose most cherished friend in her childhood had been a Jewish girl, told me over and over in my childhood, as if to pound it into my head for all my life: "The Jews are wonderful, the best people in the world"; and my Southern grandfather, to the chagrin of many of his white neighbors, was raised in the same house as a black boy whom he thought of as a brother and who became his closest friend in adulthood.

Yet in many ways my grandparents were conservatives. My maternal grandfather loathed Franklin D. Roosevelt, and my paternal grandmother loved Richard M. Nixon, an autographed picture of whom adorned her bedroom bureau throughout my childhood. When I was growing up, my parents too were political conservatives. I remember asking my mother, on the day John F. Kennedy was assassinated, whether she'd voted for him. No, she said, she'd voted for Nixon. I remember being irritated at her because she hadn't voted for the poor dead guy. But I fell into line with their politics soon enough: on Election Day in 1964, at the age of eight, I sat up watching the returns, eager to see the Johnson landslide turn around, long after my parents told me that it was all over and that I should go to bed. A year later, when William F. Buckley ran for mayor of New York, they took me on election night to Buckley headquarters, where we saw the candidate himself being borne in on the shoulders of his supporters and heard him concede defeat at the hands of John V. Lindsay. At twelve, I campaigned with a friend for Nixon, handing out brochures and buttons and bumper stickers on street corners. I was, in short, a baby conservative. But being conservative didn't have to do with hating anyone; it had to do with personal responsibility, an appreciation of democratic values, and an uncompromising hostility to Communism and all other forms of tyranny.

I was also a Christian (though an unbaptized one). My parents, though extremely irregular churchgoers and certainly not rigid sectarians, brought me up to say my prayers every night and sent me to a Lutheran Sunday school (which was selected because it happened to be around the corner). My mother, who in accordance with Southern Baptist precepts was not baptized until she had become a teenager and made her own decision for Christ, felt very strongly that it should be entirely up to my sister and me whether and when we should receive the sacrament of baptism. Hence I was not baptized as an infant. When I was about twelve years old, the pastor at the Lutheran church found out about this, was shocked, and began lobbying my mother to have me baptized at once. Before long, irked by his perseverance, she yanked me out of the Lutheran fold and, in an attempt to acquaint me with my denominational options, began taking me to services at local Protestant houses of worship—one Sunday a Presbyterian church, the next an Episcopal church, and so on. The experience sparked my imagination. I read everything I could get my hands on about religion, and became fascinated by the often abstruse differences in theology and liturgy among the various sects. Though I took these differences seriously, I came to agree with my mother that good people and sincere believers could be found in all the churches, that a loving God didn't consider the members of one church better than the members of another, and that the particulars of your belief mattered less than whether you were "a good person."

I don't recall my parents ever saying anything overtly positive or negative about homosexuality when I was a child. The subject came up only a few times in my presence, always in connection either with TV news coverage of Gay Liberation protests (which my father grumbled about) or with questions regarding the sexual status of certain unmarried friends and relatives. One time, for instance, my mother spoke of an elderly male cousin of hers who had lived all his life with another man. She spoke fondly of her cousin and his friend, and said nothing explicitly disapproving about their probable homosexuality, but she said that unless you were with them in their bedroom you could never be 100 percent sure that they were homosexual, and it wasn't fair to say that they were homosexual unless you *were* sure. Despite my mother's affection for her cousin and his friend, what I gathered from her remarks about them was that homosexuality was a very serious matter indeed; to say without proof that someone was homosexual was to charge him with a truly grievous offense.

This impression was reinforced by my reading of religious tracts and my Sunday school lessons, from which I gleaned that there was only one position a Christian could take on homosexuality: that it was sinful. There was no way to be both gay and Christian. Accordingly, on the night of the day that I realized I was gay, I didn't say the prayers that, until then, I had recited faithfully at bedtime since earliest childhood. Nor did I say them the next night, or the next; as it turned out, I didn't say them again for almost a decade. That's how sure I was that being Christian was not consistent with being gay. I knew I couldn't reject homosexuality, because from the moment that I realized I was gay, I realized also that my homosexuality was an essential part of who I was. Wrong? On the contrary, what had been wrong was the assumption, made by me and everyone around me for the first two decades of my life, that I was straight. Unnatural? For me, I knew, nothing could be *more* natural than homosexuality. And because it felt so right and natural to me, I knew that there was nothing evil or ugly about it; on the contrary, it was inextricably linked to the most true and good and beautiful emotions that I'd ever experienced. What's more, I knew instinctively that accepting my homosexuality was a matter of honor, a matter of being true to myself, a matter of being at peace with the world. If there was a God, I realized, surely His truth couldn't be diametrically opposed to the truth that was singing loudly and clearly in my heart and mind and bones. Yet all that I'd read about Protestant and Catholic belief had fixed in my mind the idea that Christianity unequivocally condemned homosexuality and that the two things were mutually exclusive; and so I rejected Christianity. Nowadays, remembering that rejection, I read the harsh anti-gay words of fundamentalist ministers and wonder: how many devout young gay Christians have denied their faith because of such people?

Clergymen who condemn homosexuality often argue that those who counsel acceptance of it have, in doing so, espoused trendy, secular, and relativistic notions of morality. Defenders of homosexuality are charged with having embraced the Now rather than the eternal, with having chosen cheap gratification over costly grace. In many instances, this is indeed the case. Instead of emphasizing that they do not find homosexuality to be inconsistent with faith, some Christians frame the question in secular terms and discuss it in the vapid, fuzzy language of post-1960s leftism, speaking of sexual freedom and the right of choice. In taking this approach, they do credit neither to their church nor to their cause. For these political categories are without spiritual meaning. As Americans we enjoy considerable temporal freedom; but those of us who are Christians believe that our only freedom is in Christ. Our rights as Americans are many, but our rights as Christians are defined by our faith. These well-meaning Christians make it seem as if homosexuality is merely another politically correct cause, another crusade to be championed in a thousand homilies by a thousand progressive-minded ministers while a thousand congregations sit on their hands and bite their tongues, wishing politics—sexual politics especially—could be banned forever from the pulpit.

In encouraging Christians to view homosexuality in this secular, political way, its apologists have been terribly misguided. For it is not secular liberalism but the truth of Christianity itself that strikes most penetratingly at the heart of what is wrong with the attitudes of reactionary Christians toward homosexuality. To present a proper Christian case for acceptance of homosexuality, in other words, it is imperative that we *not* argue for the retailoring of moral principles or religious doctrines to suit our selfish needs or the secular priorities of the times in which we live; it is, rather, to insist that it is incumbent upon Christians, *as* Christians, to distinguish principle from prejudice, well-founded teaching from groundless tradition, and to put into practice the lesson in love that was Christ's supreme commandment. Tradition is a very fine thing, but it is no virtue to adhere to unjustified, hurtful, and—yes—anti-Christian traditions merely because they *are* traditions.

Yet attitudes endure. No subject occasions such un-Christian ugliness in some Christian communities and churches as does homosexuality. Time and again, in one denomination after another, homosexuality proves to be the chief exception to the rule of Christian love. Meanwhile, many homosexuals share the view of reactionary Christians that (as an angry lesbian told the gay minister Troy Perry) "there's no such thing as gay and Christian." Kathleen Boatwright, a leader of the gay Episcopal group Integrity, notes that "the only thing dirtier than being a lesbian in a Christian community is being a Christian in a lesbian community." The gay subculture teems with hostility toward religion, and in particular toward Christianity—and the basis of this hostility is, of course, not hard to fathom. Many homosexuals were rejected by their parents in the name of Christianity; others, in their youth, went trustingly to clergymen to discuss their homosexuality, only to be condemned and betrayed to their parents. To such homosexuals, the church represents not a foundation for love and hope but a memory of hatred and rejection. Gays from non-Christian backgrounds, meanwhile, routinely equate Christianity with the religious right. Invited by an interviewee in the national gay magazine *The Advocate* to get together with some of the interviewee's Christian friends, the columnist David Ehrenstein replied, "I have met enough Christians, thank you. When people tell you over and over again that they want you dead, you tend to believe them." And, of course, there *are* professing Christians who want homosexuals dead. A study of men imprisoned for gay-bashing found that they "generally saw nothing wrong in what they did, and, more often than not, said their religious leaders and traditions sanctioned their behavior."

I can understand the feelings of both homosexuals and Christians who regard the idea of a gay Christian as a contradiction in terms. For many years, as I have said, I felt the same way. I scorned the very notion of gay Christians. I believed that such people were fooling themselves, joining a club that didn't want to have them, declaring their allegiance to two incompatible ideas.

Then something happened to me—or, rather, several things. One of them was my companion, Chris, with whom I began attending an

Episcopal church soon after we moved in together in 1988. At first I protested, apprising him of my view that Christianity and homosexuality are incompatible. I reminded him of the Jerry Falwell line: "God created Adam and Eve, not Adam and Steve." That, I told him, is how these people think: they *despise* us for being gay! "Maybe some of them do," Chris replied quietly, "but God doesn't." He reminded me that God's creation did not end with Adam and Eve; it also included David and Jonathan (of whom David sang: "Your love for me was wonderful, surpassing the love of women"). And it included many others as well—us among them.

Another thing that happened to me was John Boswell's 1980 book, *Christianity, Social Tolerance, and Homosexuality,* which I first read in 1989 and which (though my views differ from Boswell's in some respects) helped me to realize that homosexual life and Christianity were not inconsistent. Boswell and other contemporary Biblical scholars have demonstrated that there is no definitive scriptural basis for the condemnation of homosexual relationships. To be sure, a casual Bible reader, directed to certain texts by homophobic ministers, might easily be led to believe otherwise. The first thing that such a reader must understand is that society was structured very differently in Biblical times than it is today. One cannot easily draw parallels between relationships then and now. The ancients' sexual roles and sexual conventions were radically different from ours, as was their understanding of sexual emotions and sexual identity. Certain acts that most of us would consider wrong—such as Abraham fathering a child by Sarah's slave girl Hagar—are recounted approvingly in the Bible, while other actions that we would not take seriously at all are condemned as abominations punishable by death. The English language, moreover, has no exact equivalents for most of the ancient words that describe the emotions that bind men to each other or to women, and the ancients had no equivalents for some of our words.

Accordingly, Biblical passages relating to sex and sexual relationships often pose myriad problems for modern scholars. Translators paper over the ambiguities, making word choices based on their individual assumptions and prejudices. Contributing to the lack of certitude is that some words have multiple meanings or have changed greatly in meaning over the centuries. The words "sodomy" and "sodomite," for example, have at various times been used to describe almost every sort of sexual act imaginable. These words derive, of course, from Sodom, the city that was destroyed by Jehovah for its sins (along with the city of Gomorrah), as recounted in Genesis 19. That chapter describes how Lot, a householder in Sodom, plays host to two angels whom Jehovah has sent to the city to destroy it for its wickedness. Presently, the other men of Sodom appear at Lot's house, demanding to have sex with the visitors, whom they do not know to be angels. Lot refuses, and in place of the angels offers the men his daughters. "Do nothing to these men," he says, "because they have come under the shelter of my roof." The angels strike the men blind and tell Lot to save himself and his family, for they have come to destroy the city.

Though generations of readers have focused on the homosexual element of the passage, which to twentieth-century readers is probably its most startling element, homosexuality is not explicitly identified as the Sodomites' damning vice. On the contrary, a scrupulous reading suggests that it is not the homosexual nature of the Sodomites' lust that angers Jehovah so much as it is their lust itself, their intent to commit rape, and their indifference to the rules of hospitality. If this emphasis on hospitality sounds unlikely to today's readers, it only underscores the dramatic difference between ancient and modern values: for in ancient times failures of hospitality were, in fact, considered a serious transgression; this was certainly true of Periclean Athens, in which homosexual relationships, by contrast, were taken completely for granted and regarded as, if anything, a moral good. Certainly the early fathers of the church, in writing about Genesis 19, didn't read the passage as a condemnation of homosexuality, and in the King James translation "sodomite" is employed as an English equivalent for the Hebrew word for "temple prostitute," thus suggesting that seventeenth-century England may have understood the sin of Sodom as having something to do with prostitution.

So it is that in the King James Version, Deuteronomy 23:17 reads, "There shall be no whore of the daughters of Israel, nor a sodomite of the sons of Israel." I Kings 14:24 reads, "And there were also sodomites in the land: *and* they did according to all the abominations of the nations which the LORD cast out before the children of Israel." I Kings 22:46 reads, "And the remnant of the sodomites, which remained in the days of his father Asa, he took out of the land." And II Kings 23:7 reads, "And he brake down the house of the sodomites, that *were* by the house of the LORD, where the women wove hangings for the grove."

These four passages are sometimes used to condemn homosexuality. Yet if one looks at the same four passages in the most authoritative recent translations of the Bible, one discovers that they are not about homosexuality but about prostitution:*

> No Israelite woman may become a temple prostitute, nor may an Israelite man.

> Worse still, all over the country there were male prostitutes attached to the shrines, and the people adopted all the abominable practices of the nations whom the Lord had dispossessed in favour of Israel.

> He expelled from the land such of the male prostitutes attached to the shrines as were still left from the days of Asa his father.

> He also pulled down the quarters of the male prostitutes attached to the house of the Lord, where the women wove vestments in honour of Asherah.

Indeed, in the entire Old Testament, only two passages refer explicitly to homosexual acts:

> You must not lie with a man as with a woman: that is an abomination. (Leviticus 18:22)

> If a man has intercourse with a man as with a woman, both commit an abomination. They must be put to death; their blood be on their own heads! (Leviticus 20:13)

The first thing that should be said about these passages is that the word "abomination" is used liberally in the Old Testament; it is, for example, an abomination to sacrifice a bull or sheep with "any defect or serious blemish" (Deuteronomy 17:1). Second, it should be noted that these passages are part of what Biblical scholars call the Holiness Code, which is concerned not with the "intrinsic wrong" of various actions, as John Boswell puts it, but with questions of "ritual purity." Boswell notes that in the Septuagint, the pre-Christian Greek translation

*These and all subsequent Bible quotations are taken from the Revised English Bible.

of the Old Testament by Jewish scholars, "the Levitical enactments against homosexual behavior characterize it unequivocally as ceremonially unclean rather than inherently evil." As Peter J. Gomes has written, "The code explicitly bans homosexual acts. But it also prohibits eating raw meat, planting two different kinds of seed in the same field and wearing garments with two different kinds of yarn. Tattoos, adultery and sexual intercourse during a woman's menstrual period are similarly outlawed." With the advent of Christianity and its spread to the gentiles, the Holiness Code was increasingly seen as archaic and irrelevant to the new faith.

Outside of the Holiness Code, there is no mention of homosexual relations in the Old Testament. This seems surprising, for Leviticus and Deuteronomy in particular are bursting with lists of abominations punishable by death, many (but not all) of them sex-related. For instance, it is required that rebellious sons (Deuteronomy 21:21), unvirginal brides (Deuteronomy 22:20), adulterers (Leviticus 20:9, Deuteronomy 22:21), and those guilty of incest (Leviticus 20:12 and elsewhere) all be put to death. If a man sleeps with a woman and her mother, all three must be burned to death "so that there may be no lewdness in your midst" (Leviticus 20:14). There are other punishments, moreover, that would strike the average contemporary reader as harsh and unfair, and of which few Jews or Christians today would approve. An unbetrothed woman raped by a man must become his wife and stay with him forever (Deuteronomy 22:29). Bastards and their descendants, "even down to the tenth generation," are denied temple membership (Deuteronomy 23:2). The Old Testament endorses slavery but not tolerance, directing the Israelites "to demolish completely all the sanctuaries where the nations whom you are dispossessing worship their gods" (Deuteronomy 12:2). And it authorizes slaughter and rape: "If the town does not make peace with you but gives battle, you are to lay siege to it and, when the Lord your God delivers it into your hands, put every male in it to the sword; but you may take the women, the dependants, and the livestock for yourselves, and plunder everything else in the town" (Deuteronomy 20:14). Some of the Old Testament's sex-related edicts would seem downright bizarre to a contemporary Jew or Christian:

No man whose testicles have been crushed or whose organ has been cut off may become a member of the assembly of the Lord. (Deuteronomy 23:1)

When two men are fighting and the wife of one of them intervenes to drag her husband clear of his opponent, if she puts out her hand and catches hold of the man by the genitals, you must cut off her hand and show her no mercy. (Deuteronomy 25:11–12)

What all these passages underscore is not that God is cruel and unreasonable but that the Bible was written by men who lived in a particular time and place with values that differed dramatically from our own. To say this is not to deny that the Bible is, as many of us believe, inspired by God; it is simply to point out that the actual words of the Bible were set down by human beings, and that the scriptures, as they have come down to us, could therefore not help bearing the marks of human frailty, ignorance, and prejudice. These passages also underscore something else—namely, that to contend that the Levitical proscription of male homosexuality should apply to Christians today while ignoring its context is to speak out of either ignorance or hypocrisy. Those who decide that this prohibition is to be taken more seriously than the other edicts in the Holiness Code do so not because there is anything in the Bible to indicate that they should but because of their own prejudices. Their hostility to homosexuality, in short, isn't derived from the Bible; on the contrary, they are merely quoting the Bible selectively to support their own pre-existing biases. As Troy Perry has written, "If we as Christians are going to blindly accept some parts of the Bible, then we have to take them all! You must consider that there are scriptures which say clearly that it is an abomination to mix fabrics—in other words, one is forbidden to wear cotton and linen at the same time. There are scriptures that state clearly that you may not eat shrimp, lobster, oysters, or have your steak cooked too rare."

What of the gospels? Gomes puts it succinctly: "There is no mention of homosexuality in the four Gospels of the New Testament. The moral teachings of Jesus are not concerned with the subject." As for the rest of the New Testament, three passages from Saint Paul have sometimes been translated in this century in such a way as to suggest that Paul was referring to homosexuality. I Corinthians 6:9 and I Timothy 1:10 state that people guilty of two particular types of conduct will be excluded from the Kingdom of Heaven. As a result of uncertainty over the exact meaning of the words for these types of conduct in the time of Saint Paul, however, different translators have rendered those words in very different ways. In some translations, the practice forbidden by these passages is effeminate behavior (which in the ancient world was not associated with homosexuality); in others, masturbation or child molestation or child prostitution. (Boswell's book contains a long, scholarly appendix examining the historical use and meaning of the words in these two passages.)

The New Testament passage most often cited in connection with homosexuality is Romans 1:26–27: "God has given them [the Romans] up to shameful passions. Among them women have exchanged natural intercourse for unnatural, and men too, giving up natural relations with women, burn with lust for one another; males behave indecently with males, and are paid in their own persons the fitting wage of such perversion." Boswell, reading the verses in the context of the chapter of Romans in which they appear, observes that Paul's chief concern here is not with sexuality but with theology. "There was a time," Boswell writes, "when monotheism was offered to or known by the Romans, but they rejected it. The reference to homosexuality is simply a mundane analogy to this theological sin; it is patently not the crux of the argument. Once the point has been made, the subject of homosexuality is quickly dropped and the major argument resumed."

Paul is saying, in other words, that as Romans rejected the worship of one God for the worship of many gods, so they rejected opposite-sex for same-sex relations. Paul's concern here is with the *unnaturalness* of this exchange. As Boswell notes, "the persons Paul condemns are manifestly not homosexual: what he derogates are homosexual acts committed by apparently heterosexual persons. The whole point of Romans 1, in fact, is to stigmatize persons who have rejected their calling, gotten off the true path they were once on." In Paul's time and place, to be sure, this analogy between theology and sexuality worked because only heterosexuality was viewed as "natural." It was not understood that to some people it is homosexuality, not heterosexuality, that comes naturally, and that for those people, engaging in heterosexual relations would be as much a rejection of their true calling, a deviation from the true path, as homosexual sex would be for a heterosexual.

When one reads the Bible on these matters, it is important to recognize that sexuality is a branch of scientific knowledge like any other. The

Bible is a book of spiritual teaching, not of scientific revelation. God did not use the Bible to explain to the ancient Hebrews how to build an airplane or construct a telephone system or manufacture antibiotics; in the same way, He did not use it to correct ancient misconceptions about human sexuality.

The point that emerges, then, from a careful study of the Biblical passages that are invoked in attacks on homosexuality is that one cannot divorce them from their historical and textual settings. The unfortunate fact is that anti-gay bigots have had their own motives for wrenching certain lines out of context, with the consequence that the idea of homosexuality as a violation of Christian teachings has in recent centuries become deeply ingrained in the minds of most people in the Western world. To be sure, Biblical scholars differ on the specific interpretations of the passages I've discussed. Whatever their differences, however, the indisputable fact remains that this *is* an issue about which intelligent, serious, and responsible scholars can disagree. In such circumstances, it would seem obvious that the Christian thing to do is to accept rather than condemn, to love rather than hate. The lesson of Jesus is one of love, not of denunciation of love.

Certainly one could make a long list of things that are more inconsistent with both the spirit and the letter of Christ's gospel than homosexuality: being rich, for one. Though Christ says nothing in the gospels about homosexuality, he does say unequivocally that it would be "easier for a camel to go through the eye of a needle than for a rich man to enter the kingdom of heaven." But Christians accumulate wealth and are celebrated for it. One can safely say that most of the people who cheered Pat Buchanan's homophobic remarks at the 1992 Republican convention consider certain millionaires to be good Christians and great Americans. My aim here is not to denounce wealth but to note that the kind of person who condemns homosexuality on the grounds of Christian morality while accumulating wealth is blinkered and selective. Such a person is not defending moral principles but is, rather, defending habits of mind with which he is comfortable and that he is too passive or frightened to allow to be brought into question. That some people have fixated on the Levitical passages about homosexuality while ignoring Christ's explicit condemnation of wealth and his exaltation of love—which he celebrates without qualification or exception—is a reflection not of those people's Christianity but of their un-Christian prejudices.

• • •

Over the first few weeks during which I warily accompanied Chris to church, I came to understand exactly how wrong I had been about homosexuality and Christian faith. Gradually I came to see that Chris's and my love for each other, far from being inconsistent with Christianity, was in fact the supreme testament in my own life to Christ's love. Our love made me feel to the depths of my spirit the truth of Christianity, the truth of the proposition that we were placed here, above all, to love and praise; it made me understand that human love is a reflection of divine love and that love is at the heart of the meaning of everything. When, in November of 1990, I was baptized at our church in New York City, Chris served as one of my two sponsors. If I had fallen away from Christ because of my homosexuality, it was my homosexuality that led me back into the fold.

Chris and I feel quite welcome at our home parish, as we have at many of the other Episcopal churches we've visited in New York and elsewhere. Yet it's odd to sit there every Sunday knowing that these priests, who would bless my cat or my car if I asked them to, wouldn't be able to bless my union with Chris without risking severe punishment by the bishop. Indeed, most American churches today find themselves in a quandary, trapped between the traditional view of homosexuality as evil and a growing recognition that committed homosexual relationships are as deserving of respect as any other. Many clergy in the mainstream Protestant denominations—Episcopal, Presbyterian, Methodist, Lutheran—now occupy a philosophically inconsistent middle ground: although they object to the ordination of open homosexuals and the blessing of gay unions, they welcome gays into their congregations and treat gay couples with respect. This makes no sense. If homosexuality is a transgression, why respect the relationship of a gay couple? If it isn't a transgression, why not accept gay ministers and bless gay unions? The illogic of these ministers' position was demonstrated by a recent ruling by the highest court of the Presbyterian Church that while "a person who is no longer engaged in a homosexual way of life" may be hired as a minister, "a self-affirmed practicing homosexual may not be invited to serve in a Presbyterian Church position which presumes ordination." This decision nullified the hiring of a lesbian, Jane Adams Spahr, as co-pastor of a Rochester, New York, church. "This decision says either lie or repent," Spahr commented. "I will not lie, and I will never repent. We are talking about who it is that God made me." The ruling, which was in accordance with a 1978 policy statement by the church's General Assembly barring the ordination of "unrepentant" homosexuals, overturned two lower church courts that supported Spahr's hiring. The sole dissenter on the high court was W. Clark Chamberlain of Houston, who put his finger on the illogic at the heart of the decision. He wrote: "The position of the majority is not consistent. If Jane Adams Spahr is a sinner, why is she not to be disciplined? If she is in good standing, why can her call not be fulfilled?" Precisely.

Casual hypocrisy of this sort is rife in Christendom. Homosexual clergy are ordained all the time by bishops who know that they are homosexual and in the presence of congregations that also know, but the fact is kept out of the public record and nobody makes waves. In many churches, there is a gentlemen's agreement tacitly understood by all parties (and often spelled out tactfully by helpful clerics to young postulants): if you agree not to say you're gay (even though everyone involved knows that you are), they agree not to ask about it. If Spahr, of all the gay and lesbian Presbyterian ministers, became the subject of judiciary proceedings, it was not because she was gay but because she was *publicly* gay, connected with a gay organization. My own observations suggest that in the Episcopal Church, anyway, a large minority—if not an actual majority—of newly ordained ministers these days are gay. "Discreet" homosexual relationships are a long-honored tradition (not to mention a long-standing joke) in the Episcopal Church. Richard L. Huff, in a 1992 letter to the *New York Times*, writes of two Episcopal priests' attempts to seduce him in the 1960s when he was a college student aspiring to the priesthood. He says that "the experience drove me from the church, from the priesthood and from Christianity." Years later, what has emerged from this experience is the conviction that "the Episcopal Church should lead the way in openly permitting ordination of gay priests. It is the mendacity of ordaining gay men or women, yet acting as if it does not happen, that erodes the credibility and honor of the church and leads to the disillusionment and exodus of individuals like me. . . . The poison of hypocrisy regarding the gay clergy undermines the church. It is time to be rid of it."

The hypocrisy of the Presbyterian and Episcopal churches on this score, however, is dwarfed by that which may be found in the Roman Catholic Church. The irony of anti-gay Catholics' frequent equation of homosexuality with pederasty—even though sexual abuse of children is no more common among gay men than among straight men—lies in the fact that pederasty *is* especially prevalent in the ranks of the Roman Catholic priesthood. (An estimate reported widely on network news programs placed it at about 6 percent.) The Church has been intransigent, of course, in its declarations that homosexuality is unnatural; yet what this statistic underscores is that it's not homosexuality but the Church's sexual attitudes that are unnatural.

The usual argument for the Church's rule of clerical celibacy (which did not obtain in the early Church) is that it removes the distraction of family life, thus making a priest better able to focus on his duties and to view his congregation as his family. But human nature doesn't work this way. A loving, committed human relationship isn't a distraction from work but a support to it; it doesn't hinder, but rather enhances, one's responsiveness to the problems of others. My acquaintance with several inspiring Episcopal priests has made it clear to me that it is possible to be called to the priesthood without being called to a lifetime of celibacy— and, indeed, that being a good priest is not inconsistent with being married, female, or gay. The sort of repression encouraged by Roman Catholic sexual teachings only makes child abuse more likely, for when a gay man rejects the option of living monogamously with another man, he is, like any prisoner, liable to succumb sooner or later to temptation in whatever form it presents itself. Many a young gay Roman Catholic, tormented by guilt over his homosexuality, remains closeted, becomes a priest in order to avoid the issue of marriage, and, unable to control or otherwise gratify his sexual desires, eventually abuses schoolboys.

Vows of celibacy don't produce more godly priests, then; they produce more child abuse. It is not only unrealistic but heartless to expect someone who is not called to celibacy to forsake physical intimacy throughout his entire life without becoming bitter and spiritually twisted and succumbing to sexual desire. Parents who insist that they would never allow their children to be taught by an openly gay man—a man who, precisely *because* he is openly gay, has no reason to reach into his classroom for a sex partner—willingly place their children in the hands of priests who have no one *but* children to turn to as sexual partners. Why do such parents behave so illogically? Because they are clinging to extreme, fantastic stereotypes—the saintly priest without a shadow of a sex drive, the predatory homosexual who is *all* sex drive. The 1992 Vatican directive that pronounced anti-gay discrimination acceptable in the hiring of teachers and coaches was ironic, given that openly gay teachers and

coaches are far less likely to make sexual overtures to children than are
closeted Catholic priests.

In a letter to the *New York Times*, the Reverend Leonard F. Villa
provides a good example of the kind of thinking that underlies Roman
Catholic teachings on homosexuality. Writing in response to an article
about child sexual abuse by Roman Catholic priests, Villa blames such
abuse on the fact that

> We live in a sex-saturated society, wherein alternative life styles are
> trumpeted in popular culture, and homosexuality is advanced as a right
> and a positive good. This agenda has been imported into some semi-
> naries and programs for the religious and the clergy by so-called dis-
> senting theologians, which has succeeded in many cases in breaking
> down inhibitions to deviant behavior and distorting consciences.
>   You [i.e., the *New York Times*] have supported this agenda editorially
> and given these same dissenting theologians a forum to attack the
> church's moral teachings. When these bad ideas produce bad conse-
> quences, proponents of alternative life styles use these cases of pedo-
> philia, not to question the bad morality they support, but to advance
> their final goal: to attack and weaken the church.

By blaming the sexual abuse of children by priests on contemporary
theology and pop culture, Villa only demonstrates that certain church-
men simply refuse to acknowledge how sexual desire works and to speak
honestly about the nature of the problem. The problem is not that today's
society is sex-saturated; it's that man is a sexual being. A priest doesn't
need a theologian or a TV show to put the idea of sex into his head.
Sexual abuse of children by priests didn't begin in recent times, and is
probably no more common now than it ever was: the only difference is
that the victims of such abuse nowadays feel more free to tell their
stories, and stand a better chance of being believed, than would have
been the case a generation or two ago.

Unfortunately, Villa is typical of many Roman Catholic priests in his
equation of homosexuality with pederasty and in his attribution to homosexuals of a motive that the great majority of them would utterly reject:
"to attack and weaken the church." Villa charges gays with hostility
toward his Church, but gay Roman Catholics know where the hostility

really lies. Having honestly sought a meeting ground for their faith and their God-given sexual nature, they have been cruelly repudiated by a Church that refuses to deal frankly with sexual matters. To me, one of the most dramatic contrasts in all of Christianity is that between the gay Episcopal group Integrity, which holds eucharistic services and meetings in Episcopal churches, and whose 1992 convention was addressed by the head of the church in America, Presiding Bishop Edmund Browning, and the gay Roman Catholic group Dignity, which is not even permitted to meet in Roman Catholic churches.

Yet even in the Roman Catholic Church there are hopeful signs. All Roman Catholic priests do not see eye to eye with Leonard F. Villa. More and more of them, recognizing that to respect loving homosexual relationships is not to betray Christ but to serve him, have repented the Church's maltreatment of gay Roman Catholics and have struggled to restore them to the fold. A recent article in the *Los Angeles Daily News* recounted an "epiphany" that helped alter the Reverend Jack Beattie's feelings on the subject. One day in 1989, we are told, Father Beattie

> was called to the City of Angels hospice, where a young gay man was in a coma and dying from AIDS. When Beattie arrived, he found the man's friends sitting around him, one of them stroking his forehead.
>
> Beattie prayed with them, and celebrated the Sacrament of the Sick, also known as the Last Rites. As he left the hospice, the priest suddenly had to pull over to the side of the road.
>
> "Quite literally, the hair on the back of my head stood up," he said. "I remember sitting there and saying I was just there in the presence of God—for where there is love there is God."
>
> Beattie believes the church has failed the gays and lesbians.
>
> "One of the things we have got to do as a church," he said, "is simply apologize and beg forgiveness of the gay community."

One last point in connection with homosexuality and religion: America is not a theocracy. However many churches denounce homosexuality, the American republic is founded not on the Bible but on the principles of democracy, the idea of individual liberty, and, in Jefferson's words, "the pursuit of happiness." In church, one may believe what one will and condemn what one will. But to attempt to place restrictions on individual liberty and the right of others to pursue happiness is, quite simply, un-American.

• • •

Professional opponents of homosexuality, from fundamentalist Christians to secular Jews, have their own way of talking about the subject. They even have their own short lexicon consisting of words that they have learned to use over and over again in order to distort the truth. They have taught these words, moreover, to countless ordinary Americans who don't really know anything about homosexuality. As a result, these words crop up with extraordinary consistency in newspaper articles, in letters to the editor, and in news reports about gay issues. If *Nightline* or *Donahue* does a gay-issues program, the chances are that the representative for the anti-gay position will use most of these words at least once. Among them:

• *Choice.* In a television interview during the 1992 presidential election, Dan Quayle was asked whether homosexuality was a matter of choice. Quayle said, "My viewpoint is that it's more of a choice than a biological situation." He added, "I think it is a wrong choice. It is a wrong; it is a wrong choice. I do believe in most cases it certainly is a choice."

A *New York Times*/CBS News poll taken in March 1993 showed that America is evenly divided on this question. Forty-four percent think that people choose to be gay; 43 percent think that homosexuality is something that people "can't change." Jeffrey Schmalz, in a *New York Times* article about the poll results, noted that there was a strong connection between respondents' opinions on this subject and their attitudes on a variety of gay-related questions. People who believe homosexuality to be a matter of choice are far more likely than those who see it as unchosen and unchangeable, for example, to regard homosexual relations between adults as morally wrong, to believe that such relations should be illegal, to disapprove of permitting gays to serve in the military, and to object to having a gay doctor.

For many, this seems to be the main question about homosexuality: is it something that one chooses? I've never quite understood how anyone could believe that it is. Why, if you weren't really more attracted to your own sex than to the opposite sex, would you decide that you wanted to spend your life as a homosexual? It makes no sense, especially given all the additional trouble that homosexuals have to live with. Why would you do it? To be ornery? So that you can live in danger of getting beaten up by gay-bashers, of being called "faggot" on the street by teenage boys, of losing your job or home because you're gay? Or is Dan Quayle suggesting that all men are in fact more attracted to other men than to women, but that only some choose to act upon it? If he believes it, on what evidence does he base his belief?

To describe homosexuality as a matter of choice is not only wrong; it's absurd and obscene. It denies the torment of every teenager who was ever rejected by his family for being gay; it denies every gay teenage suicide; it denies the existence of the millions of married men who lead lives of quiet desperation, hiding their homosexuality from their wives and children. What makes people like Quayle, who presumably have been around enough to know a few homosexuals, say such things? The motivation, I think, is a refusal to face the truth about homosexuality—for to face that truth would bring people like Quayle closer to recognizing fully the unfairness and brutality of their own prejudices. If people like Quayle accepted that homosexuality is not a matter of choice, then they would have to recognize it as an unchangeable fact of life with which they must come to terms.

The simple answer to Quayle is: "Take my word for what I feel." A longer answer is that gays *do* face a choice—but not the choice to which Quayle refers. As Eric Marcus writes in *Newsweek*, "I *did* have a choice, but not between homosexuality and heterosexuality. I could choose to live in the closet, maybe even marry a woman and pretend to be who I'm not, or I could be honest about who I am and live my life openly—no easy thing to do. I didn't choose to be gay, but I did choose to tell the truth."

Perhaps one reason why some people are so fixated on the notion of homosexuality as a choice is that choices can be reversed. Anti-gay activists routinely cite statistics on gays who have been "changed back" to heterosexuality by "therapists." But this is nonsense. It's no more possible to turn a homosexual straight through therapy than it is to turn a heterosexual gay. Sexual orientation is an essential element of a person's identity. Any homosexual who knows what it is like to emerge from years of denial and to accept one's own sexuality knows very well what has happened to people who claim to have been "changed." What has happened, quite simply, is that these people—who wouldn't be trying to "change," of course, if they had ever fully accepted their sexual identity—have returned to a state of denial. What is cruel about this situation is that these "ex-gay" individuals are encouraged to marry and have families. This is unfair to the spouses and children: for the "ex-

gay" individuals are not "ex-gay" at all; they are still gay, and they are
emotional cripples as well, who are lying to everyone, most of all
themselves.

The belief of many people that homosexuality is a choice underlies
much of the misguided discourse on the subject, particularly as regards
the effect of gay rights on children. In one essay after another, commentators suggest that gay rights and openness about homosexuality
are somehow incompatible with the best interests of children, and that
some balance has to be found. "Americans have not yet had the full and
open public debate about whether society has an interest and responsibility to foster heterosexuality," writes Catherine O'Neill in a typical
Los Angeles Times essay. "While opposing discrimination, we have not
agreed that homosexuality is a life model that we will present [to chil-
dren] on the same level as male-female relationships." But the issue
that O'Neill raises is in fact a false issue, a non-issue. Homosexuality
is not something that can be "fostered" or offered as a "life model."
Why? Because *it's not a matter of choice*.

It is because many parents do not understand this fact that they resist
the idea of gay-tolerance lessons in the schools and describe such lessons
as an attempt to "teach homosexuality." During a demonstration in front
of New York's Board of Education headquarters, for instance, Monsignor
John G. Woolsey, the director of the Family Life office of the Archdiocese
of New York, told a reporter: "These people believe that homosexuality
should not be taught to their children as a viable, positive lifestyle."
Parents seem to fear that homosexuality is being offered to their children
as an option—an item, as it were, on a menu of possible "lifestyles."
But it's *not* an option, because it's not a choice. To teach a young person
about homosexuality is merely to tell him that homosexuality exists,
that homosexuals should be treated with the same respect as anyone
else, and that if he or one of his friends happens to grow up to be
homosexual, he shouldn't feel terrible about it. Such lessons are good
for children, not bad. (Monsignor Woolsey's refusal to accept that a
homosexual life may be "viable" and "positive," by the way, would appear
to reflect a belief, contrary to current Roman Catholic teaching, that
homosexuals have some other choice than to be homosexual; for it would
be heartless and un-Christian for a man who understood that sexuality
isn't a matter of choice to suggest that a homosexual orientation dooms
an individual to an existence neither viable nor positive.)

To be sure, a tiny proportion of homosexuals do claim to have chosen to be gay. Why? Because, I think, they are unable to accept the fact that some things in life can't be controlled. Perhaps somewhere on this earth, moreover, there are a few people who *have* chosen, for some inconceivable psychological reason, to spend their lives having same-sex rather than opposite-sex relations, even though they would prefer the latter. But if this is truly the case, then these people aren't really homosexuals, because deep down their primary attraction is not to their own sex; rather, they're straight people who are betraying their own true nature, in the same way as gay people who marry members of the opposite sex.

Even the Vatican acknowledges that homosexuality is not a matter of choice.

• *Recruit.* As General Thomas Moore remarked on *Donahue,* "They can't reproduce, so they have to recruit." This notion was popularized by Anita Bryant during her 1970s "Save Our Children" campaign. "Since homosexuals cannot reproduce," she wrote in her autobiography, "they must recruit, must freshen their ranks." The fiction of "recruiting" is connected to the fiction of "choice": if gays can choose to be gay, then they can also influence others to make the same choice. It's a scary image: the gay man as vampire, inducting young people into the corrupt brotherhood everywhere he goes. But what makes the image powerful, I think, is that for some parents it may also be strangely comforting; because if people become gay through "recruiting," then homosexuality is something that comes from outside, something from which one's children can be protected by keeping homosexuals away from them and by prohibiting teachers from mentioning the subject. The truth is precisely the opposite: sexual orientation comes from inside. It's probably entirely innate, and in any event is fixed by an extremely early age and has absolutely nothing to do with exposure or lack of exposure to homosexuals. Raising a child who is destined to be straight in an all-gay household won't turn him gay. Keeping a child who is destined to be gay from ever hearing the word "gay" won't make him straight. (It'll just make him very confused when he reaches adolescence.)

Yet many people cling to the illusion of recruitment. Will Perkins, the leader of the anti-gay group Colorado for Family Values, says: "From up until the time I was in the eighth or ninth grade, I didn't really like girls, wasn't interested in them. If I had a counselor who was predisposed in that way, he could have easily convinced me: 'You're one of us. We like guys.' " First of all, no responsible school counselor would ever say such a thing to a student: it's not the job of such a person to determine a student's sexual orientation, straight *or* gay. Second, it's ludicrous to suggest that a heterosexual teenager who has lived his entire life in a society that tells him he's straight will be "turned gay," in effect, because one person tells him he's gay.

• *Advocate, promote.* Similar to the idea of gay "recruitment" is the idea that measures taken to guarantee gay civil rights, for example, are designed to "advocate" or "promote" homosexuality. In an interview a week after the 1992 Republican convention, Dan Quayle told a reporter that he accepted the right of homosexuals to "choose" their "lifestyle," and even to teach school, "as long as they don't advocate it [homosexuality] as preferable." And George Bush, as I've noted, expressed the hope that a hypothetical gay grandchild "wouldn't become an advocate for a life style that in my view is not normal."

Bush and Quayle are typical of many in asserting that they aren't attacking homosexuals but are rather simply expressing disapproval of gays who "advocate" or "promote" homosexuality. But this is absurd. Just as homosexuality is not a matter of choice, it is not a matter of advocacy or promotion. Either you're gay or you're not. You can advocate equal rights for homosexuals, but the idea of advocating homosexuality makes no more sense than advocating lefthandedness.

• *Unnatural, abnormal.* "I think you'll all agree with me," said Senator Strom Thurmond to a panel of gay military officers at the Senate Armed Services Committee hearings on gays in the military, "that homosexuality is not the normal lifestyle."

Homosexuality, say many heterosexuals, is abnormal, unnatural. Yes, it is—for them. Just as heterosexuality is unnatural for homosexuals.

To a heterosexual man, being with a woman feels natural. And the idea of being with a man feels very unnatural. It's the opposite with a gay man. To a gay man, being with another man feels natural. And to him, it *is*. It's *his nature*. If a gay man feels pressured to marry by society or his family or himself, the feeling that he has about such a marriage is comparable to the way a heterosexual man would feel if he were forced to sleep with another man. In either case, a man would be doing something that felt unnatural to him. In Mary Renault's 1959 novel *The Charioteer*, a homosexual merchant marine named Ralph Layton, who for several months has slept only with women, sleeps with

a man again and thinks, "Thank the Lord, back to normal at last."
Precisely; for a homosexual, turning from a female to a male bed partner
does feel normal. Eric Marcus writes, "President Bush said I'm not
normal. I don't know what he means. Bush's left-handedness isn't normal either, if 'normal' means 'in the majority.' But like being left-handed,
being gay doesn't diminish my humanity, my normal wish to love, be
loved, contribute and prosper."

• *Lifestyle.* In a *New York Times* op-ed, Kay S. Hymowitz writes that
the Rainbow Curriculum in New York City represented an attempt "to
incorporate the teaching of homosexual life styles in New York City's
public schools" and that it drew opposition from blacks and Hispanics
"who were offended by the equation of gay and lesbian life styles with
African-American or Latino traditions."

"Lifestyle" is a convenient term. It enables people to deny the equality
of individuals who happen to be gay with individuals who happen to be
straight by pretending that the matter at issue is not individual rights
or personhood but a certain way of life. It sounds better to say that you
don't want your children taught about "the gay lifestyle" than to say
that you don't want your children to learn tolerance.

People like Hymowitz speak of a "gay lifestyle" as if it were some
monolithic concept. But, as I've said, there is as wide a variety of "lifestyles" among homosexuals as among heterosexuals. Some homosexuals lead wild lives; some lead quiet, conservative lives. To quote a *Wall
Street Journal* reader's irate comment on the phrase: "Why is it that as
a gay man I have a *life style*, while a straight man has a *life*?" "Would
somebody please tell me what a gay lifestyle is?" Eric Marcus writes.
"One may choose a country-club lifestyle, a Western lifestyle, a city
lifestyle, but there is no such thing as a gay lifestyle—just as there is
no such thing as a heterosexual lifestyle. Homosexual lifestyles, like
heterosexual lifestyles, run the gamut. They defy classification. And the
only way I can 'promote' my sexual orientation is to show other gay and
lesbian people by my example that you can be homosexual, live outside
the closet and lead a full, happy, family-centered life."

• *Equivalent.* Opponents of gay rights complain about the danger of
gay relationships being viewed as the "moral equivalent of traditional
marriage." What does this mean? It's as if "marriage" were some abstract
concept and not a very real thing—a contract between two people. We

are speaking here, after all, of civil arrangements, not religious sacraments. Some people marry in churches or synagogues; others are married by justices of the peace or by judges at City Hall. Under civil law, though certainly not in the eyes of people of various faiths, these marriages are all equally valid, all *legally* "equivalent." Moral equivalence does not enter into the matter: the point of civil rights legislation is not to make statements about what sort of social arrangements are or aren't morally equivalent with one another—that isn't the province of the law— but to guarantee equality of rights under the law. Marriage is recognized by the state not because some religions consider it a sacrament but because it reinforces civilized values by enhancing the reliability of workers and the stability of homes. Committed gay couples exist by the millions, and it is unquestionably in the state's interest that homosexuals live in such couples rather than live alone and sleep around; why shouldn't the state, then, recognize those relationships as it does heterosexual commitments? For the state to do so would not deny to anyone the right to consider his or her marriage morally superior to my domestic partnership—or, for that matter, to anyone *else's* heterosexual marriage.

For my part, I wouldn't want to live in a relationship that was the "moral equivalent" of most of the marriages with which I'm familiar. Half the husbands I know cheat on their wives. Some beat their wives. Some couples argue constantly; some hardly speak to each other. Some of the husbands are dominated completely by their wives, some of the wives are slaves to their husbands. Some get along passably with each other but have very superficial relationships. Some seem to have nothing in common but sex. Not in a million years would I want a relationship that was "morally equivalent" to such marriages. Nor would I ever suggest that because my relationship is more trusting and loving than someone else's marriage, or because my companion and I are more compatible than this or that married couple, that I'm somehow more virtuous than somebody else. No, I'm just extremely lucky. In any event, I can't imagine being a straight man and denying a gay couple the same rights that I have as a married person on the grounds that their relationship isn't "morally equivalent" to mine. What audacity! What arrogance! What stunted humanity!

• *Agenda.* "I think there are a lot of people who are sick and tired of having this homosexual-agenda stuff shoved down their throats," said a supporter of Oregon's anti-gay Measure 9. "There's an agenda to promote homosexuality as a desirable lifestyle," said a mother on the *Jane Whitney* show (thereby using, in one short sentence, three words from the anti-gay lexicon).

Homophobes like to argue that gay-rights supporters have an "agenda." It's one of those words that politicians use in campaigns. They have a "cause"; their opponents have an "agenda." The word makes it sound as if you're at war with shady characters who have a sinister secret plan. "What agenda?" a homosexual said on one of the talk shows. "I don't want to be thrown out of my job or my home just because I'm gay. That's my agenda." "We have an agenda," said Urvashi Vaid, former director of the National Gay and Lesbian Task Force. "It's civil rights." Or, as Martina Navratilova observed on *Nightline:* "Wanting to adopt a child is not a political agenda."

• *Special rights, special privileges, special protection.* When Governor Pete Wilson signed California's gay-rights bill in September 1992, the Reverend Lou Sheldon, chairman of the Traditional Values Coalition, said that Wilson had "opened the door for all kinds of special rights for perverted, sexually-addicted people."

What special rights is Sheldon talking about? Well, he and other anti-gay activists raise the specter of affirmative-action quotas and recruitment programs for gays in government jobs, the military, college admissions, and the like. But quotas and recruitment programs do not figure in any of the gay-rights bills that have passed various state and local legislatures. Those bills seek not to create "special rights" but to protect people from unfair prejudice and to expand existing rights to those who have been denied them. The question, then, is one not of special rights but of equal rights. The gay-rights movement, in short, is not a matter of gay people demanding special rights on account of their homosexuality; it's a matter of gay people demanding that their homosexuality not be used as an excuse to deny them equal rights. The term "special rights" was coined, of course, because it is easier to win support for a crusade against special rights than for a war on equal rights. (A friend of mine once said, "The term 'gay rights' should be changed to 'happen-to-be-gay rights.' Because that's what we're talking about here: treating those who happen to be gay in the same way we treat those who happen to be straight.")

This is not to suggest that some gays—like some blacks before them— wouldn't seek to establish affirmative-action programs to benefit their own minority group. But I don't think such programs would stand a chance. The great majority of homosexuals, I suspect, would strongly oppose them; I know I would. Quota systems subordinate individual identity to group identity; they reinforce the tendency to view someone who happens to belong to a minority group not as an individual but as a member of that group. The aspirations of most homosexuals lie in precisely the opposite direction: more than anything else, we want people to see past the "gay" label, and past whatever associations that label may carry in their minds, and to view us as individuals.

• *Family.* Nothing has been more vile than the use of the word "family" as a club with which to beat gays. At the 1992 Republican convention, while teenage members of the Republican Youth Coalition (which is under the control of the Republican National Committee) waved signs reading "Family Rights Forever, Gay Rights Never," Dan Quayle proclaimed that "Americans try to raise their children to understand right and wrong only to be told that every so-called 'life-style alternative' is morally equivalent. That is wrong. The gap between us and our opponents is a cultural divide. It is not just a difference between conservative and liberal, it is a difference between fighting for what is right and refusing to see what is wrong."

But what is most assuredly wrong, where homosexuality and the family is concerned, is to raise your child to be the kind of teenager that harasses gays—the kind of teenager that, if he turns out to be gay, will be so overwhelmed with guilt and self-hatred that he'll be incapable of living as a decent, contented, and self-respecting adult. If Murphy Brown had a homosexual child, he'd probably end up fine; it's people with attitudes like those reflected in Quayle's speech whose homosexual children end up as runaways, prostitutes, and teen suicides.

• *Endorse, approve.* On May 27, 1993, during a live broadcast of *CBS This Morning,* a Virginia minister asked President Clinton about the issue of gays in the military. In his response, Clinton startled and dismayed many gay supporters by borrowing the words "endorse" and "approve" (not to mention "promote" and "lifestyle") from the anti-gay lexicon. "Most Americans," said Clinton, "believe that the gay life style should not be promoted by the military or anybody else in this country. . . . We are trying to work this out so that our country does not appear to be endorsing a gay life style. . . . I think most Americans will agree when it works out that people are treated properly if

they behave properly without the Government appearing to endorse a
life style."

Opponents of gay rights argue that they are being asked to "endorse
homosexuality" or to "approve of the gay lifestyle." But to speak of
homosexuality as something of which one can approve or disapprove,
something that one can endorse or refuse to endorse, is to distort its
nature, to pretend that it is a matter of choice. One can approve or
disapprove of somebody's actions, opinions, beliefs; but it is meaningless
to speak of approving or disapproving of another person's innate characteristics. To say that one approves or disapproves of somebody's homosexuality is comparable to saying that one approves or disapproves of
somebody's baldness or tallness.

• *Politicize.* Many people say they're not anti-gay; they just don't like
to see gays "politicizing" their sexuality. In a sense, I agree: I don't like
it when gays reduce their individual identities to a political idea. But
often what people mean when they complain about gays "politicizing"
their sexuality is that they don't see why there should be such a thing
as a gay-rights movement or gay-rights laws. So accustomed are these
people to statutes that distinguish between gay and straight and that
criminalize gay sex that it doesn't occur to them that it is not gays but
these anti-gay statutes that do, in fact, "politicize" their sexual orientation.

• *Practice, activity, behavior, conduct.* To quote Admiral Thomas Moore,
former chairman of the Joint Chiefs of Staff: homosexuality is "a filthy,
disease-ridden practice." To quote a letter distributed by Mary Cummins, school board president for District 24 in Queens, New York, to
22,000 parents: "We will not accept two people of the same sex engaged
in deviant sex practices as 'family.'" And to quote a letter to the *New
York Times* from J. L. Reilly of Littleton, Colorado, in support of Colorado's anti-gay Amendment 2:

> Just as the state and society have expressed disapproval of other forms
> of personal conduct deemed undesirable—prostitution, solicitation,
> drug use, tobacco smoking, public indecency, bestiality and adultery,
> to name a few—so too has homosexuality been identified as inappro-
> priate for legal protection. . . . Like most other states Colorado outlaws
> prostitution, solicitation, and other sex-related activities. Coloradans
> have concluded that certain sexual activities, even among consenting
> adults, are not worthy of legal protection or social acceptance.

Words like "practice" and "activity" draw attention to what gay people do, or supposedly do, in bed. To many homosexuals, the fixation of some homophobes on this subject seems curious, to say the least. The fixation is, I suppose, understandable: when two heterosexuals meet each other, it usually doesn't occur to one of them to imagine the other having sex. But when a heterosexual who doesn't know many homosexuals meets someone whom he knows to be gay, that person's sexuality becomes, for the heterosexual, the cardinal fact about him, subsuming every other attribute. The heterosexual can't *help* imagining the homosexual in bed—and he doesn't like what he sees.

Because the thought of homosexual sex affects so many heterosexuals so strongly and negatively, it is in the interests of opponents of homosexuality and gay rights to focus attention on bedroom matters. By using such dehumanizing words as "practice" and "activity," anti-gay activists reduce profound personal relationships to graphic peep-show images. These words isolate the sexual act; they strip it from the context of life and love and partnership and hold it up for all to see, naked, scandalous, and clinically explicit. Most homosexuals want to fall in love, to be part of a couple, to make a life with someone else. Sex is usually an important part of the picture, but it's *only* a part. Yet heterosexuals who speak of "activity" either can't see, or don't want others to see, beyond that part. Words like "activity" and "practice" also accomplish something else: they downplay recognition of the homosexual as a kind of person whose sexual orientation cannot be changed, while implying a connection between homosexuality and such objectively self-destructive (and reversible) behavioral phenomena as heavy drinking and drug taking. Canon Barger and his "rehabilitation" model to the contrary, homosexuality is not a bad habit or addiction of which a gay person can and should be broken; it's about the whole way that one experiences love and human attachment in this world, if one happens to be gay.

For all the propagandists' emphasis on "activity," moreover, in reality such institutions as the armed forces, the Boy Scouts, and the clergy of many Protestant denominations terminate membership on the basis not of sexual activity but of sexual orientation. If a soldier is discovered having sex with another man, he may be permitted to stay in the Army so long as he testifies that he's not homosexual—that the liaison, in other words, was an example of what is called "situational homosexuality." If a soldier is not discovered having sex with another man but simply admits that he is homosexual, he will be discharged. Such policies point up the hypocrisy of the anti-gay activists' emphasis on "activity"; for, in one institution after another, the real target is not individuals (gay or straight) who may have done certain things in bed but individuals whose natural sexual orientation differs from that of the majority.

Many heterosexuals use words like "behavior" to describe homosexuals' personal lives in a way at which they would take grave offense if someone spoke thus about them. In a *Commentary* essay on the homosexual English novelist E. M. Forster, for example, Cynthia Ozick writes that "the Gay Liberation argument that homosexual activity is a positive good in a world afflicted by overpopulation would not have won Forster over." Her opinion of Forster and "the Gay Liberation argument" aside, what startles one about this sentence is the phrase "homosexual activity." What Ozick shares with her husband is, one presumes, a loving home; what two men living together share is "homosexual activity." One is dismayed to see Ozick, a sensitive and intelligent writer, using so unspeakably cruel, insulting, and diminishing a phrase.

Some opponents of gay rights follow the Roman Catholic Church's formula: the Church, recognizing that homosexuals are born gay and can't do anything about it, opposes "homosexual conduct," not "homosexual orientation." Referring to Commander Gomulka's aforementioned position paper on homosexuality, Captain Ellis, the Marine Corps chaplain, said that it was not intended to be "hostile toward persons who are homosexuals—just hostile toward homosexual behavior." Yet to recognize homosexual orientation as naturally occurring and morally neutral, while insisting that acting upon that orientation is, in every instance and without exception, abnormal, unnatural, and perverse, makes no sense. If homosexual "behavior" comes as naturally to gays as heterosexual "behavior" comes to straight people, then how can heterosexual sex in marriage be seen as a blessing, a virtue, and a force for good, while homosexual sex within a committed long-term relationship is seen as an evil, deviant urge that must be resisted?

When decent, well-meaning people say that they don't mind homosexuals but are simply "opposed to homosexual behavior," all I can think is that such unintentional heartlessness could only be the result of a failure to consider, or an inability to imagine, how things look through my eyes. After all, I have a pretty good idea how things look to them, because like most homosexuals I've had to make my way from their point of view, which was thrust on me, to the one I have now, as my need to understand myself demanded. In short, while I've seen homosexuality through their eyes—having been raised to do so—they've never seen it through mine.

Homosexuality, at the deepest, truest level, is not a matter of *doing* something. It's a matter of *being* something.

3

"Everything

I do

is gay"

"The only time I ever feel ashamed of being gay," says a friend of mine, "is on Gay Pride Day."

I know what he means, though my own emotions on that day are, at worst, closer to dismay than to shame. Every June, on the appointed Sunday, I stand on the sidewalk somewhere along Fifth Avenue in midtown Manhattan, sometimes alone and sometimes with friends, and watch the march file past, each group behind its identifying banner: the gay senior citizens, the separatist lesbians, the Dykes on Bikes, the People With AIDS coalition, the recovering alcoholics who call themselves Clean and Sober, the interracial couples who call themselves Men of All Colors Together (formerly Black and White Men Together), the gay and lesbian student organizations from various colleges and universities, the local chapters of direct-action groups like ACT UP and Queer Nation, the disco-blaring floats advertising various bars and dance clubs, the volunteers from Gay Men's Health Crisis and God's Love We Deliver, the Parents and Friends of Lesbians and Gays, the gay Catholics, the gay Episcopalians, the gay Jews, the Gay Fathers, the gays in leather, the gay swimmers . . .

My feelings are always mixed. There's a certain comfort in being among so many people who have all experienced self-discoveries similar to one's own, and who have all had to deal with the same slights and cruelties that homosexuals have to put up with from people who want to inflict pain or who don't care or who just don't know any better. The march also provides safety in numbers: no danger of gay-bashing here. And it affords a spectacle of quiet heroism: many of the marchers are dying. (In some cases you can tell, in some you can't.) Watching them file past, I know that I'm looking at thousands of untold stories of extraordinary courage.

Yet on that appointed Sunday in June there is always for me, as well, a certain disquiet. Year by year, I find myself increasingly vexed by certain aspects of the march. Part of me doesn't want to attend it. If at its best the event hints at the diversity of the gay population in America, altogether too much of it is silly, sleazy, and sex-centered, a reflection of the narrow, contorted definition of homosexuality that marks some sectors of the gay subculture. On Gay Pride Day in 1991, for instance, I was perplexed to see that among the handful of V.I.P.s on the reviewing stand at Forty-first Street was Robin Byrd, an X-rated movie actress who generally appears in public wearing a string mesh bikini. Byrd's weekly public-access TV program showcases the talents of youngsters, some of them teenage runaways, who work in Times Square strip clubs. Did the organizers of the march, I wondered, really want the world to think that *this* was what being gay was all about?

Byrd may also have been on the reviewing stand a year later, but I didn't see her. On Gay Pride Day 1992 I positioned myself a half-mile or so north of the reviewing stand, near the corner of Fifth Avenue and Fifty-fourth Street. This intersection is three blocks north of Saint Patrick's Cathedral, opposite which a few dozen protesters traditionally congregate behind blue police lines, yelling anti-gay epithets and waving homemade signs on which they have scrawled the usual scriptural quotations. It is customary for marchers passing this group to chant, with rather dignified restraint, "Shame! Shame! Shame!" For some reason, on Gay Pride Day 1992 a group of protesters left their assigned spot while the march was still going by. As they headed up the Fifth Avenue sidewalk past me, toting signs that read "Jesus Forever—Repent," the Queer Nation contingent was about to reach Fifty-fourth Street. The two groups clashed near the northeast corner. "Shame! Shame! Shame!" the Queer Nation members chanted, breaking ranks and heading for the sidewalk as a dozen or so policemen moved quickly to form a human barricade. The Queer Nation marchers and the anti-gay protesters exchanged verbal abuse for a few moments; then the protesters resumed walking up the sidewalk and the Queer Nation contingent peeled away to continue marching down the avenue. Everything seemed in order until one Queer Nation member, a short leather-clad young man with a bushy mustache who was at the moment no more than six or eight feet from me, suddenly stopped and turned around to shriek happily, at the top of his lungs, at the departing protesters: *"Jesus was a faggot!"*

I shook my head in disappointment. Now what, I wondered, was the point of *that*?

Apart from that episode, there were the usual sights. Bearded men in dresses. Young men masquerading as Marilyn Monroe, Mae West, Barbara Bush, Joan Collins. Fat men in bathing trunks. Two friends, one dressed as a priest and the other as Jesus. A couple of dozen young fellows in a truck that displayed two banners, one reading "Gay Whores" and the other "Legalize Prostitution." (I recognized one of the young men from my health club, where he always swims in the fast lane.) There was a float blaring dance music and bearing the name of the radical New Alliance Party, some of whose members marched behind and alongside the float, chanting threateningly with raised fists: "N.A.P.! We got to build a New Alliance Movement!" And there were three— count 'em, three—middle-aged members of NAMBLA, the North American Man-Boy Love Association, two of whom carried the organization's banner while the third held up a sign proclaiming the joys of pederasty.

It must be emphasized that most of the marchers were not at all shocking. There were several times more Gay Catholics than Gay Whores, more men in tennis shorts than in underpants. And NAMBLA was the tiniest group of all. Yet there was plenty to make John Q. Public do a double take—plenty, indeed, that appeared to have been designed to accomplish precisely that. It seemed as if people who wore suits and ties on the 364 other days of the year had, on this particular morning, ransacked their closets for their tackiest, skimpiest, most revealing items of clothing. There were hundreds of bare chests, bare bottoms, mesh pants, nipple rings, leather shorts, and tight designer briefs without anything covering them. Couples who almost certainly didn't go in for public displays of affection on an ordinary Sunday made sure to pause every block or so during their progress down Fifth Avenue to kiss or grab each other's crotches or rub their bodies together in a simulation of sex. There was more sashaying and queeny posing in a couple of hours than one could expect to see in a solid month of gay bar-hopping. Smart, talented people who held down respectable jobs in the corporate world or the fashion industry, on Wall Street or Publishers' Row, seemed to have done their best on this special day to look like tawdry bimbos, bar boys, and beach bums. Time and again, glimpsing this or that un-conventionally attired or coiffed or made-up marcher, I found myself

feeling momentarily as if I'd stumbled into a private costume party and
seen something I wasn't supposed to see. Unfortunately, however, this
wasn't a private party; it was a public spectacle.

And therein lay its illogic. The signs that some of the participants
carried—signs demanding equal rights, more money for AIDS research,
and so on—suggested that the march was intended, at least in part, to
be a political statement directed at the heterosexual population. But if
this was the case, what could explain the grotesque appearance and
vulgar behavior of so many marchers, who were, quite frankly, a public-
relations nightmare? The facts of the matter, after all, seemed obvious:
the Gay Pride Day march provided a first-class opportunity to exhibit
the real face of gay America, to demonstrate that the gay population is
in every way a cross-section of the country—black and white, rural and
urban, rich and poor. If the gay population put that real face forward
on Gay Pride Day, it wouldn't look alien to anyone. But instead, the
march represented gay America by means of what seems at times to be
a veritable circus parade, a parade that too often underlined the sexual
aspect of gay life—and underlined the most sordid elements of that
sexual aspect. It presented homosexuals less as human beings than as
sexual beings.

That, indeed, is the hallmark of the gay subculture: the notion that
life, for homosexuals, naturally revolves around sex more than it does
for heterosexuals. This notion is hardly surprising, given that this particular subculture is the creation of people who are united not by ethnicity, religion, or profession but by sexual orientation; yet one of this
notion's unfortunate consequences is an annual march that, instead of
giving the world a representative picture of gay life, offers a strange and
demeaning caricature thereof. Looking at some of those marchers, I
couldn't help thinking that the subculture mentality had worked upon
them in such a way that they virtually considered it their responsibility
as gay people to reduce themselves to stereotypes every Gay Pride Day;
however much they might or might not have to do the rest of the year
with the subculture and its ethos, however far they may have grown
away from it and into themselves, it was clear from their dress and
deportment that, on some level, they had never rejected completely the
subculture's definition of what it meant to be gay—and today, apparently,
was their Holy Day of Obligation, their day to be as gay as they could
possibly be.

Most homosexuals in the New York area, of course, weren't anywhere near the march. Most hadn't even considered coming; they *never* came. Where were they? Well, some were doubtless enjoying a leisurely brunch; some were spending Sunday with their families; some were puttering around the house, or walking in the park, or taking in a movie. I'd seen at least two dozen gay men at church that morning, every last one of them elegantly turned out in suit and tie and polished black shoes, and would be astonished, to say the least, to see any of them in the march. I hadn't mentioned the march to any of them, but I'd talked about it enough with gay friends to have a pretty good idea how they'd react: with a wince, a grimace, a rhetorical question or two: "Who'd want to be part of that tacky display? Why should I participate in something whose sole purpose is to make a dirty joke out of who I am?"

I can't say I felt very differently. I could never bring myself to take part fully in a march that included the likes of NAMBLA. Yet most years I did go so far as to include myself in the ranks of the thousands of spectators who, after the last marchers had passed, tagged along at the end all the way down to Greenwich Village. For I felt that if the image of homosexuals that the march projected was ever to be set right, those of us who were displeased with it in its present form couldn't keep away entirely. We had to do *something*.

That day, as on every previous Gay Pride Day, I found myself reflecting on the march's ramifications. In the evening, people in New York and around the country would turn on their local news and see a few seconds of this or some other gay march. I'd watched enough of those reports to have a pretty good idea what the producers would choose to show: some leathermen, maybe the Barbara Bush and Marilyn Monroe impersonators, almost certainly the young man dressed as Jesus. In the succeeding weeks and months, moreover, long after the young stockbrokers and magazine editors had stowed away their flamboyant Gay Pride Day accoutrements for another year and slipped back into their everyday Brooks Brothers togs, anti-gay propagandists would put together videotapes showing these young professionals looking very, shall we say, unprofessional. These videotapes, featuring the most outrageous parts of this and other recent gay marches, would be advertised in right-wing political magazines and various church publications and would be sold and shipped to purchasers around the country. These purchasers, in turn, would make copies for friends and relatives or show them at neighborhood get-togethers, at church socials, at P.T.A. meetings. From Maine to California, men and women would watch these videotapes and shake their heads in disgust, not only at the individuals portrayed in them but at what they presumably represented. To those men and women, this was the face of homosexuality.

Standing there as the march went by, I didn't have to imagine the reactions of small-town middle Americans to the Gay Pride Day march. This was, after all, a Sunday in June in midtown Manhattan, and there were tourists all over the place. From my spot on the Fifth Avenue curb, I watched one out-of-town family after another hurry across the avenue or up the sidewalk, maps and cameras and shopping bags in hand, on their way from one metropolitan attraction to another. It was clear that the Gay Pride Day march did not figure on these people's sightseeing itineraries but had, rather, taken them by surprise. In every instance, I saw nothing on their faces but shock, revulsion, and a desperate desire to get away from Fifth Avenue as quickly as possible.

One family in particular stands out in my memory: a husband and wife and their tall, gangly, shy-looking son, who was about thirteen and who, it occurred to me, might well wake up one morning four or five years hence and realize he was gay. It distressed me to think that this march would probably shape that family's most vivid image of homosexuality. If the boy did eventually prove to be gay, the memory of this day could only make it harder for him to recognize and come to terms with his homosexuality and for his parents to understand and accept the truth about him. That shouldn't be the way things worked. If the march had any legitimate purpose, it was to make things easier, not harder, for young gay people and their families. Things would be hard enough for them as it was.

That afternoon, on a float for a drinking establishment called the Crowbar, I noticed a sign: "Greetings from the Planet Gay!" The sign, I felt, summed up the whole day: too many of the people involved in the march *did* think of themselves as living on another planet—or, at least, thought of their sexual identity as being something from another planet. They had been provided here with an extraordinary opportunity to educate the heterosexual population about homosexuality, to destroy backward myths, to win friends and supporters for the cause of gay equality; instead, much of the march simply served to reinforce myths, to confirm prejudices, and to make new enemies for homosexuals. If Jerry Falwell or Pat Robertson had wanted to orchestrate an annual spectacle designed to increase hostility toward gays, I reflected, they could hardly have done a better job than this.

It seemed to me, indeed, that the sort of pride on display in the Gay Pride Day march was, in many cases, not so much pride in the sense of "self-respect" or "dignity" than pride in the sense of "arrogance," "conceit," "hubris." Real pride, after all, is a hard-won individual attribute. It doesn't come from being gay, or from belonging to *any* group. It can come, however, from dealing with the fact of your homosexuality in a responsible and mature manner, from not using it as a club to beat other people with or as an excuse to behave irresponsibly or unseriously. The more loudly someone declares his pride, the more it should be suspected; for real pride is not shrill and insistent but quiet and strong.

After the last marchers had passed my post at Fifty-fourth Street, I went home for a quick bite, then took the subway three miles downtown to Greenwich Village, where I found a place to stand near the door of a small red-brick Episcopal church called Saint Luke in the Fields. From that spot, a few yards from the corner of Hudson and Christopher streets where the parade route ended, I watched the marchers pour into the intersection, meet up with friends, and disperse to different parts of the Village. Every so often one or two of them would come and stand near the entrance to Saint Luke's. Gradually a small crowd formed. Sometime after six, with the marchers still pouring into the intersection after their long walk down Fifth Avenue, the church doors opened and we all filed in for the annual Gay Pride Day evensong service.

It was in most ways a typical evensong. While the yells and laughter and music of the march wafted in through the windows, the organist played a Brahms fugue and a chaconne by Dietrich Buxtehude. The cantor sang an anthem in German. And the congregation sang three hymns. The singing was unusually loud and deep and fervent: most of the people in attendance were men who had strong voices and loved to sing and meant what they were singing. The second hymn was "Engelberg," number 477 in the Episcopal hymnal:

> Thou cam'st to us in lowliness of thought;
> by thee the outcast and the poor were sought;
> and by thy death was God's salvation wrought.
> Alleluia.

Toward the end of the service, the pastor welcomed us and spoke on Saint Paul's text: "Nothing can separate us from the love of God." There were prayers for people who had died of AIDS, who were dying of it, who were infected with the AIDS virus, who were worried that they might be infected with the AIDS virus, and who loved and cared for those who were dead or dying or infected. The prayer leader paused to allow the congregants to recite names aloud, and all around me names floated up to God. "James. Robert. Steven. Jane. David." Suddenly I realized that for the first time all day I was feeling pride: not pride in myself for being gay, but pride in these fellow human beings for being brave and having faith, for walking into church on a beautiful summer evening at the end of a wild and raucous parade to pray and sing hymns and recite the names of their dead and dying loved ones.

A few days later my mother dropped by my apartment. She had just had lunch with a Roman Catholic friend who had seen a bit of the march on her way to work. The friend had said that it was "disgusting." I told my mother that, yes, some parts of the march *were* disgusting; a few participants seemed eager to confirm every fundamentalist's ugliest stereotypes about homosexuality. But I also described to her the service at Saint Luke's. I wished her friend could have seen that, too—although it occurred to me that, after having seen the parade, she might well have considered the service the most profane spectacle of all.

The marchers who make the Gay Pride Day march embarrassing to many homosexuals and disgusting to people like my mother's friend represent the same small but vocal minority of the gay population that has, for a generation, played no small part in shaping and sustaining most heterosexuals' notions of what it means to be homosexual. I've noted that many heterosexuals speak of the "gay lifestyle" as if there were only one way to be gay; but it must also be said that some gays, encouraged by the subculture to think that they are obliged as homosexuals to adopt certain ways and views and tastes, themselves speak of the "gay lifestyle." I've remarked that many heterosexuals think of homosexuality in terms of "practice" or "activity"; but this is at least partly because subculture-oriented gays center their lives on their sexual orientation and because a generation of gay activists have made the right to engage with abandon in certain kinds of sexual activity their

principal cause. One day in December 1992, I walked past Saint Patrick's
Cathedral in New York during an ACT UP protest presumably connected
to the Roman Catholic Church's opposition to pro-tolerance curricula
in the public schools. "Teach gay sex!" the signs read—as if fostering
young people's tolerance of homosexuality, or informing them of the
existence of gay parents, necessarily involved teaching about bedroom
matters. Nothing could be more emblematic of the subculture's view of
homosexuality than this reduction of gay identity, gay life, and gay
culture to gay sex. I've said that being gay isn't a matter of what one
does, in bed or anywhere else, but of what one *is;* too often, alas, the
gay subculture acts as if what one does in bed is the *quintessence* of
what one is.

It's ubiquitous. Walk into a gay bar or club; read a gay newspaper or
magazine; watch a gay entertainment or information program on PBS
or public-access television—do any of these things, and you'll find yourself confronted again and again with the gay-subculture convention of
reducing everything to sex. To a subculture initiate, this sort of thing
can come as a surprise. You may be standing near the piano in a gay
club, sipping your beer while the pianist plays "On the Street Where
You Live," when the next thing you know he's standing up on his piano
bench and baring his posterior. Why? Because this, to him, is part of
what it means to be gay.

Or consider a telling line from a *Baltimore Sun* article that appeared
on April 25, 1993, the day of the March on Washington. In the article,
Arthur Hirsch reported on a mass gay wedding ceremony that had been
held in the capital the day before. "Couples took vows, exchanged rings
or other gifts, kissed passionately and were pelted with flying rice,"
wrote Hirsch, who proceeded to discuss one of the couples:

> For Mitch Goldstone and Carl Berman of Irvine, Calif., the ceremony
> underscored their commitment. In June, they will celebrate their 10th
> anniversary together.
>
> "We own a business together; we share our lives together," says Mr.
> Goldstone.
>
> The public ceremony yesterday, he says, was "a powerful expression
> of our commitment for justice and equality."
>
> So that others might know, Mr. Goldstone took a piece of blue chalk,
> knelt down to the pavement of Constitution Avenue and drew a heart
> and within it the message: "Carl does Mitch."

Not "Carl *loves* Mitch," mind you, but "Carl *does* Mitch." It seemed clear that these two men shared a deeply committed relationship. Yet Mr. Goldstone nonetheless felt compelled to reduce that commitment to the level of the physical act of sex and to refer to it in vulgar language. Why? Because this, to him, is part of what it means to be gay.

In spring 1993 I received in the mail a review copy of a heavily promoted new book: Frank Browning's *The Culture of Desire: Paradox and Perversity in Gay Lives Today*. The publicity materials assured me that Browning, a gay reporter for National Public Radio, had written a serious study that would illuminate the subject of homosexuality in America for gay and straight readers alike. Yet the cover photo alone was enough to raise my doubts. The picture jolted me, for it seemed to reflect a determination to reinforce all the negative stereotypes about homosexuality. It showed two barechested young men who were at most twenty-five years old. They stood one behind the other, directly facing the camera. The one in front was something out of a sex fantasy: blond and beautiful, with a perfectly developed upper body, he stood with his legs apart, his jeans unbuckled, and the top of his underwear showing, Marky Mark–style. He was centered directly on the spine, so that when you placed the book on a shelf with your other books you could see him among the staid titles, face and navel and crotch. Enhancing his role as sex object rather than human being was the fact that you couldn't see his eyes; his head was bent forward, and instead of staring out at the camera, he looked down at his partner's upper arm, which was hooked over his shoulder and which he clutched sensually with both hands. It was his partner, standing behind him, who stared into the camera, and this was the most disconcerting thing about the picture, for the look in his eyes was chilling. He looked disturbed, psychotic. There was the slightest suggestion of danger—one could easily imagine him tightening his grip around his beautiful partner's neck and choking him to death. In any event he looked like someone whose life took its meaning from dehumanized sex and nothing else, and who by meeting your eyes suggested that you shared his obsession.

This picture made me angry. And what made me angrier was looking at the small photograph of Frank Browning on the inside back flap. For Browning didn't look like either of those young men. He was fiftyish, bald, sane-looking, intelligent-looking, with a neatly trimmed white beard and mustache. *This*, I couldn't help thinking, was a far more representative picture of gay America than that sex fantasy on the front

cover. America needed to know that. Why didn't people like Frank
Browning and his publishers understand?

Soon after the publication of *The Culture of Desire* there appeared
another heavily promoted gay book, Michelangelo Signorile's *Queer in
America*. If the cover of Browning's book reinforced the stereotypical
equation of homosexuality with lewdness and promiscuity, the back
cover of Signorile's book—on which the author, in black T-shirt, his
arms crossed, stared defiantly out at the reader—bolstered the image
of gay-as-radical. Meanwhile, the front cover, which featured a map of
the United States that had been flipped over so that the East Coast
appeared on the left and the West Coast on the right, graphically con-
veyed the subculture's view of gays as the utter opposite of heterosexuals—as weird, "queer," totally Other. As if all this weren't enough, the
invitations to Signorile's book party offended in much the same way as
Browning's front cover. As reported in *New York* magazine in May 1993,
the invitations depicted a nude man with the logo of Random House
(Signorile's publisher) on his derrière. When Random House executives
complained, the party organizer said: "It's ironic they're publishing a
book on being out of the closet and objecting to gay images." Yet what
did this silly and vulgar picture have to do with the life of gay people
in America? Why couldn't the party organizer see that to describe such
a picture as a "gay image" was to reduce the lives of people who happen
to be homosexual to a dirty joke?

The subculture shapes the thinking of gays and straights alike. Its
influence is in evidence when the heterosexual actress Sarah Jessica
Parker comments facetiously that she is "basically a homosexual man.
I love clothes. I love good, fine fabrics. I work out. I'm concerned about
my looks. I'm vain." It is in evidence when the designer William Ivey
Long says: "I think being gay is like being on the spice rack. It's not
the real food. It's just the spice." It is in evidence when the gay activist
and writer Michelangelo Signorile tells *Newsday*: "I think all gay men
have a bitchy queen inside them." It is in evidence when a flier accompanying a glossy catalog containing photographs of pouty men in skimpy
underwear and swim togs announces that the catalog "celebrates the
gay perspective on style and living." It is in evidence when a January
1993 *Advocate* cover commemorates the inauguration of the first pro-
gay-rights President and Vice President by placing the faces of Bill

Clinton and Al Gore on the bodies of a tanned, bare-chested couple in cutoffs, their arms around each other, and with the headline "Will Clinton & Gore go all the way for gay rights in 1993?"

When in 1990 Thomas M. Disch, *The Nation*'s drama critic, pointed out that virtually every gay-related play staged in New York that year contained a scene involving female impersonation, he was taking note of a subculture-influenced phenomenon. The ubiquity of transvestism bothered him—not because there is anything terrible about cross-dressing, nor even because cross-dressing (men "becoming" the women their parents thought they wanted to be) is the ultimate emblem of the subculture's view of homosexuality as an absurd and estranging fate, but simply because its ubiquity in gay New York theater didn't say much for the subculture's imaginative breadth.

Many gays who are casual about other matters can be astonishingly mindful not to violate the rules of subculture taste and opinion. A few years back, during a conversation with a stranger in a Lansing, Michigan, gay bar, a friend of mine said a few words in praise of Carly Simon. The stranger, in all seriousness, replied: "Do we like her?" My friend had been in enough gay bars to understand what the stranger meant. He wanted to know whether Carly Simon was—like Madonna, Bette Midler, Joan Rivers, and Barbra Streisand, among others—on the gay subculture's unwritten list of approved entertainers and artists.

Many subculture-oriented gays—and subculture-influenced heterosexuals as well—speak of a distinctive "gay sensibility" or "gay spirit" or "gay soul." They believe that there are such things as inherently gay tastes in everything from art and literature to clothing and decor. It *is* true that from an early age, often long before he realizes that he is gay, many a homosexual will find himself amused by certain movies or touched by certain songs or captivated by certain female performers that may not interest his heterosexual friends at all or that may appeal to them in a strikingly different way. Or he may fall in love with opera, whose male fans are disproportionately gay (though opera fans represent a tiny percentage of the gay population as a whole). It is on the widely— though by no means ubiquitously—shared fascination of many homosexual men with certain cultural phenomena, their tendency to respond to those phenomena in certain ways, and the inclination of some homosexual writers, composers, and artists to make certain types of cultural contributions rather than others, that the notion of a "gay sensibility" is based. It is this notion that is being adduced when, say, the writer

Paul Monette maintains that his teenage "Liz Taylor fetish . . . marked me as a budding queen."

Is there indeed such a thing as a "gay sensibility"? Yes and no. Yes, these special cultural affinities exist. But it is wrong to suggest, as the subculture does, that they are inherent in homosexuality or that they take the same form or exist to the same degree in every gay man. In fact—and this is an important distinction, fine though it may seem— these affinities grow not out of homosexuality per se but rather out of the experience of being homosexual in a society where homosexuality is a marginalizing attribute and where culture, both high and low, tends not to acknowledge its existence explicitly. In such a society, a gay person cannot help being deeply aware of, and having a profound sense of himself as an exception to, the generally accepted ordering of things. The intensity with which a particular gay man experiences these cultural affinities will vary depending on a number of factors, including the level of his intelligence, the range of his imagination, the nature of his individual taste and cultural education—and, one might add, the degree to which he feels himself to be (or permits himself to feel, or indulges his own sense of being) marginalized, ignored, excluded.

Because this special kind of cultural interest derives from a sense of marginalization on the basis of romantic or sexual attraction, its objects tend to be cultural phenomena that defy or lampoon or are at least conspicuously conscious of the mainstream society's sexual, romantic, and domestic assumptions; or, alternatively, cultural phenomena that so mindlessly embrace those assumptions that they are, to a gay admirer, unintentionally funny. Likewise, some gay men make icons of female performers who are not just women but are, in sundry ways, *about* being women. Wordlessly, and for the most part subliminally, these icons make fun (gently or viciously, as the case may be) of the general audience's assumptions about sex roles and sexual identity, and perhaps even about femaleness or heterosexuality or heterosexual romance, thereby making their gay male audiences feel accepted, included, embraced, flattered. If Billie Holiday in her songs and Bette Davis in her movies render a vision of heterosexual relationships and of distaff heartache that can (like opera) be melodramatic to the point of ludicrous self-caricature, so a woman like Marlene Dietrich or Joan Collins seems with every glance, for instance, to snort at the game of the sexes. As

Dietrich's or Collins's elaborate makeup and meticulous lighting and posing, moreover, form a flattering contrast with the naturalness of male beauty, so the neurotically exaggerated mannerisms by means of which a Judy Garland puts over a torch song, or the aggressive sexiness of a Mae West, make gay men's discreet public signals of mutual attraction seem like a mark not of oppression but of refinement and restraint. And so on.

The attraction of many gay men to such entertainers, then, can contain elements of both love and contempt. The icon may be admired for her intelligence and irony and willingness to laugh at herself, or she may be mocked for the utter seriousness with which she takes a sappy script or a lachrymose lyric or her role as a sex goddess. Whether a given gay man happens to be a devotee of a given gay icon, of course, depends on various factors both innate and environmental. Gay men who were taught by their parents to feel contempt for homosexuality and who have never developed very much self-esteem may derive a strong psychological boost from seeing heterosexuality or female sexuality ridiculed. In such cases, when watching a movie or listening to a song becomes nothing more than an excuse to laugh contemptuously at women or heterosexuality, or (even worse) a way of snuggling comfortably inside the cocoon of homosexuality, an attraction to gay icons is neither psychologically healthy nor morally admirable.

Indeed, the problem with "gay sensibility" tastes, which in the case of most gay men exist in conjunction with lively interests in a wide range of cultural phenomena, resides in the fact that for some subculture-oriented gay men, these tastes take the place of, or are confused hopelessly with, a capacity for genuine aesthetic response. Such men experience all culture, to the degree that they experience it at all, in this manner—which is to say that they are able to respond to mainstream culture only as members of a marginalized minority. While there's nothing wrong, then, with "gay sensibility" tastes, they shouldn't be the chief component of *anybody's* cultural equipment. Nor should it ever be forgotten that such tastes are essentially a celebration not of homosexuality but of gay marginalization—which is something that should be lamented, not celebrated.

"All gay men," says a character in Paul Rudnick's off-Broadway play *Jeffrey,* "are obsessed with opera."

I don't like opera.

Certain gay people who love opera like to say that all gay people love opera. They say that we love it because, as people who have been compelled to keep our emotional lives under wraps, we find the overblown emotion of it liberating. This is doubtless true of many so-called opera queens. Yet one gay opera fan of my acquaintance objected strongly to this whole line of argument about gays and opera. "It demeans opera," he said, "and it demeans those of us who happen to be gay but who also happen to love opera for *itself,* not for some psychological boost it supposedly gives us as gay people. To be a gay opera fan is not necessarily to be an 'opera queen.' Opera is art. I don't respond to it as a gay man who identifies with divas or finds the melodrama wonderfully campy or thinks that the whole thing speaks in some special way to me as a homosexual; I respond to it as a human being who's capable of appreciating beauty."

A couple of generations ago, homosexuals received little respect from government, the media, the medical establishment—or themselves. The majority passed as straight, keeping their homosexuality secret from their families and professional colleagues, satisfying their sexual needs furtively in gay bars and waterfront pickup spots, and (often) looking down upon those few homosexuals—some of them "obviously gay"— whose lives seemed to revolve around their homosexuality and who (in many cases) often referred to one another as "girls" or "women" or "sisters." (Meanwhile, many heterosexuals referred to them as "boys"— as in the patronizing title of Midge Decter's 1980 *Commentary* piece on Gay Liberation, "The Boys on the Beach.") Such homosexuals were, then, in agreement with the heterosexuals around them on one point: whatever male homosexuals were, they weren't *men.*

During the years between F.D.R. and L.B.J. a few small, covert gay organizations were founded, a handful of demonstrations were held against anti-gay bigotry, and the occasional gay-rights lawsuit was tried. But the pre-1960s subculture was essentially apolitical: these boys, for the most part, just wanted to have fun. If few of them thought to complain that they might be arrested at any moment simply for being the way they were and for seeking the company of others like them, it was partly because they assumed that things would always be thus and partly because deep down, thanks to the notions about sexuality on which they had been brought up, many of them couldn't bring themselves to believe that they didn't *deserve* to get arrested.

Gay Lib turned things around. Triggered not by a landlord's eviction of a gay couple but by a police raid at a bar, the gay-rights movement focused from the beginning not on domestic-partnership rights but on sexual freedom. Homosexuals might have striven to help heterosexuals to see things through their eyes and thereby to enable their own full integration into mainstream society; instead, unable to imagine such integration ever taking place, the homosexuals who led conservative lives (and who fit most easily into the mainstream world) tended to keep a low profile, while the most extreme elements of the homosexual population participated in demonstrations, building a wall around themselves instead of reaching out.

While the great majority of homosexuals remained invisible, accordingly, the world became increasingly familiar with the radical political ideas and sexual mores of those few gays who, in taking on the Establishment, had also begun to forge for their subculture a set of shared assumptions about politics, society, sex, and religion that were resolutely at odds with the received ideas of the mainstream culture. Those gays promulgated the idea that homosexuals are a distinct social unit, joined not only by a common sexual orientation but by a common political ideology, sexual morality, and cultural philosophy, and that it is reasonable, accordingly, to speak of "gay politics," "gay culture," and (yes) the "gay lifestyle," as if all gay people lived and thought—or, if they don't, *should* live and think—in a certain way. (To be sure, there is a certain range of permissible styles and tastes within the gay subculture: not everyone is expected to be into leather, say, or drag. But one is expected to choose, as it were, from the menu.)

So it is that when young people discover themselves to be gay, they find their way to subculture institutions—bars, community centers, direct-action groups—where, at least somewhat estranged from their past by self-knowledge, and eager to bring their sense of identity into full focus, they are extremely susceptible to the subculture's pressures to conform. A few years ago, a friend of mine came out to his fundamentalist family and moved to New York, where he fell in with a group of drag queens whom he met in a Greenwich Village bar. He liked them very much, but it soon became clear to him that he would never be fully granted their friendship and trust unless he sacrificed much of what made him different from them—for instance, a respect for middle-class values, a passion for baroque music, a suspicion of radical politics, and (mostly) an utter lack of interest in wearing women's clothing—and became one of them. "I knew," he says, "that there was a place in my heart for them, but there was no place in their hearts for me, as I was then. There *would* have been such a place for me, if I'd put on a dress and joined the club. Otherwise, I knew there would always remain a distance."

The temptation was not inconsiderable: my friend felt alone, confused, in need of a family's unconditional love and support. But just as he had resisted the pressure to conform in the fundamentalist community of his youth, so he resisted the similar pressures exerted by those drag queens. Not every gay person, however, is that strong—especially when he or she is in the extremely lost, lonely, and vulnerable position of having just emerged from the closet. Little wonder, then, that so many young people in the 1970s allowed themselves to be convinced that being gay didn't mean falling in love and settling down with someone of the same sex, but meant spending one's life in bed with a large number of anonymous partners—a situation that not only eventuated in widespread spiritual emptiness and sexual obsessiveness but also, of course, made it possible for AIDS to spread more widely and quickly in the United States than it probably would otherwise have done.

The apparent ease with which so many young homosexuals were persuaded to lead promiscuous lives can indeed be explained in large part by the degree to which young gay people feel alone and confused in the years preceding their recognition and acceptance of their homosexuality. For such young people, promiscuity can be a buoyant, desperate overresponse to their sudden sense of freedom and self-knowledge, a swing of the pendulum away from loneliness and an attempt to shore up a sense of sexual identity and to find in the embrace of strangers a brief sense of acceptance and closeness in the wake of a family's rejection. Randy Shilts is partly right, too, to attribute the promiscuity of the '70s to the fact that "in an all-male subculture there was nobody to say 'no'—no moderating role like that a woman plays in the heterosexual milieu." And a psychotherapist named Marjorie Rosenberg is also partly correct when she maintains that "social tolerance of [gay] promiscuity produced its increase" in the 1960s and '70s. But this isn't the whole truth of the matter, and indeed, in her suggestion of a necessary connection between tolerance and promiscuity, Rosenberg is downright misleading. For while gay promiscuity was tolerated in the

'70s, American laws and social attitudes continued to make it more difficult for homosexuals than for heterosexuals to live in monogamous relationships. As the statistics on whorehouses in Victorian England demonstrate, it is relatively easy to carry on a busy sex life, gay or straight, in almost any culture; no one needs anybody's consent in order to sneak off every night to have clandestine casual encounters with strangers. But one *does* require a degree of understanding and approval—on the part of one's family, friends, neighbors, employers, and co-workers alike—in order to live safely and serenely in an open, committed same-sex relationship. And that's a *big* part of the reason for the gay-subculture promiscuity of the 1970s.

A landmark document of the pre-AIDS era is Edmund White's illuminating 1980 book *States of Desire: Travels in Gay America*. The book purported to be a representative survey of homosexual life in the United States. In fact, it was an account of White's encounters with certain homosexuals, a disproportionate number of whom were gay activists, pornographers, transvestites, and other people whose lives revolved around their sexuality. Most abundant of all were the young hustlers whom White met in gay bars and bathhouses and with whom his dealings were, in many cases, more than merely reportorial. It seems singularly bizarre, yet is symptomatic of the subculture's routine equation of sex with culture, that White, one of our most brilliantly gifted novelists, should have written not only this book but the first edition of *The Joy of Gay Sex* as well: it's as if Saul Bellow or John Updike had written *The Joy of Sex*. Rereading *States of Desire* now, one wishes that it had at least been given a more honest subtitle; calling it *Travels in Gay America* was not much less outrageous than writing a survey of inner-city pimps, prostitutes, and drug addicts and calling it *Travels in Black America*. One of the book's few mentions of nonstereotypical, nonsubculture gays occurs on page 141, where someone tells White about a group of gay engineers: "You'd never believe those fellows are gay. They talk about nothing but oil drilling, offshore rigs and freight forwarding." (At this point in the book, to be sure, after 141 pages of anecdotes about gay-bar and bathhouse life in San Francisco, Seattle, and several other Western cities, this reader would have welcomed a bit of dialogue about freight forwarding.)

Implicit throughout the book is that the subculture's approach to gay

life is the only one that makes sense. Indeed, the Edmund White of
States of Desire is more than merely an observer and practitioner of the
fast-and-loose life; he is an ardent proponent of the gay-subculture philosophy of sex and a harsh critic of the old ways. He ridicules the "self-
hatred" of gays who "pair off" into permanent couples. Gay Lib, he
asserts, has moved past "love" into a Brave New World in which promiscuity vanquishes possessiveness and jealousy. He prides himself on
his liberalism but defends exploitation of minors in the form of teen
prostitution and man-boy love; at one point he speaks of a thirty-six-
year-old man's "lover," age twelve. Of such relationships, he says that
"it does no good to disown questionable elements in gay life; we must
defend them." Thus moral considerations and the welfare of young
people take a back seat to gay solidarity; in accordance with the rules
of the subculture, a man's obligations to the abstract idea of the good,
and to virtuous people of whatever sexual orientation, are subordinated
to his determination to defend the actions of other people, good or bad,
who happen to be gay, on the grounds that anything they do is by
definition a part of "gay life."

To be sure, White is too smart to accept the gay-subculture philosophy
without reservations. He admits his discomfort with the fact that, as he
sees it, "the collapse of other social values (those of religion, patriotism,
the family and so on)" has forced sex "to take up the slack, to become
our sole mode of transcendence and our only touchstone of authen-
ticity." He adds that "I can picture wiser people in the next century
regarding our sexual mania as akin to the religious madness of the
Middle Ages—a cooperative delusion" and expresses the hope and expectation that "sex will be restored to its appropriate place as a pleasure,
a communication, an appetite, an art; it will no longer pose as a religion,
a reason for being." (He makes no mention, naturally, of sex as an
expression of love.) The irony of these statements is that it would not
be another century, but would be only another year or so, before the
AIDS crisis began to effect a dramatic change in gay-subculture attitudes toward sex. Indeed, White's book was a case of sadly ironic timing:
published on the brink of the AIDS epidemic, it glorified the very way
of life that precipitated that crisis.

A few years after *States of Desire*, another gifted novelist, Andrew
Holleran, wrote a piece entitled "Notes on Promiscuity." By turns per-

ceptive and exasperating, the piece both reflects and reflects upon gay-subculture attitudes toward promiscuity; it is at once a critical exami-nation and a defense of the subculture's sexual philosophy. Here is note number 1, for instance: "If a young man is promiscuous, we say he is *sowing his oats;* if a young woman is promiscuous, we say she is a *slut;* if a homosexual of any age is promiscuous, we say he is a *neurotic example of low self-esteem.*" Holleran's point, of course, is that prom-iscuity among gay men is viewed differently by most people than is promiscuity among straight men. True enough, but he ignores the fact that most heterosexual men who are "sowing oats" don't have sex with several partners a night, as many gay men did in the bathhouses of the 1970s and early '80s; if heterosexual men did such a thing, most people would call *them* neurotic, too. (Besides, continuing to be promiscuous into middle age and beyond can hardly be described as "sowing oats.")

Here is Holleran's note number 8: "Sex is a pleasurable experience repeated many, many times during our lives that, if experienced with the same person each time, is considered responsible, adult, mature; if experienced with a different person each time, is considered promis-cuous." Why? Because sex experienced with the same person each time is presumably an expression of affection, part of a relationship; with a multiplicity of partners it tends toward sheer animal gratification. Note number 12: "It takes time to become promiscuous. Married couples reading stories about AIDS are astounded to learn that a homosexual man has slept with eight hundred men; to the homosexual reader, this does not seem *that* bizarre." Maybe it didn't seem bizarre to the sub-culture-oriented readers of the gay magazine *Christopher Street* in which this list originally appeared, but to most homosexuals it certainly does. Here is note number 19:

> When a friend asked me, "Why are gay men promiscuous?" I started to reply, "Because they don't marry and have children, because they feel guilty about being gay, because they're men, because men are like dogs, because they're lonely, because everyone would have as much sex as he could if he could, because sex is the most transcendent experience"—then I saw my friend lighting another cigarette, and said, "Why do you smoke?"

Yes, and how about: because they confuse liberation with childish aban-don, as if no responsibility went along with it; and because, having been brought up to believe that being gay was itself inherently decadent, they didn't feel that they had any further to sink by running wild. (Of course, it is not fair to ask "Why are gay men promiscuous?" because even in the 1970s far from all gay men *were* promiscuous.)

Here's note number 38: "The nature of promiscuity came clear to me the night at the baths when I looked back at the doorway of the room whose occupant I had just fallen deeply in love with after the most wonderful, intense, earth-shattering, intimate, and ecstatic sex and watched another man walk into his room and close the door behind him with a little click." How's that? "Deeply in love"? The ultimate tragedy of 1970s gay promiscuity, aside from the fact that it eventuated in AIDS, was that intelligent, sensitive men like Andrew Holleran could confuse great sex with great love, and have scads of the former yet end up alone. "Promiscuity," he writes in note number 40, "entails a double standard: We want to be promiscuous ourselves, but we want the people we sleep with to want only us." Precisely, and this observation cuts to the heart of why promiscuity can cause so much pain and ultimately be dehumanizing: to sleep with hundreds of partners a year makes it easier to deny the individuality and the distinctive histories of those partners, and to impose one's fantasies on their unfamiliar faces and bodies. That they are doing the same thing doesn't mitigate the offense. Taken to an extreme, then, sexual liberation can mean deliverance not from cruel shackles that inhibit sensual delight but from human responses and responsibilities.

Randy Shilts's book about the AIDS crisis, *And the Band Played On,* documents the astonishing ways in which gay-subculture leaders' refusal to abandon the ideal of sexual liberation contributed—along with the apathy of the medical establishment, the media, and the federal government—to the spread of AIDS in the early 1980s. Even after it was clear that anal sex could spread AIDS, for example, a gay newspaper in Toronto ran an article on "rimming [anal-oral contact] as a revolutionary act." A San Francisco gay organization condemned an order requiring health warnings in bathhouses as "a direct attack on the social and economic viability of our community"; gays who supported bathhouse closings were accused of being "collaborators" in an attempted "annihilation of gay life"; and a gay writer who suggested that gays abstain from sex "until it once again is safe" was labeled a "sexual

Nazi." Meanwhile, bathhouse owners (one of whom cynically told an AIDS doctor: "We're both in it for the same thing. Money") were hailed as heroes of the gay community and the bathhouses themselves cele- brated as gay cultural centers and "leaders in AIDS education." For fear of gay-subculture backlash, medical and other authorities pussy- footed around. The American Association of Physicians for Human Rights told gay men that they could continue to have sex, though they should check their partners first for AIDS symptoms and might want to have fewer partners. An early Gay Men's Health Crisis pamphlet read: "Have as much sex as you want, but with fewer people and HEALTHY people." And a young man who tested positive for the AIDS virus was told by his psychological counselors "that it's important for me to have sex."

Shilts speaks of how the lessons learned from all this foolishness incited the gay community's "collective redefinition," which he de- scribes as a "profound" development. Indeed, the gay subculture did undergo extensive changes in the 1980s. Many subculture-oriented gays, suffering the ravages of the AIDS epidemic, learned that prom- iscuity was not all that it was cracked up to be. Libidinousness was not liberating; the road of excess did not lead to the palace of wisdom. (One suspects that this realization might have come eventually, even without AIDS, as the promiscuous young men of the 1970s grew into lonely middle-aged men in the 1980s and '90s.) Men who had once spent much of their time cruising the streets in search of anonymous sex now devoted free hours to volunteer work at Gay Men's Health Crisis and ACT UP meetings. Bar and dance-club attendance fell off, while at- tendance at health clubs and twelve-step programs and houses of wor- ship rose. Many gays who had lived empty, dissolute lives found faith and inner strength and a sense of responsibility.

The days are gone, then, when one in four gay men in San Francisco went to bathhouses at least once a week for anonymous sex, and when everybody in certain corners of certain gay ghettos seemed to have slept with everyone else. There is considerable truth in William A. Henry III's observation, in a 1992 *Newsweek* cover story, that AIDS "turned an often hedonistic male subculture of bar hopping, promiscuity and abundant 'recreational' drugs—an endless party centered on the young and the restless—into a true community, rich in social services and political lobbies, in volunteerism and civic spirit." Yet one should not underestimate the degree to which the subculture's belief in the liberating power of sex still holds sway. The personals and escort-service ads in publications like the *Native* and *The Advocate* make it clear that not everyone has abandoned anonymous sex; certainly young gay people still get the impression, from much of what they read in these publications and hear in gay bars and on gay cable-television shows, that sex is emancipating. When I first came out to a gay friend in the early 1980s, AIDS was already in the news and the dangers of anonymous sex almost universally recognized, but that didn't prevent my friend from giving me the standard gay-subculture advice—to go to a bathhouse. I hadn't expressed any interest in having anonymous sex, or (I might add) in contracting a deadly virus, but that didn't matter: in the gay subculture, bathhouse sex was an essential rite of passage; you *needed* to sleep with a lot of strangers—so the theory ran—in order to grow accustomed to the idea of homosexuality and to know and like and accept yourself as a gay person. So it is that many young homosexuals become promiscuous not because they really want to but because they are encouraged to believe that that's what one does, what one *must* do, when one is gay. In doing so, alas, they make themselves captives, in freedom's name, of a way of life to which they have never aspired.

If for some elements of the subculture, then, AIDS has occasioned a mature and purposeful dedication to the fight for a cure, for others it has only given a strange new twist to the doctrine of gay sex as liberating and revolutionary. On a recent public-access TV program in New York City, a young man could be seen stripping his clothes off while a deep and eerily passionless voice, recorded along with the dance music, slowly intoned over and over again: "Nothing makes them stop. This AIDS thing's not working." These two sentences articulated a favorite subculture fantasy—namely, that AIDS is part of a government conspiracy designed to keep homosexuals from having sex—and encouraged the tendency, among still-promiscuous gays, to congratulate themselves and one another for continuing, after more than a decade of AIDS, to engage in patently self-destructive sexual behavior. The chant's subtext is plain: gay sex is always a revolutionary act, and the only true means of asserting one's identity as a gay person; not to engage in it, under whatever circumstances and for whatever reason, is to capitulate to the enemy and, ultimately, to extinguish one's selfhood. So it is that some elements of the subculture turn the truth completely around, identifying randiness in the age of AIDS not with the risk of death but with life, and abstinence not with self-preservation but with self-annihilation.

• • •

These days, such thinking figures importantly in much gay activism. There are, of course, many activists who work intelligently and responsibly to win gay rights; but all too often, a gay man will turn on the television or pick up the newspaper to find himself embarrassed by people who, purporting to speak or act on his behalf, celebrate sexual adventurousness and proclaim that every time they have sex they're striking a blow against the Establishment. For such people, gay activism doesn't mean self-sacrifice but self-indulgence; in addressing the general public, they seek not to illuminate but to inflame. Their goal is not to make it less problematic for homosexuals to live in stable homes and committed relationships but to liberate homosexuals—and as many heterosexuals as possible—from a world of stable homes and committed relationships into a world of sexual anarchy and political radicalism.

Like many an anti-gay propagandist, these activists make gay sex, not gay rights, the issue that drives their rhetoric: they're exactly what the protagonist of Larry Kramer's play *The Normal Heart* is talking about when he complains that "the gay leaders who created this sexual-liberation philosophy in the first place have been the death of us" because they fought "for the right to legitimize promiscuity" instead of "the right to get married" and have thus "created . . . generations of guys who can't deal with each other as anything but erections." While most homosexuals are busy pursuing lives and careers in the larger world, these activists appear on the op-ed pages and talk shows, presenting themselves as spokespeople for the gay community and shaping the public's ideas about homosexuality in unfortunate ways.

One such activist is Donna Minkowitz, a contributor to *The Advocate* and *The Village Voice*, who in a 1992 *Advocate* column urged gays to "take the offensive" on gay rights. Entitled "Recruit, recruit, recruit!," the article began with a reference to Minkowitz's recent appearance on the *Montel Williams* show, on which she was introduced as "a gay woman who says it's all about recruiting." Gays don't recruit children, Minkowitz argued in the column, "if the phrase is taken to mean we sexually abuse the young in order to make converts for our community. But I am increasingly impatient with the old chestnut that our movement for public acceptance has not increased and will not increase the number of gay men and lesbians in existence." She quoted John D'Emilio to the effect that "there are *more of us* than there used to be," and made it

clear that she agreed. She went on to say that "other right-wing asper-
sions also have grains of truth in them"—that homophobes are correct,
for example, in saying that gays are

> a sexually adventurous, gender-defying bunch. We have also come up
> with configurations for relationships and families that go a long way
> toward solving the problem that has kept heterosexuals sad for cen-
> turies—how to combine emotional fidelity with sexual freedom. One
> of the right wing's goals in making these attributes into smears is to
> force lesbians and gay men to abandon the most defiant, least heter-
> osexual aspects of our lives. If we become the straightest gays in world
> history, they've already won half their battle.

Homophobes are right, too, she insisted, when they say that gays
"threaten the family, male domination, and the Calvinist ethic of work
and grimness that has paralyzed most Americans' search for pleasure."
She agreed with Pat Buchanan: the battle over gay rights *is* a "cultural
war" for "the soul of America," a war in which gays "have been on the
defensive far too long." Instead of trying to seem innocuous, we should
"advertise our potential to change straight society in radical, beneficial
ways," to "revolutionize straight lives." Above all, heterosexuals can learn
from gays "that pleasure is possible (and desirable) beyond the sanctions
of the state." In some cases, that may mean heterosexuals learning "to
live out their hetero desires to the fullest"; in other cases, it may mean
heterosexuals discovering, well, the joy of gay sex. "Remember that most
of the line about homosex being one's nature, not a choice, was articulated as a response to brutal repression. . . . it's time for us to abandon
this defensive posture and walk upright on the earth. Maybe you didn't
choose to be gay—that's fine. But I did." Her concluding line: "Provoke
the Right."

Even by gay-activist standards, Minkowitz is far out: she admits that
the things she says "piss off many, if not most, of the lesbian and gay
activists I know." But her article should not be dismissed out of hand,
because it demonstrates the radical extremes that the subculture is
willing to embrace. Of all the gay writers in the United States, it is
Minkowitz who was chosen in 1992 to write a study of "gay and lesbian
culture" for a new series of books for gay and lesbian teenagers published

by Chelsea House. One can only lament the selection of Minkowitz for this unprecedented project—and worry about the gay teens who will turn to her book in an effort to understand themselves. For to judge by Minkowitz's *Advocate* essay, she defines homosexuality in such a way as to exclude upwards of 95 percent of homosexuals. To begin with, she falsely links sexual orientation with other categories to which it has no innate connection. By speaking of "the most defiant, least heterosexual aspects of our lives," for example, she implicitly characterizes homosexuality as an act of defiance and equates being gay with being rebellious. In warning homosexuals against "becom[ing] the straightest gays in world history," she draws a connection between two different senses of the word "straight"—(a) heterosexual and (b) dreary, whitebread, bourgeois—and thereby suggests that heterosexuality is innately dull and that homosexuality is innately adventurous and exciting. In arguing that gays can introduce heterosexuals to "pleasure . . . beyond the sanctions of the state," moreover, she draws a connection among homosexuality, hedonism, and political subversiveness. Throughout the essay, phrases like "join our ranks" reinforce the idea of homosexuality itself as a club, a movement, a political party whose role is to teach the world how to *party*.

But being gay is not a political act. Homosexuality is not a movement. The number of self-accepting and uncloseted gays has certainly increased in recent years, but there is no reason to believe that homosexuals make up a larger percentage of the population than they ever did. To suggest otherwise is to do none of us any good, and all of us much harm. Minkowitz says that she chose to be gay. But homosexuality is not a matter of choice: to be homosexual is to be, by nature, more attracted to one's own sex than to the opposite sex. If Minkowitz did "choose," then she's not really gay at all; she's a straight woman who for some political reason, or more accurately for some psychological reason that she explains to herself as a political reason, has decided to live as a gay woman. Either that or she is a genuinely gay woman whose feminist politics of self-empowerment render her incapable of dealing with the plain fact that there *are* things in life that we can't choose and who, in order to feel good about her homosexuality, needs to believe that in identifying herself as a lesbian she is not accepting her fate but taking control of her life.

In linking homosexuality with radical politics, Minkowitz does not serve the cause of gay rights. Quite the contrary; she is using the cause of gay rights to advance her own program, which would seem to have very little to do with furthering understanding and acceptance of homosexuality as it really exists in America and everything to do with promoting radical-left political ideas and (as the gratuitous mention of her *Montel Williams* show appearance makes clear) with pursuing her reckless quest for celebrity. I say "reckless" because every time she appears on television, Minkowitz helps to undo the work of countless unsung people who are struggling intelligently for gay rights and whose goal is not to "Provoke the Right" but to build bridges. Can one imagine the plight of a small-town gay teenager whose parents get their ideas about homosexuality from watching Minkowitz on *Montel*? It's a terrifying thought. Minkowitz to the contrary, the huge majority of such teenagers don't want to be defiant, promiscuous East Village radicals; they don't want to teach the world how to have better sex. They just want to be able to love in the way that comes naturally to them, in the places where they feel at home. What Minkowitz fails to understand is that getting booked on *Montel* takes a lot less political courage than does living among hostile people who, by virtue of mundane daily encounters, gradually become less fearful and hostile. Ultimately, her motives would seem to be disturbingly similar to those of people like Oregon gay-basher Lon Mabon: like him, she gets attention by telling provocative, outrageous, and irresponsible lies about homosexuality, and thereby makes a name for herself on the backs of gay people.

Remarkably, Minkowitz would seem to think that her enthusiasm for the emancipating powers of sex, which recalls the most inane and irresponsible subculture attitudes of the 1970s, represents cutting-edge thinking. If she were alone in this enthusiasm, and if she had not been given the opportunity by Chelsea House to spread her narrow vision of homosexuality to the gay and lesbian teenagers of America, there would be little reason to pay attention to her. But in fact Minkowitz and people like her wield inordinate power in the gay subculture and command enormous media attention. One of the problems with the media in general, and with programs like *Donahue, Oprah,* and *Montel* in particular, is that a person who proffers an honest and unsensational image of homosexuality and who takes a conciliatory rather than a combative approach to gay-rights issues (and, in doing so, represents the overwhelming majority of gays) stands less chance of being given a hearing on such programs than someone who waves her fist at the camera and screams, "Recruit, recruit, recruit!"

•   •   •

Though he does not, like Minkowitz, go so far as to say that gay people make a conscious choice to be gay, the gay writer Darrell Yates Rist, in a *Nation* article entitled "Are Homosexuals Born That Way?," does cling like Minkowitz to the idea of homosexuality as a kind of rebellion that can be infectious. Rist suggests that "by some subtle pattern of erotic choices from childhood on," gay men "defiantly nurture a kind of desire, possible in every man, that might otherwise lie dormant." He adds that people "intuitively know" that "their children can be lured by queer ideas if the urge is not embedded in their brains from birth," and says that "even many of my most unbiased straight friends grow skittish with my homosexual candor—say, kissing my mate—when their children are around. For underneath it all, they too understand that sexually free ideas are infectious and that, once introduced to the suggestion of same-sex love, their kids might just try it and like it."

But homosexuality is not a flavor of ice cream that anybody can "try" and "like"; it's something that feels either natural to you or unnatural. Nor is it a matter of being in possession of "ideas" that are more "sexually free" than someone else's. (In what way, for heaven's sake, is homosexuality more "free" than heterosexuality?) The fact is that children see expressions of heterosexuality every day of their lives, from Daddy kissing Mommy to Kermit romancing Miss Piggy, and see almost no expression of homosexuality, either in real life or on television; but that doesn't keep those who are destined to be gay—a more or less uniform percentage, it would appear, in most times and places—from growing up to be gay. Likewise, while witnessing an occasional kiss between two men may help a youngster to realize that he's gay, such an experience is certainly not going to alter the sexuality of a youngster who's destined to be straight. For when such a young person sees two men kissing, it doesn't seem attractive to him but peculiar, curious, even bizarre. Rist's failure to realize this proclaims the limitation of his perspective: because *he* was fascinated as a boy by the sight of two men kissing, he assumes it works that way for all boys. But it doesn't.

Another gay writer who views homosexuality as a liberating and virtuous trait of which all people are capable is Richard Goldstein, whose pretentious, often cryptic essay "Faith, Hope and Sodomy" appeared in the June 1993 "Queer Issue" of the *Village Voice*. Gay liberation, wrote Goldstein, grasps the fullness of the human libido. It doesn't hold that everyone is homosexual, but rather that homoeroticism exists in everyone. In struggling to release this potential, it means to free us all from the violent numbness of a personality in conflict with itself. It leaves unsolved the mystery of sexual development. It leaves unanswered the question: Will I always be as I am today? Instead, it embraces everyone who honors their sexuality—whether or not they express it in sex. And armed with this faith in the goodness of gayness, it moves beyond its enemies' worst nightmare. It reproduces *and* recruits.

Spouting off about recruiting on a show like *Montel* and proclaiming the infectiousness of "sexually free ideas" and such in the pages of *The Nation* and the *Village Voice* are not, of course, the only ways in which gay activists attract negative attention and reinforce pernicious myths about homosexuality. Near the beginning of the controversy sparked by the Rainbow Curriculum, about fifty members of a group called Lesbian Avengers protested that rejection outside of Public School 87 in Middle Village, Queens. Gary Terracino reported in *QW* on the demonstration, which took place on the first day of school in fall 1992 while parents were arriving with their children:

> "Here," a protestor-cum-back-to-school-reveller said to a little boy. "Have a balloon." She handed him a bright, lavender balloon that read "Teach About Lesbian Lives."
> "I don't believe this shit!" the mother exclaimed. "Give it back!"
> By this time, several children were crying, either because of all the scary police, or their irate parents or the fact that their pretty lavender balloons had been wrenched from their grip.
> "I'm not gay and I don't want it taught to my son," a mother said from her stoop overlooking the near-melee, as she clutched her son protectively. By the tearful look on his face, it was clear that her son agreed.

Terracino went on to describe how a "young mother, pushing a stroller with sleeping child, yelled at the police to 'Shoot them!'" and how another woman "yelled at the departing lesbians: 'Marry a husband!'" And Terracino quotes one of the Lesbian Avengers' explanation of the group's goal: "To bring awareness to the community here about lesbian visibility, lesbian vulnerability, in a sense. And I think we did that."

In its confrontational approach and its goal of "visibility," this Lesbian Avengers demonstration was typical of many gay-activist events nowadays. Visibility? Those Middle Village parents know very well that lesbians exist. Only in this celebrity-crazy, promotion-happy age could a political activist speak of "visibility," in and of itself, as a goal. What such activists as the Lesbian Avengers seem not to realize is that there are good and bad ways of being visible. What they should be seeking is not simply to achieve visibility but to banish ignorance about, and thus fear and hatred of, homosexuality. Among other things, heterosexuals should be made to recognize that being gay doesn't exclude the possibility of being a mature, responsible adult. Instead, however, the Lesbian Avengers managed to reinforce the notion of gays as reckless and infantile.

They did the one thing, moreover, that gay activists should most strenuously avoid: they made parents feel threatened, made them feel as if homosexuals want to "recruit" their kids or supplant their authority. What's more, the Lesbian Avengers created a situation that upset many of those children, the most sensitive of whom, straight *and* gay, will doubtless associate homosexuality with this scary, confusing event for years to come. As someone who happens to have attended grammar school in Middle Village, and who sensed his own differentness for a long time before recognizing that he was homosexual, I know that if I'd seen the Lesbian Avengers rallying outside my sixth-grade classroom window, they would simply have reinforced my stereotype of gays as weird degenerate hippie types whose lives revolve around their sexuality, and would have reinforced my belief that *that* could not possibly be what I was.

Like the Gay Pride Day march, protests like that staged by the Lesbian Avengers almost seem designed to antagonize parents and to scare gay children away from self-knowledge and self-acceptance. Ultimately, all that the Lesbian Avengers accomplished was to reinforce the idea that gays aren't really concerned about the well-being of children but care only about advancing their own interests; indeed, they made it possible for those mothers to walk away from the incident thinking that the lesbians had been acting out of a frustration over being childless or, perhaps, out of an underlying lack of self-esteem. For the Lesbian Avengers would seem to *want* to be seen as clowns; how else can one explain their calling themselves Lesbian Avengers and singing (as they did on their way to the protest) "When the Dykes Come Marching In"? It's as if they've subconsciously accepted the mainstream culture's harshest judgments of them and sought to defuse the pain of disapproval through self-parody. At the very least, it seems fair to say that the demonstration at P.S. 87 doesn't quite qualify as a sensible bid to win respect. Can one wonder that parents, seeing such buffoonery, don't want their children to be taught about "lesbian lives"?

This is not to deny that the self-loathing manifested by activists like the Lesbian Avengers is understandable. Many gay men and lesbians, after all, grew up in households where homosexuality was viewed as an abomination and where homosexuals were dismissed as jokes of nature. Consequently, for all the dedication with which they have organized and agitated for their rights, there is a level on which many subculture-oriented gays don't really take themselves—or anything—seriously, especially where sex is concerned. Liberated though they think themselves to be, many of them have never really liberated themselves from their parents' view of homosexuality as a joke; in order to live with themselves, they have had to adopt a worldview that sees *everything* as a joke, that laughs at everything that has traditionally been taken most seriously, from religion to the family. Much of the reason for the gay-rights movement's vociferous emphasis on "gay pride" is that, deep down, many subculture-oriented gays don't really have very much pride in themselves as individuals; for it would never occur to an individual with pride in himself to feel a need for group-oriented pride. If, in short, the gay subculture sometimes seems almost to be its own worst enemy, perhaps it is because so many of the people in it are suffering from a self-hatred so deep that they can't even begin to acknowledge it to themselves.

Though groups like the Lesbian Avengers, with their counterproductive antics, are not representative of all gay activists, they do share one unfortunate trait with many gay-rights groups: namely, a failure to recognize that boosting gay visibility, pressuring government and corporate bureaucrats, and winning the backing of individual politicians for gay-rights measures are, in the long term, of secondary importance to increasing broad public understanding of homosexuality and support for the rights of gays. This failure was demonstrated dramatically in early 1993, when gay-rights groups were caught off guard by the national outcry over Bill Clinton's plans to lift the military's ban on homosexuals. As Jeffrey Schmalz wrote in the *New York Times*, it was not until the controversy erupted that "gay-rights leaders . . . realized that having the President on their side was not enough." It is a measure of the subculture's sense of estrangement from the general public that so many intelligent people should be capable of making such an elementary error.

I was afforded a glimpse into the strategic thinking of groups like the Lesbian Avengers when I chatted not long ago with an activist whom I'll call Ned. It was an illuminating conversation. When I spoke of "building bridges" to the mainstream community, Ned said that building bridges wasn't what he was all about; in his view, the point of gay activism is for homosexuals to gain political power and thereby win the respect of the majority. I told him that this struck me as a cart-before-the-horse way of thinking; no minority group could hope to gain very much political power under a democratic system so long as the majority didn't respect it; certainly it couldn't do so by antagonizing that majority. The primary goal, it seemed to me, shouldn't be to achieve "power" but to eradicate the prejudice of individuals; and the only way to do that is to eradicate the ignorance out of which that prejudice flows. He replied that the AIDS epidemic compelled a sense of urgency on the part of gay activists; this was "no time to be polite." Point taken. Yet the question remained: while rallies and building takeovers organized by direct-action groups like ACT UP and Queer Nation had indeed proven effective in forcing bureaucracies to act on specific funding and drug-testing issues, how could such tactics win wide public support for gay-rights laws and public acknowledgment of gay relationships? Strategically, these were two utterly distinct challenges.

Ned, who in the 1960s had participated in non-gay activism, was very much a leftist. He used the word "progressive" so frequently that it sounded like a mantra. When I finally asked what he meant by it, his discursive answer gave the impression that, in his mind, "progressive" was something of a synonym for "all good things." He saw everything in terms of power relations between groups. At one point he mentioned casually that American blacks are still slaves. I said, "No, they're not." He said, "Well, I don't mean slaves, but they belong to whites in a way." I said, "No, they don't." He said that there's a permanent black under-class because the powers that be—the government and big corporations—*want* there to be one; it serves their purposes. "How?" I asked. He didn't have an answer. He wasn't used to being asked such questions.

Though he presumably discussed these matters often with friends who agreed with his every word, and also apparently spent a lot of time battling it out head-to-head with homophobes who had their own set of unexamined doctrines, he wasn't in the habit of being asked to scrutinize his own assumptions, to examine his own prejudices. The one thing about which he seemed abashed—almost ashamed, in fact—was something of which I felt he had a right to be quite proud. He spoke of it contemptuously as "mainstream" work: he spent a great deal of time on the phone lobbying City Council members, bureaucrats, and school board officials. With all of them, he said, he was polite, reasonable, and patient. Even more impressively, as a mutual friend informed me, Ned had demonstrated remarkable dedication and courage in helping to bring to justice a felon who had been motivated by homophobia. Since then, living in an urban neighborhood outside the gay ghetto, Ned had established and administered a remarkably successful program to improve gay-straight relations in his community; in a relatively short while he had accomplished more in this regard than any individual I know of anywhere.

As far as religion was concerned, Ned (a Jew) was preoccupied with the Roman Catholic Church, in particular New York's Cardinal O'Connor, and with Protestant fundamentalism. To listen to Ned talk, one would think that those two groups comprised all of American Christianity. I told him that for gay activists to take a hostile attitude toward organized religion is strategically foolish, because a majority of Americans are churchgoing Christians, and most are neither Protestant fundamentalists nor Cardinal O'Connor–style Catholics. I mentioned ACT UP's notorious disruption of a worship service at Saint Patrick's Cathedral, during which someone had tossed consecrated host on the floor. To my surprise, Ned insisted that the incident was a good thing because it got ACT UP members booked on talk shows around the country to discuss AIDS. I made the point that people don't remember those talk shows, but they remember Saint Pat's; the image of that act of desecration will stay with some people forever. I told him about a sixtyish working-class man whom I'd seen interviewed a few nights earlier as part of an ABC News focus group. The man said that he "used to feel sorry for" homosexuals, "but ever since the desecration of Saint Patrick's Cathedral I've had no use for them whatsoever." Although gay people don't want or need heterosexuals to feel sorry for them, a widespread metamorphosis of pity into hate could hardly be considered a good thing.

This point didn't seem to make much of an impression on Ned, who suggested that it would be a good idea to "take over" Saint Patrick's. When I expressed shock at this proposal, he said, "Why not?"

Ned had made many praiseworthy and eminently responsible-minded contributions to the cause of gay rights. But he also had an imprudent side that brought to mind some of his less admirable fellow activists. For the fact is that many radical gay activists don't really want the general public's tolerance or acceptance; what they want most of all is to feel, if only for an evening, an instant, that they have power; they want to be in a position to intimidate others as they believe themselves to have been intimidated. Many of them, I think, are basically decent people who are motivated by extraordinary fear and suspicion, by a profound sense of being hated that has fueled a considerable insecurity, and by an utter inability to imagine gay life as being anything other than fundamentally distinct from mainstream life. For such activists, political action doesn't entail the firm control and purposeful channeling of anger but is rather an explosion of anger; protest is a means not of achieving emancipation but of attaining a momentary illusion of empowerment. Few if any of them would ever try to burn down a church on their own; but as part of a group? Perhaps. Such is the nature of authoritarianism— and authoritarianism is a fundamental element of the extreme subculture mentality.

Consider, in this connection, what happened to a friend of mine whom I'll call Jane. Jane, a lawyer, used to do extensive *pro bono* work for Gay Men's Health Crisis, helping dying men to write their wills. One day in 1991 she was walking past New York's Federal Hall during an ACT UP demonstration when several of the protesters began heckling her, calling her an "Establishment Bitch" and other such things, presumably because she was dressed in her best downtown-lawyer garb and carrying a briefcase. Not being the type to shrink from a confrontation, Jane strode over to the protesters and demanded to know why they were addressing her in that way. They were sarcastic, insulting. "How do you know I'm not HIV positive?" she asked. She informed them that she supported their cause, described her GMHC volunteer work, and chided them for jumping to conclusions about people. Nothing that she said had the slightest effect upon their treatment of her. As far as they were concerned, the only essential facts about Jane were that she was a straight woman, a Wall Street lawyer, a part of the System—ergo, the enemy. In tormenting her as they did, these ACT UP demonstrators were not unlike any other group of male loiterers who harass female passersby; the only difference was that they were doing it in the name of a cause.

Jane, a strong woman, was troubled by her encounter with these young men—not because she felt that they posed a physical threat to her, but because their manner was so prejudicial, so inhuman. They were very much like Red Guards during the Chinese Cultural Revolution: in their minds, any action on their part was defensible because their cause was pure. Either you were one of them or you were the enemy. Could their behavior be excused as the product of frustration and despair, brought on by their own infection and illness? I don't think so. The young men who harassed Jane were, she told me, all white men in their early twenties, seemingly upper-middle-class and suburb-bred, who would have been barely into puberty when AIDS was first identified in the early 1980s and "safer sex" guidelines established.

Indeed, listening to young upper-middle-class ACT UP members discuss their reasons for such gratuitously hostile acts, one gets the impression that some of them are angry less about government inaction on the AIDS crisis than about their own sexuality: for all their bluster, they haven't completely accepted that they're gay. Most of them have never known how it feels to be a member of any minority group, let alone to go hungry or be homeless or fight in a war; all their lives they've taken for granted their health, prosperity, and privilege, and their own homosexuality is the first curve ball that life has thrown them. They haven't yet gotten used to the fact that the world is full of things they can't control, that nobody can have everything he wants, that life isn't always easy and is never fair. Accustomed to being protected from reality by their parents, and having been raised in a generation to whom children's television proclaimed the Freedom to Be You and Me without ever suggesting that human freedom has its natural limits, their natural response to such aspects of adult life as sexual self-discovery, the necessity to obey one's boss, or (for that matter) the obligation to pay rent is to assail the government petulantly as father figure rather than to deal in a mature fashion with life's ever unfair challenges.

On February 23, 1993, the *New York Times* carried an obituary for Robert Rafsky, a Harvard graduate and former public relations executive who had left his job in 1989 to work full time as a member of ACT UP.

Rafsky's obituary, which indicated that he had accomplished a great deal as an AIDS activist, made special mention of his widely televised challenge to then–presidential candidate Bill Clinton at a March 1992 fund-raising event. "What are you going to do about AIDS?" Rafsky demanded of Clinton. "We're dying!" The obituary implied a causal relation between Clinton's encounter with Rafsky and the candidate's later formulation of an AIDS policy for his administration. Yet when Rafsky extolled the virtues of ACT UP's brand of activism in a *New York Times* op-ed entitled "A Better Life for Having Acted Up," he placed emphasis (as his title suggests) not on the effectiveness of ACT UP's strategy in achieving certain ends but on the psychological value of direct-action politics for its participants.

At Rafsky's memorial service, the recollection that seemed uppermost in the minds of his friends was of an ACT UP meeting where, fed up with the suggestion that ACT UP emphasize AIDS prevention and not the search for a cure, Rafsky stood up and screamed over and over: "I want a cure!" What is interesting is that while Rafsky did make an important contribution to the AIDS cause, his fellow activists focused not on that contribution but on his rage—on Rafsky not as AIDS activist but as AIDS personality. The ACT UP–produced public-access program on which excerpts from this memorial service were aired also showed Rafsky howling to fellow gay activists, apropos of heterosexuals: "We're more important than they are!"—an attitude which is no less ugly than that of heterosexuals who take it for granted that they are more important than homosexuals.

This is the same Robert Rafsky who on *60 Minutes* was seen participating in the takeover of a pharmaceutical company's headquarters, where, quite properly incensed over the exorbitant price charged by the company for an AIDS drug, Rafsky told an employee, "You are my murderer!" Rafsky didn't know the employee's identity, didn't know what the man's job was, didn't know what part he had or hadn't played in the formulation of the company's AIDS drug policies. But none of that mattered; Rafsky was angry. The employee, he felt, was complicit in his illness. As the segment progressed, however, a remarkable fact emerged: Rafsky had been married, had accepted his homosexuality in the late 1980s, and had been infected with AIDS shortly thereafter, in 1987. At that time, of course, the epidemic had been several years old, and Rafsky had been fully aware of the ways in which the virus was spread. Yet he claimed that his infection wasn't his fault; it was the fault of society, which had made him feel bad about being gay and thereby caused him to engage in reckless sexual behavior. Now, it was clear, he was channeling that same recklessness into politics; the same self-loathing and self-destructiveness that had driven him to expose himself to AIDS was now driving him to engage in direct-action activism, which, whether productive (as much of it was) or counterproductive (as much of it was), he found worthwhile because it "gives me a reason for living."

Likewise, Ned's way of explaining his involvement in gay politics focused on self-esteem. He said that he originally got involved because he had nothing in his life to feel good about; and he consistently talked about activism in terms of how it made him feel about himself. There was also, in his case, something of a persecution complex at work. Several times during our conversation he referred to homophobes "coming to get us" or "rounding us up" as if we were in imminent danger of some such concerted action. This sort of paranoia is not uncommon in the gay subculture—which, of course, makes sense; as Randy Shilts has noted, "humans who have been subjected to a lifetime of irrational bigotry on the part of a mainstream society can be excused for harboring irrational fears."

When Ned said that he'd like to burn down every church on earth, I replied that the remark disturbed me very much as a Christian; I explained that it was as unsettling as hearing someone say that he'd like to burn down every homosexual's house. Politically, I added, it was foolish to make such a remark, and as a gay person I was angered to think that someone presuming to speak for me could say such a thing. Ned countered that he had been addressing the comment only to me; he'd never make it in public. I said, "Why say it if you don't mean it? I have to assume you *do* mean it." He replied, "I say a lot of reckless things; it's a matter of which day you catch me on." He seemed not to be aware that when one is an activist, one is viewed as representing a wide variety of people whom one doesn't even know and to whom one has taken on a serious responsibility.

Every member of a marginalized group faces two antithetical options. Either one can decide to behave in an especially responsible manner so as not to make things worse for other members of the group, and so that bigots may be helped to see the error of their ways; or one can take the attitude: "OK, if in your view I'm not a co-equal member of the race, then I refuse to assume the responsibilities of one. I'll just do whatever feels good, whatever I think is best for *me*." It seems to me that if many gay activists are motivated by a powerful sense of responsibility to other homosexuals (and to humankind in general), too many of the participants in direct-action gay activism are only doing what feels good, what they believe to be best for them. For these people, activism is less a matter of intellectual and moral commitment than of visceral experience; it is less about achieving specific goals at some future time than about losing oneself in the euphoria of the present moment—about, that is, involvement in the protest itself. It is ecstatic, irrational, existential, orgasmic; indeed, I have often felt that for those with powerful memories of long-ago encounters in parks and bathhouses—and, what's more, for many who are too young to have such memories—such activism serves as a substitute for self-destructive promiscuous sex.

Michael Portantiere summed up the attitudes of many homosexuals toward ACT UP in a letter to the now-defunct gay weekly *QW* about an AIDS rally in Times Square. "I was standing with a group of gay friends," wrote Portantiere, "when ACT UP began to act up." His friends all "found ACT UP's behavior annoying and counterproductive. A question I heard repeated several times was: 'Why is ACT UP disrupting an AIDS rally?' " Stephen Wolf, who also wrote to *QW* about that rally, contrasted Elizabeth Glaser, a heterosexual woman with AIDS who spoke at the Democratic convention, with a demonstrator whom he observed at the rally, "shrilly blowing on his whistle." Whereas Glaser "affirmed that if one worked within the system, mastering the craft of politics, one could create a changed environment, a truly kinder, gentler world," the whistle blower "displayed his anger and his impotence, his alienation from the processes for change." Whereas "articulate, educated moderates" like Glaser "understand how the process works and learn the skills to work the process," "professional queers" like the whistle blower "tend to be inarticulate, eternal children, children whose only tactic is concocting noise to draw attention to themselves, children who turn off all their listeners (gay and straight and bisexual), having no program to put forth and no tact to present themselves." Wolf suggested that gays learn "to ignore the angry, impotent, shrill whistle blowers who confuse activism with primal therapy" and encourage "the gay men and lesbians with ideas to present and the talent to present them; the gay men and lesbians with faith in transforming the system and the skills to transform it."

To acknowledge that there is more than a bit of truth in these observations is not to deny that, in the early days of the health crisis, ACT UP's tactics represented an eminently appropriate response to ubiquitous apathy; it is merely to note that, over the years, many of ACT UP's actions came to seem inane and chaotic, their chief purpose often seeming to be the immediate gratification of the protesters themselves. Too often, involvement in direct-action groups like ACT UP has followed a predictable and unpromising pattern: get angry, get involved, get it out of your system, and get out.

It was Tony Malliaris, another letter writer, who in a subsequent issue of *QW* articulated the classic gay-subculture response to Wolf's complaint. Addressing Wolf as "you self-hating, hypocritical, misinformed piece of shit," Malliaris wrote: "I have no idea if you're HIV-positive. If you aren't, I can only hope you get the virus: being infected would do you some good. It puts a clock on your ass, makes you desperate. . . . You're a disgrace to the queer nation." Malliaris's letter might have been written to provide an illustration of exactly what Wolf says: that, understandable though it may be, the desperation of people like Malliaris—who confuse being desperate with having a rational political strategy—too often eventuates in undiplomatic statements and counterproductive actions. Malliaris's description of Wolf as "self-hating" is typical of many subculture-oriented gays, in whose view a refusal to accept the subculture's idea of homosexuality constitutes a refusal to accept one's own homosexuality; his "queer nation" rhetoric, meanwhile, only serves to reinforce the notion of gays as a segregated group, an Other—and it is this notion of gays that helps explain why many pragmatic fund-raisers and politicians who aim to reach the mainstream community tend to select as their spokespeople heterosexual women like Elizabeth Glaser and children like Ryan White rather than gay men.

To read such letters as these is to recognize quickly enough which gays have self-respect and which don't. In gay activism, the ultimate test of courage, pride, and self-respect is not how a person behaves when he is spouting off on *Montel* or participating in a public protest in Greenwich Village or taking over a building with a hundred confederates, but how he conducts himself when he's outside the gay ghetto without gay friends around him. The truth is that all too many so-called gay radicals have never integrated their sexuality into their lives in the "real" world, the places where they came from and where their families live. If in

Greenwich Village, West Hollywood, or wherever they happen to hang their caps they are "out, loud, and proud" (in the words of a recent Gay Pride Day slogan), the moment they're back with their families they seem to be—well—bowed and cowed. For example, a young movie director named Gregg Araki, whose publicity identifies him as a "guerrilla filmmaker," admitted in an interview that though he's close to his parents, he's never worked up the nerve to talk with them about his homosexuality. "I never actually came out to them in that TV-movie way; it's more an unspoken thing. I went out with a guy for three years and they met him—and mothers always know. They accept that I'm the weird kid. . . . They're very understanding." "The weird kid": now *there's* progressive thinking! Araki added that while his parents are "very supportive" of his career, "I don't like them to see my films, because they reflect a side I'm not comfortable with exposing to them." What kind of pride is this? What kind of fearlessness disappears the moment one finds oneself unprotected by the company of a like-minded crowd? It's easy to be a "guerrilla filmmaker" in Greenwich Village; what's braver is talking honestly to your parents about who you are.

As it happened, the same issue of *QW* that contained the interview with Araki also featured an essay by John Weir entitled "Homo in Heteroland." While spending a few days with his brother and sister-in-law and their children on the road to Atlanta, Weir wrote, "I was a homo in heteroland, and all my brave political opinions, my aggressive outness, my pinkness, faded away. . . . We couldn't talk about gender issues. . . . It's hard to talk political agenda when your primary focus is a two-year-old child choking on a Ninja in the way-back seat." How sad that for Weir his identity as a homosexual is tied up with talk about "gender issues" and "political agendas" and that he can't find a way to be a part of his family's world while still being entirely and proudly himself. Both Araki and Weir exemplify the way in which intelligent and gifted people can be crippled by the gay subculture's confusion of individual identity with group politics. Though they learn how to function in the subculture—and how to make defiant noises and gestures about the world beyond—such people never learn how to *live* in that larger world.

Things may be looking up on the gay-activist front. ACT UP members disenchanted with the organization's confrontational approach left to form TAG (Treatment Action Group), which, in the words of one of its founders, "provide[s] a safe and sane haven for effective treatment activists to continue their critical work unencumbered by PC zealots, New Alliance Party operatives and crackpot pseudo-scientists." An October 1992 issue of *QW* examined "the New Face of AIDS Activism," noting that during the Democratic convention "ACT UP seemed to have abandoned its role as organizer of large-scale, high-visibility demonstrations" but "remained a major force behind the scenes to promote AIDS awareness." A January 1993 issue of *The Advocate* reported that ACT UP and other such groups, "wracked [sic] by burnout, deaths, internal dissension, and their members' changing interests," had quieted down, and that many of their members had "become insiders." A Queer Nation / Atlanta member admitted that many activists now realized that "actions that got media attention and were titillating are not always effective in the long run." And a 1992 *New York Times* article explained that one reason why a bill forbidding anti-gay discrimination in New York State has languished in the legislature for twenty-one years is that "in the past, many legislators' contacts with gay groups came during angry clashes like a demonstration last spring in which the radical group Queer Nation paraded around with an effigy of Senate majority leader Ralph J. Marino, which they burned." But the bill had gained supporters during the previous year because a gay lobbying group called Empire State Pride had taken a more traditional (i.e., polite) approach.

To be sure, Senate Republicans' rejection of the gay-rights bill in the summer of 1993, after its passage by the Assembly, raised the possibility that gay-rights lobbying groups might revert to more fractious methods. Yet on the whole gay activists do seem to be learning that to oppose the fanatical rhetoric of the anti-gay crusaders with equally fanatical rhetoric is only to play into the homophobes' hands. By opposing the extreme positions of the Lon Mabons and Randall Terrys with equally extreme arguments—by bashing religious and democratic institutions, that is, and crying "Recruit, recruit, recruit!"—subculture-oriented gays succeed only in making the homophobes' positions look legitimate to many middle Americans. This is the ultimate and tragic irony of gay-subculture politics, and the lesson of it is that if gays are ever to be incorporated fully and freely into American society, the world has to be shown who the real fringe is, and who it isn't—just as subculture-oriented gays need to learn that real pride stems from individual integrity and self-respect, and not the other way around.

• • •

"Is Bruce homophobic?"

Allen Ginsberg posed that question to a friend of mine several years ago, after I published a review essay that was harshly critical of his *Collected Poems*. The question reflected a classic gay-subculture view of things: if a critic doesn't like a particular gay artist's work, he must hate gays.

Ginsberg—who has, over the decades, succeeded in selling himself to the public as *the* American gay laureate, representative in some way of the nation's homosexuals ("America," he wrote in a famous poem, "I'm putting my queer shoulder to the wheel")—may be the single most notorious example of the subculture-oriented gay artist. What he would probably never be able to understand is that if I felt compelled to speak my mind about his poetry, it's precisely because I'm gay, and thus especially vexed that he has sold himself as a gay laureate only to behave like a vulgar oaf, shedding his clothes in public and rhapsodizing about sex with minors. Ginsberg's carefully cultivated image as America's buffoonish gay bard has done wonders for his career, but has only harmed gays by fortifying homophobic stereotypes.

What does it say about a writer or artist that he was homosexual? Does it make a difference? The Gay Studies departments that have sprung up in various universities maintain that it does. They claim writers like Herman Melville, Henry James, and Willa Cather as their own, and distort and diminish these writers by interpreting them not in terms of their individual accomplishments but in terms of the subculture's ideas about sexual identity. Meanwhile, some conservative critics and teachers either recoil from the very notion that Melville, James, and Cather were homosexual or view their homosexuality as a detail that is embarrassing or unimportant or both. Or they say the sort of thing a college professor said when my companion, Chris, asked permission to do a paper on Oscar Wilde: "Oh no, he was a vile man— anyone else, not him."

In fact, knowing that a great writer was homosexual can be illuminating, though making too much of it is invariably reductive, and pays the writer's art and thought no compliment. Henry James, America's greatest novelist, almost certainly owed his slot on Parnassus at least in part to his homosexuality, which compelled him, given his exceedingly conservative sensibility, to withdraw from any prospect of intimate relations with another human being and to become a voyeur. To read his novels in sequence is to be struck by an overwhelming sense of loneliness and distance; and the more one reads of him, the more his long, nuanced, periphrastic sentences look like a protective wall thrown up between the writer and life, humanity, the world of feeling. Yet with the conspicuous exception of a handful of works with gay subtexts— notably his novels *Roderick Hudson* and *The Bostonians* and his stories "The Pupil" and "The Author of 'Beltraffio' "—homosexuality seems a relatively minor theme in James's work.

If to ignore James's homosexuality, then, is to fail to appreciate fully the scale of the man's personal tragedy and artistic triumph, to focus too tightly upon it is to be distracted from his actual literary themes and accomplishments. Gay or straight, every man or woman is an individual, and a great writer more of an individual than most. In art as in life, homosexuality is always a factor, but it never operates alone; it acts invariably in combination with individual temperament and genius, and the nature of the interaction, and the role and importance of homosexuality in that interaction, vary widely from one author to the next.

This is not, of course, to defend the traditional practice of keeping silent about the subject of famous people's homosexuality. During my childhood, I watched a number of old movies on television that celebrated the lives of people who were homosexual (though I didn't know at the time that they *were* homosexual), from Cary Grant as Cole Porter in *Night and Day* and Mickey Rooney as Lorenz Hart in *Words and Music* to Charlton Heston as Michelangelo in *The Agony and the Ecstasy* and Danny Kaye in the title role of *Hans Christian Andersen*. Though these films played fast and loose with biographical data, the most dishonest thing about them was that they never even mentioned their subjects' homosexuality. In one such movie after another, the screenwriters went to absurd and unconvincing lengths to find something to take the place of homosexuality as a plausible explanation for why the protagonist didn't marry, why he had "woman problems," why he drank too much, and so forth. Why did the screenwriters do this? Plainly, because most filmgoers of the day considered homosexuality immoral. Yet at the same time they considered the homosexual heroes of these movies to be worthy of respect, in some cases even veneration. How could this be? Could a man's sexual orientation really be trimmed away so neatly from the story of his life, like fat from a roast?

The same policy obtained in Hollywood's adaptations of literary works.

Whenever the rare novel or play with a homosexual character was made into a film, that character was omitted or turned into a heterosexual. Lillian Hellman's play *The Children's Hour,* which was about two teachers accused of lesbianism, became the 1936 film *These Three,* about a woman teacher accused of heterosexual hanky-panky. (A more faithful cinematic version of the play was released in 1961.) Richard Brooks's novel *The Brick Foxhole,* about a soldier who murders a homosexual, became the 1947 movie *Crossfire,* about a soldier who murders a Jew. And the implicitly gay narrator of Truman Capote's *Breakfast at Tiffany's* became, in the movie, Audrey Hepburn's love interest. (Producers have continued to follow this procedure: Steven Spielberg's movie version of *The Color Purple* toned down the lesbianism in Alice Walker's novel, and the movie *Fried Green Tomatoes* turned the lesbian romance of Fannie Flagg's novel into a platonic friendship between two heterosexual women.) Many old Hollywood movies, furthermore, contained homosexual stereotypes—sissyish unmarried men and tough wisecracking spinsters—though the word "homosexual" was never used, of course, and the characters weren't shown in homosexual relationships; and other movies featured homosexual subtexts (such as the strongly hinted-at attachment between Glenn Ford and George Macready, both supposedly rivals for Rita Hayworth's affections, in *Gilda*) that heterosexuals might not notice but that most homosexuals could hardly miss.

The philosophy that guided the making of biographical movies also governed, and in most American schools continues to govern, the teaching of arts and humanities. Teachers who routinely discuss the historical impact of John Adams's marriage or Wordsworth's friendship with Coleridge never breathe a word about the homosexuality of James Buchanan or Walt Whitman or Dag Hammarskjöld or Langston Hughes. It seems plain that the rule for teachers and movie directors alike should be not to go out of one's way either to mention a historical figure's homosexuality or to avoid mentioning it. In a context where it seems reasonable to bring up a heterosexual's marriage, it should be considered reasonable to talk about the personal life of a homosexual.

Gay literature is fraught with paradox. The best novel about male homosexuality—*The Charioteer*—was written by a woman, Mary Renault. One of the greatest novels by a homosexual male—Marcel Proust's *A la recherche du temps perdu*—centers on a heterosexual romance.

Until relatively recent times, of course, few writers felt free to introduce homosexual themes explicitly into literary fiction. Accordingly, many homosexual writers disguised stories of same-sex romance in order to make them palatable to a general reading public. Proust turned his lover Alfred into his heroine Albertine; the heroine in *Of Human Bondage* was based on a young male object of Somerset Maugham's affection. E. M. Forster, however, quit writing novels because he didn't feel honest writing about heterosexuals and knew he wouldn't be published if he wrote about homosexuals. "I should have been a more famous writer if I had written or rather published more," he once commented, "but sex has prevented the latter." The extraordinarily gifted Glenway Wescott, a contemporary of F. Scott Fitzgerald and Ernest Hemingway, published several books in his twenties, including an exquisite novel entitled *The Grandmothers* (1927), all of them derived from his childhood and youth in Wisconsin. Yet though he lived into his eighties, his output after the age of thirty was tiny; his only published works of fiction after 1927 were the Jamesian novella *The Pilgrim Hawk* (1940) and the short novel *Apartment in Athens* (1945). It is hard to read Wescott's posthumously published diaries, which chronicle the complicated sexual life of his middle years, without concluding that, having used up the material provided by his childhood and youth, this highly autobiographical author was hindered from writing novels based on his adult experience both by the censorious standards of the time and by his own sense of guilt about his homosexuality.

In the works of many a homosexual writer—from James and Proust to Oscar Wilde and Terence Rattigan—the author's homosexuality (latent or otherwise) is manifested not in the form of explicitly homosexual subject matter but in the form of certain qualities of style and tone and perspective that suggest the distinctive, ironic position of a homosexual who is an esteemed member of a society that disdains homosexuality. Many such authors wrote portraits of society that are richly nuanced and elliptical, mainly because their situation made them all the more aware of nuances of language and gesture and because they were constantly having to talk around the truth about themselves. Denied their natural subject, moreover, many gay writers chose instead to concentrate on, and indeed to make a fetish of, style. In recent times, of course, the burgeoning category of Gay Lit has made it possible to draw a distinction between Gay Writers and writers who happen to be gay. A Gay Writer addresses a mostly gay audience; a writer who happens to be gay addresses a general audience. In either case, something must be sacrificed. The Gay Writer probes deeply into a local truth that is of profound significance to him and other homosexuals, but not to most heterosexuals; the writer who happens to be gay avoids or disguises the depths of one important aspect of his own particular truth in order to commune successfully on a serious level with a heterosexual audience. The Gay Writer's novel says: *This is what it means to live as a homosexual man in a mostly heterosexual world that doesn't understand or sympathize*. The novel by the writer who happens to be gay says: *This is life*. Yet the Gay Novel at its best addresses a high moral question: how does one live honorably as a homosexual in a world that considers homosexuality itself dishonorable?

The Gay Writer is in a problematic position. His chief difficulty is that when it comes to the subject closest to his heart, he may well have a perspective on things that many readers would consider utterly outlandish. What is to him a gentle love story may be to them an obscene provocation; what is to him simply life may be to them an *issue*—and a highly controversial one, at that. In this the Gay Writer is truly unique. A Haitian reading Philip Roth, say, or a Mississippian reading Naguib Mahfouz may find certain aspects of the novelist's culture exotic and baffling and even irksome, but certain things are universal: envy, sloth, greed, lust, ambition, the love of beauty, the fear of death, and above all the human attachments—boy-girl romance, parental affection, marital strife—on which most novels center. But can even the most gifted gay novelist count on straight readers to respond as desired to a novel about two young men falling in love? The Gay Novel is, in short, the most ghettoized of literary categories. A white boy may read *Black Boy* but the average straight boy doesn't even want to be *seen* reading, say, Mary Renault's *The Persian Boy* or Mart Crowley's *The Boys in the Band* or John Fox's *The Boys on the Rock*. This is, of course, a one-way problem. Homosexuals grow up around married couples, heterosexual dating, male classmates discussing their designs on various girls. Every song, movie, and TV show contributes in some way to gay people's awareness of male-female relations; they don't have to be straight to understand or care about what's going on between Anna and Vronsky in *Anna Karenina* or Emma and Charles in *Madame Bovary*. To most straight people, by contrast, gay life is at best a mystery, at worst an object of revulsion, and the Gay Novel therefore a largely minority taste and, for all but a few straight readers, something other than a purely literary experience.

Each period of modern gay history has had its own typical fictions—novels that not only illuminate the way in which homosexuality was viewed during a given period both by gay and straight people but also provide a glimpse of the gay subculture at various stages.

Before the 1970s, the Gay Novel, then a rare phenomenon, tended to focus on a protagonist who learns (or fails to learn) to live with his homosexuality in a hostile and uncomprehending world. The best such novel is Mary Renault's *The Charioteer* (1959). Set in England during World War II, it is about a young British soldier named Laurie Odell who has sustained a leg injury at Dunkirk. While laid up in a rural army hospital, Laurie meets and falls in love with an intelligent, virtuous young orderly, a conscientious objector named Andrew Raynes. They quickly become best friends. But Laurie doesn't declare his love, for while Andrew is obviously in love with him as well, it is also clear that the innocent young man hasn't yet recognized his own homosexuality or the nature of his affection for Laurie.

Until now, Laurie has resisted accepting his own homosexuality; he met several homosexuals while a student at Oxford, but their silliness and sexual intemperance repelled him. Now, on leave from the hospital, he is reunited with Ralph Lanyon, a merchant seaman who had been his idol at school. He also encounters a local circle of homosexuals that he finds as repellent as he did the homosexuals at Oxford, and for the same reason: "They were specialists. . . . They had identified themselves with their limitations; they were making a career of them. They had turned from all other reality, and curled up in them snugly, as in a womb." In short, they are more or less typical midcentury subculture-oriented gays. One is, to be sure, troubled by Renault's use of the word "limitations," by Ralph's continual insistence (with which Renault plainly concurs) that homosexuality is a kind of liability, and by the symbolic handicaps of both Laurie and Ralph. Does Renault mean to suggest that homosexuality is, by its nature, confining? Perhaps, though in her later novels about Alexander the Great she plainly doesn't view *his* homosexuality in such a way. She may mean to suggest that, in early twentieth-century England, homosexuality is a drawback in practical terms because of the restrictions imposed on homosexuals by laws and social conventions. Yet she does give every indication of subscribing to the now-discredited notion of homosexuality as a disorder stemming from childhood trauma: we are clearly meant to understand Laurie's homosexuality as the product of his parents' divorce and his clinging mother, and Ralph's homosexuality as the consequence of childhood sex play to which his mother reacted hysterically and about which she made him feel guilty. (Renault also seems oddly contemptuous, by the way, of her own sex: not only do both Laurie and Ralph owe their homosexuality to emotionally immature mothers, but the other women in *The Charioteer* tend to be silly, innocuous, or overbearing.)

Discovering that Ralph shares his distaste for the subculture, Laurie recalls that a homosexual friend at Oxford "kept telling me I was queer, and I'd never heard it called that before and didn't like it. The word, I mean. Shutting you away, somehow; roping you off with a lot of people you don't feel much in common with, half of whom hate the other half anyway, and just keep together so that they can lean up against each other for support." It is Ralph who succinctly sums up the book's principal theme: "It's not what one is, but what one does with it." Because mainstream society refuses to deal at all with the fact of homosexuality, and because the subculture has established no moral standards or courting rituals for gays, Laurie, like every young gay person who rejects the loose sexuality of the subculture, is forced to "mak[e] up [his] own rules and tr[y] to piece it all together."

The most momentous moral choice that he must face is what to do about his love for Andrew, with whom he wants to spend his life. But Andrew, a devout Quaker who comes from a long line of military men, is increasingly burdened by guilt over his principled unwillingness to fight, and Laurie fears that making Andrew aware at this point in his life of his own homosexuality might devastate him. In Laurie's place, some members of the local gay circle might take advantage of Andrew's innocent love and trust, compelling him into a state of self-knowledge, and into a physical relationship, that he might not yet be able to handle. Ralph has provided Laurie with a different model of conduct. Back in school, Ralph made it clear that he was attracted to Laurie, but told him, "You're on the way to being something, and I don't know what, not for certain. So I'm not going to interfere with it." (The word "interfering" may be misleading here: Ralph's point is presumably not that one might unintentionally change another person's sexual orientation but that one does not want to hasten a natural process of sexual self-discovery that should occur in its own time for its own reasons.)

The Charioteer is a wonder of a novel. Though Andrew appears rarely and says little, he seems marvelously real, and Laurie's friendship with him approximates many gay men's dream of an innocent first love. Andrew is, after all, handsome, sensitive, intelligent, and virginal; Laurie meets him not at a gay bar or party or bathhouse but outside the institutions of the subculture, in the course of daily life; it is meeting him that enables Laurie to accept his homosexuality. Their relationship is a plausible if somewhat idealized version of the first love that many gay men have; for many gay men, when they are young and discovering their homosexuality, experience an intense but unspoken passion for someone to whom they are very close and to whom they cannot imagine confessing their love, usually for fear of being rejected. Often the setting of this love is a school or college—a place that is, like Laurie's hospital, set apart from the rest of the world, a place in which a romantic friendship that could never be transplanted successfully into the larger world can, for a time, seem viable. *The Charioteer* beautifully evokes the joy of love, the hopefulness of youth, and the exhilaration of self-discovery; and its ultimate poignancy derives from Laurie's gradual recognition of the limitations imposed on homosexuals by a homophobic world.

As a student Laurie reflects "that the world was a meaner place than he had supposed, but that one got nowhere by making a fuss about it." To read *The Charioteer* in the 1990s can be to feel that Renault accepts a bit too readily the necessity of the closet and the notion that most heterosexuals can never be made to understand and accept homosexuality. This observation aside, however, her recognition of homosexuality as a distinctive moral challenge is salutary, and her lesson in courage, stoicism, responsibility, and self-control is an admirable one. Renault's novel holds a valuable message for gays in the 1990s: don't ask for a medal; don't feel sorry for yourself. Being gay *is* an inconvenience; so are a lot of things; get on with it; if others have a problem with it, that's *their* problem. Above all, don't use your homosexuality or their contempt for it as an excuse to lower your moral standards. The important thing is to behave in such a way as to keep your own respect and that of people whose respect means something.

• • •

The Gay Liberation years of the 1970s saw the appearance of Gay Novels that, in their view of the proper relation of the gay individual to the subculture and to society in general, could hardly have been more different from *The Charioteer*. If Laurie is repelled by the sex-centered subculture, the promiscuous young urbanites in the novels of people like John Rechy tend to be thoroughgoing subculture types. Among the most celebrated, and the most thoughtful, of these '70s books is Andrew Holleran's *Dancer from the Dance* (1978), which was cited in *Harper's* as "the best gay novel written by anyone of our generation." It is the story of Malone, a handsome, brilliant, conservative young Ivy League lawyer who, recognizing after years of aching loneliness that he is gay, quits his job and dives headfirst into the subculture. "My only hope," he writes in his ledger, "is with those men circling the fountain [in Washington's DuPont Circle, a traditional gay pickup spot]. They are my fate and if I wish to have Life, it must be with *them*. What is most remarkable, I have no choice. I who have never been constrained by poverty, disease, accident, am now constrained by this. God's joke. His little joke. To keep us human. To humble the proud. And I have been so proud." In these few lines of Malone's ledger, we learn a lot about him. Like many subculture-oriented gays, he views homosexuality as a divine joke. Like many a privileged white gay American male, he fails to recognize that homosexuality is not the only socially problematic personal trait in American society. People who are female, black, Hispanic, foreign-born, Jewish, short, unattractive, fat, poor, chronically ill, or physically or mentally handicapped are also made to feel from time to time like second-class citizens, yet many manage to accept their circumstances, to live with them, and to be self-respecting and responsible.

What can one say about Malone's notion that his only hope for life is with "those men"? Well, yes, since he's gay his only hope for a rewarding personal life is with another gay man. But must his professional life and social life also revolve entirely around other gay men? And when he says "those" men, does he mean those in search not of a life partner at all but of a bedmate for the night? As it happens, Malone does find a lover: the most touching parts of the book—along with the passages about his early loneliness and about his unspoken, mortifying love for a high-school boy who works in his garden—are the descriptions of his joy in the simple routines of his life with the man he loves.

Yet Malone can't bring himself to stay with his lover for life. Betraying him, he becomes, in his own words, "a professional faggot," living for sex and making a living by selling it. What makes Malone lead such a life? Is it a love of beauty, as the narrator suggests at one point? Malone equates his promiscuous way of life with a search for love. Does Holleran want us to see it this way, too? (Here, as in the "Notes on Promiscuity," Holleran uses the words "fall in love" every time someone's head is turned by a face on the street.) Or is Malone motivated by self-hatred, self-destructiveness? For he makes it clear that he sees his homosexuality as "wrong," as a disease. Describing Malone's acknowledgment of his homosexuality, Holleran writes that "it was as if he had finally admitted to himself that he had cancer. He saw in that instant a life he could not conceive of opening before him, a hopeless abyss. Either way he was doomed: He did what was wrong, and condemned himself, or he did what was right, and remained a ghost."

Years later, a rich upper-class boy named John Schaeffer falls in love with Malone and wants to live with him forever. He is seen as facing the same choice as Malone—to remain sexless and honorable or to become a "full-time fag," leaving all morals behind—and Malone lobbies him to do the former. The implication is that there's no middle ground, no way of leading a responsible, romantically committed life as a homosexual man. As Malone tells his friend Sutherland: "Don't you think the moral thing to do is just tell John Schaeffer to go back to Princeton, his family's house in Maine, his suite of rooms, and forget this charade? There isn't what he thinks there is out there, and he might as well be told. Look where it got me!" As in *The Charioteer,* then, a young man sacrifices possible happiness with another young man who loves him because he doesn't want to ruin the other's life. The difference is that in *The Charioteer* it's Andrew's knowledge of his own homosexuality that Laurie is unwilling to force upon him; in *Dancer from the Dance,* it's an awareness of the sordidness of gay life that Malone feels he shouldn't force upon Schaeffer. But this is a bogus conflict, because gay life doesn't *have* to be sordid.

Holleran's novel is in many ways a remarkable piece of work: wistful, evocative, beautifully written. Though the book's vision of gay life seemed mostly alien to me when I first read it in 1981—and seems even more alien in the AIDS era—every now and then there's a line that makes one say: "Yes! That's exactly how things are. Why hadn't I ever thought to put it that way?" For all its grubby anecdotes about sex, the book might fairly be described as moral fiction. It asks the question: how does one live as a gay man in this world? Alas, the only answer it takes seriously enough to explore is that of the gay subculture. Throughout most of the book, Holleran seems to be suggesting that if you discover yourself to be gay, and value love and beauty and life itself, you are condemned, like it or not, to feel and think and behave like the people in this book; otherwise, you're what the book describes as one of those dull midtown types, playing a role unsuited to your true inner nature, all bottled up and fraudulent and living for money. What this amounts to is an endorsement of the false dichotomy propounded by the gay subculture: out, proud, and promiscuous versus closeted, ashamed, and repressed.

Both Holleran's narrator and his protagonist make numerous generalizations about homosexuals that are true of many subculture-oriented gays but decidedly untrue of homosexuals in general. "As homosexuals tend to do," the narrator says of Malone after his plunge into the subculture, "he had simply ceased to communicate with his former world." Malone contends that "the vast majority of homosexuals are looking for a superman to love and find it *very* difficult to love anyone merely human, which we unfortunately happen to be." The narrator speaks of "the great homosexual disease—the sanctity of the face seen and never spoken to" and draws a connection between homosexuals and romantics: "It was the most beautiful illusion of homosexuals and romantics alike: if only I'd loved that one . . ." "What is gay life," says Malone at one point, "but those bumper cars at an amusement park, that crash and bounce off each other?" The narrator refers to dawn as "that most insulting moment for the homosexual, when the sky goes white above him, and the birds begin to chatter, and still on his knees he looks up from the cock he's been sucking to see the light, like a man making love in a dark bedroom when the door has been flung open." The novel speaks for and of the most confused and wayward element of the gay population. And yet it implies that such gays represent the essence, the apotheosis, of gayness.

What is Malone's tragic flaw? That he's gay? Or that he has certain qualities of character—self-hatred, self-destructiveness, a desperate hunger for love, a devotion to beauty so overpowering that it causes him to devote his life to pursuing and possessing it—that, in combination with the values and imperatives of the gay subculture, prove lethal? To read Malone's story is to be told, over and over, that the two things are one and the same; to be gay *is* to have those qualities of character. Given this, it is little short of remarkable that Holleran sandwiches Malone's story, with its insistence on the subculture's narrow view of homosexuality, between an opening and closing section that place the subculture's view in its proper context. These opening and closing sections consist of a series of letters between the novel's putative author, in New York, and a gay friend who has moved from Manhattan to the Deep South. Holleran presents this "author" as the ultimate subculture type. "*I have been a full-time fag for the past five years,*" the "author" tells his correspondent. "*Everyone I know is gay, everything I do is gay, all my fantasies are gay.*" He sees non-subculture gays as both more boring and more successful than himself and his kind:

> *Most fags are as boring as straight people—they start businesses with lovers and end up in Hollywood, Florida, with dogs and double-knit slacks and I have no desire to write about them. What can you say about a success? Nothing! But failures—that tiny subspecies of homosexual, the doomed queen, who puts the car in gear and drives right off the cliff! That fascinates me. The fags who consider themselves worthless because they are queer, and who fall into degradation and sordidness! It was those whom Christ befriended, not the assholes in the ad agencies uptown who go to St. Kitts in February!*

The "author"'s friend observes: "The point is that we are not doomed because we are homosexual, my dear, we are doomed only if we live in despair because of it." The friend goes on to recall a Gay Pride Day march at which he realized, to his astonishment, that there were thousands of other homosexuals in New York who *didn't* live the way they did:

> Do you realize what a tiny fraction of the mass of homosexuals we were? . . . I used to say there were only seventeen homosexuals in New York, and we knew every one of them; but there were tons of men in that city who weren't on the circuit, who didn't dance, didn't cruise,

didn't fall in love with Malone, who stayed home and went to the country in the summer. We never saw them. We were addicted to something else: something I lived with so long it had become a technique, a routine. That was the real sin.

These letters are plainly designed to put the novel's story in perspective—to make it clear that "doomed queens" like Malone represent only a "tiny subspecies" of homosexuals, and to acknowledge that homosexuality is seen in the novel through the small, clouded, and warped lens of the subculture.

Perhaps the most touching thing in *Dancer from the Dance* is its very last word. Until the end, we never know the names of the "author" and his correspondent; their animated letters are all addressed to "Ecstasy" or "Madness" or "Vision" and signed with grand (and consistently Gallic) female names like Hélène de Sévigné and Madeleine de Rothschild. But the final letter, by the author's friend, is signed, simply, "Paul"—which suggests that, far away from the gay ghetto, he may be developing the courage to emerge from the prison of group identity and to grow into self-acceptance as a gay individual. Yet it's too easy for a casual reader to miss the point of these letters and to fail to realize that the narrator is intended to be unreliable. One shares Holleran's sympathy for people like Malone; yet one is dismayed by Holleran's inability, when he looks at non-subculture gays, to see anything more than a lot of dull people leading conventional lives. To most homosexuals, I'm sure, there could be few lives less appealing than Malone's.

If many gay novels of the 1970s centered on subculture-oriented types like Malone, the 1980s and early '90s gave us plenty of novels, among them David Feinberg's *Eighty-sixed* and Paul Monette's *Afterlife*, about men living with and dying of AIDS. The 1980s also brought a succession of minimalistic fictions by and about the post-AIDS generation of gay men. If in the typical 1970s novel the gay person's family is invisible, in these works—of which the stories and novels of David Leavitt are representative—families appear frequently. If Malone, upon accepting his homosexuality, severs his ties with parents and friends and abandons all career ambitions, Leavitt's protagonists shuttle back and forth between home turf and the gay ghetto, struggling to reconcile the two sides of their lives. If Malone, after a brief interval of monogamy, plunges into the lowest depths of the subculture, pursuing a life of countless one-night stands, Leavitt's heroes go through a period of sexual adventure but then fall in love, become monogamous, and look forward to a quiet, contented domestic life.

A *Vanity Fair* piece by James Wolcott about Leavitt's 1989 novel *Equal Affections* provides a remarkable illustration of the gay subculture's influence on sophisticated liberal views of homosexuality. Writes Wolcott: "Gay fiction has hung up its G-string. Gone are the days when a John Rechy hero would flex a biceps to feed a fistful of vitamins into his mouth, fortifying himself for a night on the man-prowl. . . . Kinky is out, kindness is in. Perhaps the writer who best reflects this shift from sexual outlaw to Care Bear is David Leavitt." Wolcott proceeds to describe Leavitt as "a gay yuppie: a guppie" who "shares a house on Long Island with his lover, life partner, spousal equivalent, and significant other, Gary Glickman, an author too." Having employed this litany of synonymous terms (he seems to have forgotten "companion") in order to ridicule gay monogamy, Wolcott proceeds to wax ironic about Leavitt's and Glickman's domesticity. The two men, he says, "heed a homing instinct." They're "nesters." They "hole up in a wired cocoon." And so, he explains, do the characters Danny and Walter in *Equal Affections*. Wolcott can't imagine anything more ludicrous, apparently, than two men living together in a middle-class suburban home. Danny and Walter are, he says, "a gay version of that nice young couple down the block." After quoting Leavitt's catalog of their household appliances, Wolcott comments snidely:

> What, no waffle iron? But don't make the mistake, O ye of little faith, of thinking that living in an appliance warehouse is an apolitical act. As Danny's sister, April, says, "Sometimes I think the most political thing a gay man or woman can do is to live openly with another gay man or woman." Norman Mailer once identified one strain of feminism as girls-may-hold-hands-in-the-suburbs. Gay lib in *Equal Affections* boils down to boys-may-hold-hands-in-the-suburbs.

Wolcott's point could not be clearer: if Leavitt's novel is a dud, it's not because of his deficiencies as a literary artist but because he has rejected the extremes of subculture sexuality and sexual politics and has chosen instead to lead an ordinary middle-class domestic life. "It needn't be this way," Wolcott laments. "Gay writers from Isherwood to Vidal have had constant companions in their private lives without allowing that to preclude a greedy thirst for gritty swigs of experience." If Leavitt couldn't achieve the "expanse" of a novel "as beautifully alive as Isherwood's *Down There on a Visit*," then, it's not because he doesn't have Isherwood's gifts but because the composition of such a book "necessitated a mental and physical voyaging-out."

A "greedy thirst for gritty swigs of experience"? A "mental and physical voyaging-out"? What is Wolcott chiding Leavitt for? Apparently for not doing drugs or drinking to excess; for not spending his nights haunting the bars and cruising the waterfronts; and for not having outrageous sex with plenty of strangers (preferably menacing ones with scars on their cheeks and knives in their boots). In short, Wolcott is chiding him for not buying completely into the gay subculture—for not being Malone. In Wolcott's view, Leavitt is a fake, a traitor, a sellout who's not living up to his social obligations. It appears not to have occurred to Wolcott that to ridicule gays for not being rebels is as offensive as ridiculing women for not being housewives or ridiculing black men for not being Pullman porters.

Wolcott makes a point of telling us that he isn't ascribing Leavitt's limitations to his homosexuality. He claims that "it isn't the gay element of being a guppie that holds Leavitt and Glickman back, it's the yuppie element, the protective coloration of being contented consumers." Yet one can't imagine him making the same argument about heterosexual writers who marry and live quietly in the suburbs. It's only when a gay writer chooses such a life that someone like Wolcott finds it ridiculous— for in Wolcott's view, to be homosexual is above all to be *sexual*, to focus one's life on carnal gratification. Gays aren't *supposed* to be bourgeois; their proper role in American society is to live dangerously, sleep around, walk on the wild side. The ultimate irony of all this is that Wolcott's review of *Equal Affections* appeared in *Vanity Fair*, the Yuppie bible of the 1980s. Wolcott's implicit message to his Yuppie readers is that it's fine for them to be Yuppies as long as they're straight, but it's *not* fine for gays. The sad thing about Wolcott's piece is that, of the hundreds of thousands of affluent young urban heterosexuals who read it—most of whom probably have openly gay friends and take homosexuality in their stride—it is likely that few were startled by Wolcott's assumptions or disturbed by his conclusions. For among urban liberal heterosexuals today, the prevalent ideas about homosexuality are, to a remarkable extent, those of the gay subculture.

Recently, for example, an intelligent New York liberal of my acquaintance admitted that he considers certain traits and mannerisms to be innately gay and that gays who don't "look gay" or "act gay" are denying something that is a natural part of them. I wondered: does this mean that Tchaikovsky lisped? That Michelangelo swung his hips when he walked? Apropos of gay ghettos, the liberal asked: "Don't you think gays naturally want to be around other gays?" I wondered how this question would sound to him if one substituted the word "Jews" or "blacks" here for "gays." He suggested that it was unrealistic for gays to aim for acceptance by the larger society; people, he argued, just aren't capable of that kind of understanding. I wondered how he would've reacted a few decades ago if I'd mounted a similar argument against combating anti-Semitism or racism.

Such conversations serve as a reminder of how bizarre even tolerant urban liberals consider homosexuality to be: they find it easier to deal with a gay person as a picturesque, easily identifiable aberration than as someone who in every other respect but sexuality is not necessarily different from anyone else. Such liberals tend to feel more comfortable, in other words, with the idea of gays as a marginal group who have their own distinctive culture and mannerisms and ghettos than with the idea of gays as a diverse assortment of individuals who are spread out all over the landscape, who have wildly varying tastes and philosophies of life, and who are (most of them) not immediately identifiable as gay. To such liberals, there is nothing more truly and disquietingly radical than the idea of a gay population that is *not* separate, *not* easily recognizable—and *not* radical.

If Wolcott's piece on Leavitt offers a depressing example of the sort of thinking about homosexuality that one finds among many liberal literary journalists, the offenses of such people pale alongside those of the growing number of academics who have, in recent years, become "specialists" in the field known as Gay Studies or (in some purlieus) Queer Studies. To be sure, Gay Studies is not necessarily an indefensible idea. It is, of course, wrong to speak of great homosexual writers or artists of the past as being the special heritage of gay people. Every writer or artist—male or female, black or white, gay or straight—is part of the common human heritage; the obvious corollary to the misguided idea that a gay writer belongs especially to gay readers is that a straight writer's work belongs *less* to a gay reader than to a straight reader.

This said, however, one cannot help adding that Gay Studies courses for gay students do make a bit more sense, in theory, than, say, Black Studies courses for black students. Most black students have grown up among blacks; black culture may in fact be the *only* culture with which they are familiar; part of the purpose of educating them should be to broaden their awareness, to acquaint them with the world beyond the one in which they have grown up. Gay students, by contrast, generally do not grow up among gays. A properly constructed course in Gay Studies might provide such students with an opportunity to contemplate the distinctive social, psychological, and ethical issues posed by the fact of being homosexual in a society that doesn't accept homosexuality and to recognize the breadth of personal and professional options open to them.

Yet this isn't how Gay Studies actually works. In practice it is less a traditional field of objective intellectual inquiry than a collective attempt to use the methods of contemporary cultural theory to advance the gay subculture's view of homosexuality. Specifically, it is a means of reinforcing gay segregation, the idea of gays as a victim group, and the notion of a defining, all-subsuming "gay identity" or "gay sensibility." Gay Studies scholars are inclined to agree with anti-gay reactionaries on one point—namely, that gays will never be accepted as full and equal members of society, will never be allowed their places at the table. Indeed, these scholars tend to dismiss the idea of society as consisting, metaphorically speaking, of a single big table; rather, in accordance with the ethos of multiculturalism, they are inclined to visualize society as consisting mostly of smaller tables, each assigned to an accredited victim group, and to see the people who sit at those tables not as individuals who should be rewarded according to individual merit and effort but as members of their respective groups who enjoy certain membership privileges. Instead of recognizing the many things that unite people with one another across lines of race, ethnicity, class, gender, and sexual orientation, then, these scholars are preoccupied with the differences that divide group from group; instead of recognizing that the greatest artists, gay or straight, transcend sexual orientation, they "celebrate" gay art and culture by wildly overstating the value of relatively slight works that exemplify the "gay sensibility."

The greatest single influence on Gay Studies today is the late French theorist Michel Foucault, an enthusiast of sadomasochism who analyzed sexual relations almost entirely in terms of power. While acolytes of the French deconstructionist critic Jacques Derrida write about literature as if aesthetic feeling were foreign to them, Foucault's followers write about sexual relations as if love didn't exist and sex were purely a drama of dominance and submission. At present the biggest name in Gay Studies is perhaps that of David M. Halperin, an MIT professor (and co-editor of the new Gay Studies journal *GLQ*) the title essay of whose 1990 book *One Hundred Years of Homosexuality* is a prototypical piece of Gay Studies scholarship. The essay's title alludes to the fact that the word "homosexuality" was coined only a century ago and that, prior to that time, people didn't think of heterosexuals and homosexuals as two different kinds of people. Halperin accepts this fact; yet, curiously, having established that the idea of "homosexuals" and "heterosexuals" as essentially different types of person is a twentieth-century sociocultural fiction, he proceeds with his argument as if he has established something quite different, namely that homosexuality—and, indeed, any kind of sexuality—is itself a sociocultural phenomenon that must be discussed not in terms of the complex personal emotions that bind actual individuals to each other but in terms of generalizations about ideology, power, and social structures. As he puts it,

> We must acknowledge that "sexuality" is a cultural production no less than are table manners, health clubs, and abstract expressionism, and we must struggle to discern in what we currently regard as our most precious, unique, original, and spontaneous impulses the traces of a previously rehearsed and socially encoded ideological script.

In short, the personal is political. Halperin proffers this idea as if it followed logically from what he has been saying. It is, however, not a reasonable conclusion but an absurd leap. Indeed, his method is preposterously circular: having declared at the outset that he intends to focus on the sociocultural structures of sexuality, he does so only to conclude that sexuality is a sociocultural phenomenon. It is rather like stating at the outset of an essay that one will discuss only Japanese automobiles, and, at the end of it, concluding that all automobiles are Japanese. Though Halperin admits in a footnote that he is "interested here not in erotic phenomenology but in the social articulation of sexual categories and in the public meanings attached to sex," he acts throughout the entire book as if love and passion—and, indeed, everything that gives a human dimension to sexual relationships—do not exist. Halperin says that to omit the social context when discussing sexual relations is to distort; but to omit the human dimension, even if one acknowledges its omission, is also to distort—and dramatically so. If one were to derive a logical conclusion from Halperin's observations, it would be that, since the homosexual is *not* a particular type of individual who shares a variety of innate characteristics with other homosexuals, the idea of a "gay brotherhood" that transcends common humanity is absurd. Instead, Halperin's logical contortions lead him to quite the opposite point of view: that since homosexuality *is* (as he claims) a political construct, then it is perfectly reasonable to talk about homosexuality in political terms, positing the idea of gay solidarity and describing homosexuality as a political movement.

One of the curious things about Gay Studies scholarship is that many of its practitioners mix the pretentious, hyperacademic, and dehumanizing discourse of a David M. Halperin with silly, pointless jabber, campy pop-cultural references, and outpourings of tacky personal anecdotes that frequently appear to be of minimal relevance to the supposed subject at hand and that seem to belong less to the seminar room than to the barroom. The customary justification for such self-indulgence is that anything a gay scholar has ever done or thought is relevant in a work of Gay Studies scholarship precisely because he *is* gay: if it happened to him, it is by definition a Gay Idea, a Gay Experience, a piece of Gay Testimony to be entered into the Gay Book of Life. Far from being abashed over their gratuitous autobiographical ditherings, Gay Studies scholars routinely describe their narcissism in heroic, hyperbolic terms; by writing about themselves, they explain, they are "breaking the silence," "bursting open the closet door."

Case in point: in a chapter of *The Columbia History of the American Novel* that is presumably supposed to be devoted to Gay Literature, Rutgers University professor Ed Cohen tells us about "the unarticulable pain" of his boyhood, about his youthful fascination with Dr. David Reuben's *Everything You Always Wanted to Know About Sex* (the title of which he gets wrong), about the inflammatory bowel disease that during his teenage years "kept me moving between toilets and hospitals in an unconscious attempt to give material form to the emotional pain that flowed through me," about how James Baldwin's *Giovanni's Room*, the first " 'gay' book" that Cohen ever read, gave "exquisite shape to something I could recognize as akin to my own pain," and so forth. The word "pain" is ubiquitous in this essay, and Cohen makes it clear throughout that, in his view, the proper role of Gay Literature and Gay Studies is that of therapeutic tools.

Though only a handful of colleges and universities have introduced Gay Studies programs, humanities professors around the country who happen to be homosexual are increasingly identifying themselves with the Gay Studies movement. The Modern Language Association's division of gay and lesbian studies now has over five hundred members. The organization's 1992 convention featured over two dozen sessions with such titles as "Henry James and Gay Studies," "Lesbian Tongues Untied," "Outing Goethe and His Age," "Gay Subjects, Mass Culture," "Lesbians at the Opera," "Gender and Gay and Lesbian Studies in Native American Literature," "Status of Gender and Feminism in Queer Theory," "The Invisible Woman: The Obscuration of the Lesbian Writer," "Lesbianism and Eighteenth-Century English Literature," and "Homosexuality and National Identity: Latin America, 1900–30."

More and more American institutions of higher education have begun offering courses in Gay Studies. Among them is the City College of San Francisco, the chairman of whose Gay and Lesbian Studies Department describes it as an "activist" department whose goal is to proffer a "critique" of "normalcy" and to mount an assault on the "dominant culture." To be sure, some of the course offerings seem legitimate. For example, "Anthropology of Homosexualities" examines "the roles and statuses of homosexuals in various cultures throughout the world." (One would not be surprised, of course, to learn that the course reflected the subculture's tendency to soft-pedal Third World homophobia and to exaggerate, by contrast, the difficulties faced by gays in the Western world.) Also plausible-sounding are courses in gay and lesbian relationships, which could presumably help young gay people to navigate their way through a society in which living as a gay couple poses special legal and social problems. Other offerings sound sensible at first blush, such as physical education courses "in which sexual minority students can expect to feel comfortable, supported, and safe." Yet why should it be better for homosexual students to be openly gay, rather than closeted, if this openness results in the segregation of gym classes according to sexual orientation? How will homosexuality ever be more generally accepted if gay students separate themselves out in this manner? To emerge from the closet, after all, is precisely to sacrifice a degree of comfort and safety in order to live openly in the world.

Other elements of the San Francisco program are more obviously misguided. One course after another is plainly informed by the subculture's view of homosexuality as something innately characterized by certain views, interests, tastes, and mannerisms. A typical course, entitled "Lesbian and Gay Style and Sensibility," "examines personal, cultural, and political styles from drag to disco and from butch/femme to lipstick from the late 1800s to the present." An essential part of the department's goal would appear to be the reinforcement of stereotypes. What else could explain why a course in "Retail Floristry 85: Introduction to Flower Arranging" should be taught as part of Gay and Lesbian Studies? And another part of the department's goal is clearly to engage in cultural segregation. A course on "Lesbians and Gays in Modern American Art and Culture," which "surveys the contributions of lesbian and gay people to modern American art and culture in fields as diverse as painting, photography, dance and poetry," is described as follows: "Concentrating on major figures from Walt Whitman to Gertrude Stein to Andy Warhol, this course makes clear that lesbian and gay people have not only been at the forefront of modernism in America, they were in fact responsible for it."

What, one wants to ask, of Ezra Pound, T. S. Eliot, Wallace Stevens, William Carlos Williams, Henri Matisse, Pablo Picasso, and Igor Stravinsky? Presumably, the point of this sort of course is to counteract the traditional reluctance of teachers to mention the homosexuality of the great men and women who figure in their lessons. But just as it is wrong for teachers to go out of their way to conceal such facts, so it makes little pedagogical sense for them to pluck the gay names out of literary and cultural history and to make a course out of it. Gay artists and writers do not exist in a vacuum; to pretend that they do, and to isolate their sexuality from the many other factors that influence their work, is to isolate, to ghettoize, to give insufficient weight to questions of literary and artistic value, and to suggest that homosexuality is of necessity a more determining consideration than it usually is.

• • •

Proclaiming itself "America's first gay college in America's first gay city," the Institute of Gay and Lesbian Education in West Hollywood, California, was founded in February 1992 and began offering courses in the fall of that year. Its faculty consists of some forty professors from UCLA, USC, and the California Institute of Technology. Several courses in its catalog sound legitimate: "Sexual Orientation and the Law"; "The Science of Human Sexuality." One sounds especially interesting: "Homo-Sexual Ethics," which explores "the philosophy of a wide variety of moral issues concerning sexual orientation, activity, and relationships." But there are plenty of offerings whose manifest subculture orientation is less than encouraging. A course in women's music is entitled "Music, Politics, The Body and Lesbian Reflection." A course entitled "Telling Our Stories: Gay and Lesbian Issues in Contemporary Art" is concerned with "the exciting potential of contemporary art to address key issues relevant to gays and lesbians. Contemporary art, through multiculturalism, now provides the opportunity for gay and lesbian artists to investigate our lives, to tell our stories." Several dubious assumptions are in evidence here: namely, that art is primarily a matter of addressing "issues"; that gay and lesbian artists cannot function properly outside of a multicultural context; that all gay lives and stories are essentially the same life and story; that art is, at its best and most meaningful, a form of political testimony on behalf of a victim group.

And then there's "Queer Space: Gays and Lesbians and Their Built Environment," the course description of which reads as follows:

> Queer Space explores sexuality in the city. This is not a travel guide to Los Angeles. Instead of looking at bars as architecture or parks as open space, we want to understand how these places shape our sexuality and how our sexuality creates them. What are the forces that create lesbian/gay/bisexual cities or neighborhoods? How do we experience these forces? Mainstream history tells us that these places are created by our choices to live and work as gays/lesbians/bisexuals. We would like to challenge this notion in exciting discussions about our collective and individual experiences in the gay city of Los Angeles.

Several of the West Hollywood faculty members are identified in the catalog as associates of left-wing organizations whose names seem to take for granted an equation between politics and culture. One professor, for example, "has taught in the Feminist Studies Workshop"; another describes herself as "a radical Lesbian feminist of white European descent" and the co-founder of a New Music ensemble called "Ovaryaction." Multiculturalism abounds. One faculty member is "a founder of Colors United Action Coalition"; another is "committed to American Indian and gender matters."

Politically correct and multiculturalist rhetoric can be found as well in the mailings of the City University of New York's Center for Lesbian and Gay Studies. In September 1992 the Center sponsored a day of lectures and discussions on "Crossing Identifications: Identity and Ethnicity, Gender, Law, Politics, Race, Sexuality, Theory"—pretty much the whole multicultural menu. During the 1993–94 academic year, the Center plans to support scholarly research into the themes of "Race and Class in Lesbian and Gay Communities." Martin Duberman, the prominent Gay Studies scholar who heads up the Center (and who is the editor of the aforementioned Chelsea House series of books for lesbian and gay teenagers), has said that the Center's goal is to become "the lesbian and gay equivalent of The Kinsey Institute"—thereby implying that cultural studies, for people who happen to be gay, must always be reduced to questions of sexual mechanics.

To peruse the course offerings of these various programs is, indeed, to recognize that Gay Studies has far less to do with culture, language, or literature than with sexuality, sexual behavior, and "lifestyle." A Gay Studies classroom would seem to be not a place for learning but, instead, a place where gay people get together and talk about being gay. Gay Studies might have a valid purpose if it could help students better to understand certain heretofore neglected aspects of Marlowe's plays, say, or Raphael's paintings, or Benjamin Britten's music. In reality, however, far from probing and questioning and attempting to understand, Gay Studies imposes reductive, politically correct ideas upon its subjects, mindlessly celebrating gay solidarity and the untying of lesbian tongues, for example, instead of seeking to understand major historical figures as individuals in whose lives and work sexuality functioned in very different ways. As I have observed, enthusiasts defend Gay Studies not for its educational value but, essentially, as a form of therapy: it helps gay students to "claim their identity," to "imagine an alternative queer world," and so forth. Yet homosexuality is not (or should not be) a fixed, defining identity; for each gay person it should be *part* of a distinctive individual identity. Yet this idea is anathema to the subculture, and therefore to Gay Studies.

In a letter to *The New Republic* defending Gay Studies, Gary Schmidgall provides insight into the discipline's therapeutic focus. Schmidgall quotes Nietzsche to the effect that "one thing is needful: that a human being attain his satisfaction with himself—whether it be by this or by that poetry and art; only then is a human being at all tolerable to behold." Schmidgall goes on to say that "programs designed to encourage gay and lesbian students to discover the 'art' and 'poetry' of self-satisfaction would, I should think, be impossible to object to. Acknowledge the existence of fairies, and the grove of academe will become decidedly less gloomy." In both its language and its reasoning, this is a thoroughly typical Gay Studies apologia. First of all, by using the word "fairies" Schmidgall reduces all homosexuals to an offensive subculture-oriented stereotype that is very much at odds with most homosexuals' views of themselves. To speak of students achieving "self-satisfaction" through Gay Studies, moreover, is equivalent to saying (as many do) that black students should concentrate on black history and culture to achieve self-esteem; yet rather than help students to grow intellectually by enabling them to recognize all of the human cultural heritage as their possession, such thinking fosters a constricted, group-based sense of identity. Finally, by suggesting that Gay Studies will make the academy "less gloomy"—to be homosexual, apparently, is by definition to be cheerful and vivacious—Schmidgall implicitly equates the two senses of the word "gay," much as Donna Minkowitz conflates two different meanings of "straight."

"Some homosexuals," Andrew Holleran writes in his book *Ground Zero,* "disapprove of their homosexual self. That self-repudiation is something that has never been addressed fully in gay life; it may lie beneath so many layers of apparently well-adapted behavior that the problem of people who have counted themselves out on some deep level, lowered their ambitions, stayed away from arenas in which they felt they could not succeed, is similar perhaps to that of blacks. No one even sees the self-hatred."

That self-hatred can be found across the spectrum. Over dinner not long ago, a gay acquaintance who works for a conservative think tank in Washington, D.C., told me bluntly, "I *hate* homosexuals." Over breakfast recently, I explained to another gay acquaintance who once belonged to ACT UP why I objected to certain aspects of the Gay Pride Day march. He misunderstood what I was saying, and flabbergasted me by replying casually, "I hate homosexuals too. I think we *all* hate us." But that wasn't my point at all. I don't hate gays. Yet a lot of gays do—and *that's* what I hate. I hate to see people cocooning themselves in victimhood and straightjacketing themselves in stereotype. I hate to see adults who have been the victims of ignorance and prejudice not taking care that what they do and say makes things easier instead of harder for young people who are only beginning to learn what it means to suffer from that selfsame ignorance and prejudice. If I feel any rancor toward some of the people in the Gay Pride Day march, my rancor is directed not at their homosexuality but at their self-disgust, at their lack of self-respect, at the self-hatred that underlies so much of their noisy "pride." I don't hate seeing people in leather or drag; what I hate is the thought that to some of them, the leather or drag is the cornerstone of their identity. What I hate is seeing people being less than they can be, people who, with every word and gesture, seem to proclaim that they despise themselves for being gay. And I hate the fact that such people have succeeded in convincing many heterosexuals that they speak for all gays and that their own less attractive qualities are inherent attributes of homosexuality.

It seems deeply ironic to me that on January 27, 1993, an elderly heterosexual senator from Ohio named Howard Metzenbaum did more for gay rights with a brief, eloquent oration opposing the military's ban on gays than, say, Donna Minkowitz has done in a lifetime. Yes, the subculture has its heroes—among them the early ACT UP members who heroically reversed callous government and pharmaceutical company policies on drug testing, availability, and pricing, and the AIDS sufferers who took on the forces of political correctness to say things that needed to be said about promiscuity and bathhouses. But in recent years the most exemplary heroes of gay rights have been distinctly non-subculture types like ousted Naval Academy cadet Joseph Steffan, ousted Sixth Army soldier of the year José Zuniga, and ousted Air Force sergeant Thomas Paniccia—people who, in their pride, prudence, and dignity, and in their determination to achieve equal rights to live, love, and serve their country, are far more representative of the majority of gays than are the Donna Minkowitzes. It is homosexuals like Steffan, Zuniga, and Paniccia who help heterosexuals like Howard Metzenbaum—and, through him, countless other Americans—to learn the truth about homosexuals and to see where justice lies.

On the afternoon of April 25, 1993, I stood at a phone booth at the corner of Pennsylvania Avenue and E Street and, as the Michigan contingent of the March on Washington filed past, spoke to my companion, Chris, in New York. He told me that I had missed a rather unpleasant episode the night before. Sometime after one A.M., a group of about ten drunken young straight men had linked arms and paraded down our block in a parody of a gay march. "We're here, we're queer, get used to it," they had chanted. They had also screamed out the words "homo" and "faggot."

As I stood on that streetcorner, I reflected that the March on Washington, even more than the annual Gay Pride Day marches, was intended to combat the widespread prejudice that lay behind such familiar acts of mockery. Would it really do so, however? Over the course of my day in Washington, I went back and forth on this question. In some ways, it seemed to me, the March *was* different from the standard Gay Pride Day march in New York. "Everybody looked so *wholesome*," my father told me the next day, having seen a few moments of the march on the evening news. In fact the contingents from places like Idaho and Nebraska did lend the event a certain fresh-scrubbed, middle-American winsomeness that you didn't find in the Fifth Avenue parade. To be sure, there were a few leathermen and drag queens and a lot of barechested women; when I watched *The 700 Club* on TV a couple of days later, I saw that its producers had managed to find and to videotape a half dozen or so sadomasochists whipping one another. But such people formed an even smaller proportion of the crowd in Washington than they did in the annual New York march. I found myself thinking that no American unblinded by hate could look at the majority of the D.C. marchers without realizing that these were decent, reasonable Americans who wanted only to be respected for who they were. Actually, compared with the parades I'd seen in New York on Saint Patrick's Day, Puerto Rican Day, and other such festivals, the March on Washington was eminently civilized, good-natured, orderly, peaceful, and tidy. I'd never felt safer, and I'd never seen so many people leave behind so little litter.

Yet when Chris, back home in New York, turned on C-SPAN for coverage of the March on Washington, what he saw wasn't the march itself but the speakers who addressed the crowd on the Mall. And what he heard, he reported to me, was a strange combination of the enlightened and the ignorant, the ennobling and the offensive, the conciliatory and the antagonistic. Eloquent speakers like the English actor Ian McKellan alternated with vulgar comediennes, one of whom described Hillary Clinton as "fuckable." Eartha Kitt led the crowd in a rousing rendition of "God Bless America"; a radical lesbian told the crowd that America was irredeemably corrupt and that they should therefore not consider it their country. A speaker who began by saying "I come to you talking in the name of love" went on to proclaim, quite unlovingly, the need to "eradicate" the Christian right. (Her combination of love talk and hate talk, Chris observed, made her sound very much like the kind of malevolent fundamentalist bigot she was condemning.)

Of course, I heard a lot of the platform talk myself. One speaker was introduced as "the only drag queen to run for President"; another was praised for being "a real rabblerouser." Several minutes were devoted to a comedienne's witless, tiresome imitation of the conservative activist Phyllis Schlafly. A brave, intelligent speech by the first openly gay member of the Canadian parliament was followed by the master of ceremonies' asinine comment "I just love Canadian boys!"

As on Gay Pride Day, I found myself growing increasingly frustrated. Hundreds of thousands of gay Americans had invested time and money (and, in many cases, had risked friction with their families or employers) in order to travel to the nation's capital to make a statement about something that mattered deeply to them. All these people, all this commitment: organized properly, such a gathering might have done a great deal to illuminate for heterosexual Americans the circumstances of their gay fellow citizens.

Yet what had the organizers of the event placed before the nation? Obscene comics. Fire-breathing radicals who spoke for only a tiny segment of the gay population. Jesse Jackson. (What was *he* doing here?) It was as if the march's organizers were out to confirm every last stereotype about homosexuals. Certainly for me that day in Washington drove home a couple of very important facts: first, that the gay-rights movement's leaders were far more radical than the gay population itself; and second, that those leaders weren't really very good leaders at all. For one thing, many of them made a point of putting down middle-class values and Christianity and the institution of the family—not caring, apparently, that in doing so they were putting down the lives and values of countless gay people who lived in places like Alabama and Montana and Nevada and who had made considerable sacrifices to attend this march. They were implicitly putting down all those groups that surrounded me on the Mall with their banners—the Gay Mennonites, the Gay Lutherans, the Gay Mormons. As Chris said, "The people who carry on about 'the struggle' aren't the ones who are really *living* the struggle." He and I both noted, moreover, that while the marchers were overwhelmingly male, the people on the platform tended to be radical feminists who, in voicing their hatred for the American system of government, most assuredly did not speak for the great majority of the marchers. (As Randy Shilts has observed, one indication of the vast difference between the typical gay activist and the gay man-in-the-street is that whereas the National Gay and Lesbian Task Force, a relatively moderate gay-rights organization, opposed the Gulf War, the huge majority of gay Americans supported it.)

I kept comparing the event with the 1963 March on Washington for black civil rights. On that occasion, Martin Luther King, Jr., had given the speech of his lifetime and had imbued not only his followers but every scrupulous American with a sense of the seriousness of his mission and the rightness of his cause. He hadn't called for revolution or denounced American democracy or shared the podium with stand-up comics. Despite the later revelations about Dr. King's plagiarism, womanizing, and homophobia, the fact remains that on that day in 1963 he gave voice to a vision of racial equality that struck at the conscience of America, bringing out the best in his followers and speaking to the more virtuous instincts of his antagonists.

By contrast, the April 1993 March on Washington was at once an earnest exercise in political petition and a carnival. Lacking a first-class leader to remind them of the seriousness of their purpose, many of the participants lost sight too easily of that purpose and instead looked upon the event as an opportunity to burst out of their accustomed silence about their sexuality and to let loose with inappropriate sexual references. (To be sure, because most gays are largely closeted and rarely find themselves in a crowd of homosexuals except in a gay bar or dance club, and because the spectacle of a city full of gays enkindles in most gays an understandable exuberance and perhaps even a joyful illusion of acceptance, security, and inclusion, it is hard for many, under such circumstances, to realize that a frivolous party mood is not in their best interests.)

The Florida contingent of the march, for instance, had worked out its own variation on the familiar gay-rights chant: "We're here, we're queer, we're *dee-li-cious!*" They alternated this with a song: "It's a queer world, after all." One woman wore a sticker on her back that read: "This bitch loves big tits." The members of one group held up calculatedly impudent signs ("SUCK COCK for Jesus"; "None of my best friends are straight") and, as they passed the White House, chanted "Where's Bill? Where's Bill?"—a sarcastic reference to the President's decision to be out of town during the march. Why, I wondered, didn't this movement have leaders who understood that if it weren't for the image problems created by the irresponsible antics of people like these, the President might well have found it less politically problematic to associate himself with their cause?

For me, the march made it clear that American gays had to make a decision. Were we satisfied with our present situation as a marginal, misunderstood, and widely despised minority, and did we therefore regard events of this sort as celebrations of, by, and for ourselves alone? Or were we fed up with being marginalized and unaccepted and did we therefore view such events as serious political demonstrations that were aimed at effecting a real change in the views of the majority and in which frivolous, self-indulgent nonsense would be frowned upon?

The schedule of platform speakers at the march suggested that its organizers saw it as being both things at once: a private party and a public protest. Even the next day's *New York Times* headline captured this inconsistency: "As Gay Marchers Gather, Mood Is Serious and Festive." But it didn't make sense for a march to be both of these things. At a party there was room for frivolousness and self-indulgence; a serious protest required restraint and self-discipline. (This complaint applies as well, of course, to the annual Gay Pride Day march, which participants routinely refer to as both a march and a parade, as if the terms were interchangeable.)

One thing about the March on Washington was remarkable and deeply moving to me: the huge numbers of people in attendance. Gays filled the streets of the capital; hardly any heterosexuals were in evidence. When I returned to New York that evening by train, virtually every seat was occupied by a gay person. Walking to the club car for a beer, I passed dozens of exhausted and sunburned young men and women, their heads resting casually on their partners' shoulders as they dozed. It was something that straight people do on public conveyances without giving it a thought but that most gay people wouldn't dare do under ordinary circumstances. I think that sight touched me more than anything else I saw over the course of the day. It was a brief glimpse of what it might be like to live, without fear, in full equality. To see all those gay and lesbian couples on the train, moreover, was to be reminded that, despite its lack of leaders, the gay-rights movement has many heroes—hundreds of thousands of them, across the country, who in small but brave and meaningful ways bring illumination every day to those among whom they live and work and worship.

4

"The only
valid
foundation"

There are few things as fascinating as the psychology of a gay person who doesn't yet know that he is gay.

In 1986, Robert Bauman published *The Gentleman from Maryland: The Conscience of a Gay Conservative,* a memoir of his career as a Republican congressman and closet homosexual. It is a remarkable story: by day, Bauman voted against gay-rights legislation and flatly told constituents who disagreed with him that he considered homosexuality an abomination; by night, he hung around in gay bars and picked up young men. He admits the contradiction but never quite explains it satisfactorily; his behavior seems, to say the least, hypocritical.

Yet one is hesitant to judge such a case too harshly. I know from my own experience that even in the face of the most seemingly incontrovertible evidence, it can take a long time to recognize that that big, solemn-sounding word "homosexual"—or, by the same token, that silly-sounding little word "gay"—applies to oneself.

Joseph Steffan, who was ejected from the Naval Academy after recognizing and admitting that he was gay, notes in his book *Honor Bound* that "I grew up thinking that a homosexual was a man who wanted to be a woman. He wanted to have sex with other men, or with young boys if he could get them. Homosexuals all talked with a lisp and swung their hips when they walked, trying to act womanlike, and I hated them. I had hated them all my life, for as long as I could remember. No one had taught me to hate them; no one had ever explained it."

Like Steffan, I have rueful memories of my childhood attitudes toward homosexuality. I didn't actually hate homosexuals—I don't think I hated anybody—but I do remember accepting the stereotypes without question: gays were men who wanted to be, or thought they were, women; they liked to sew and cook and gossip; they were silly and frivolous; and their lives revolved around sex. I never harassed homosexuals as a kid, but it didn't particularly bother me when, in my early teens, I heard friends of mine yelling out anti-gay remarks—"hey, faggot," "hey, homo"—at a bouncy, limp-wristed college-age neighbor of ours. It never occurred to me that anyone I cared about might be gay—let alone that I might be gay myself.

Yes, I always realized that there were differences between me and most other boys. One of the differences was that while they loved team sports, my favorite athletic activity, and the only one at which I didn't feel awkward, was swimming. Also, while I loved science and geography and excelled in math, I spent much of my time reading, writing, and playing the piano—pastimes that few of my male friends shared.

It was during my early years that I first began to notice another difference between myself and my male classmates—a difference that was unrelated to my interests in writing and music and swimming. Many of those classmates were beginning to be attracted to girls; I, on the other hand, found myself preoccupied with certain boys, my absence from whom during summer vacations upset me so much that I was incapable of enjoying myself.

What the hell was going on here? My father was a doctor and medical editor, and since by the age of fourteen I had secretly read every word in his extensive medical library that related to the subject of adolescent sex, I knew very well that most boys experience during puberty a period of attraction to other boys. Thus I decided that I must simply be going through a "phase."

Yet as time went by and the "phase" didn't come to an end, that excuse came to seem less and less tenable. This was all right, however, because I had another theory—namely, that my interest in boys was a lingering effect of the sex play in which I'd engaged regularly for several months with a junior high school classmate (who is, I might add, now a husband and father). Yes, that must be the answer; at times I was convinced of it. To be sure, my medical reading had also taught me that sex play between adolescent boys was extremely common; so this explanation, over time, likewise became less convincing.

Yet I remained undaunted, for I had plenty of other hypotheses at the ready, all of which I ran through in my mind every time I found myself drawn to a good-looking boy. The first of these hypotheses was that I wasn't really attracted to other boys; rather, I was just curious about their bodies. (After all, I told myself, I was an extremely inquisitive boy.) The second hypothesis was that my attraction to other boys was a manifestation of my inordinately sensitive and sentimental nature. If, in other words, I was fascinated by another boy, it was not because I was sexually attracted to him but because I had exaggerated and romanticized my own quite natural feelings of friendship for him. The third hypothesis was that what I imagined to be an attraction to other boys was in reality an envy of their looks, their grace, their poise: I was, after all, a terribly insecure boy. The fourth hypothesis was that my interest in these boys was essentially not sexual or romantic but aesthetic. By nature and vocation, I told myself, I was an admirer of beauty; and if I could admire the beauty of a poem or a landscape or a piece of music, why not the beauty of another boy?

At no time in the course of all this fervent rationalization did my unconscious mind allow my conscious mind to entertain even for a moment the notion that I might, quite simply, be homosexual. For if my attraction to other boys felt to me like the most natural thing in the world, the word "homosexuality" seemed to connote everything unnatural. I was *me*, and there was nothing with which I was more familiar than myself; the word "homosexuality," by contrast, sounded like something more alien than Malawi or Mongolia or the moon. What, after all, could be more foreign to an ordinary middle-class American boy than the concept of homosexuality? The famous people whom I knew to be homosexual, and who were held out as representative homosexuals by both the gay subculture and the mainstream culture, were grotesque characters with whom I couldn't identify in the slightest. Liberace? Truman Capote? Yes, I played the piano and wrote stories and plays, but otherwise I wasn't remotely like either of them.

Nor were there open homosexuals in my own life with whom I could identify. My one obviously gay teacher in junior high school was a campy fellow who every morning would put a foot up on his desk and flamboyantly lift his trouser cuff to show the class his sock; every day, you see, he wore a new pair, deliberately chosen for its colorful, tacky pattern. The students found him ridiculous and clownish—an image with which he seemed thoroughly satisfied. I knew I wasn't like this absurd man;

there wasn't any teacher in the whole school with whom I identified less. Nor could I relate to my one flagrantly gay high-school classmate. Fat and effeminate and quip-happy, this boy was like no one I'd ever known. He spent the entire homeroom period waving his arms about and gossiping gushily with girls, around whom he had an unself-conscious ease, utterly free of sexual tension, that seemed exotic to me. Though I don't think I ever expressed it to myself in so many words at the time, the implication of all this patter seemed to be that sexuality was a joke—indeed, that *everything* was a joke.

No, I couldn't recognize even a trace of myself in people like the history teacher and the gossipy boy. And what other images of gay men were there in my world? They were all but invisible in the books I read and in the movies and television shows I watched. As I've noted, I'd seen plenty of old movies on TV about historical figures who had been homosexual, but the filmmakers had kept those people's homosexuality a deep dark secret. Despite the changes that movies underwent in the late 1960s and '70s, with the introduction of sex and nudity and pro-fanity—and despite the fact that homosexuality in the American cin-ema, in the words of the late film historian Vito Russo, came "out of the closet and into the shadows" with the 1961 movie *Advise and Con-sent*—homosexual love, as an explicit theme, remained almost entirely taboo in Hollywood. To be sure, I did see a couple of movies when I was young in which homosexuality figured, and I remember them vividly. One was *Inside Daisy Clover* (1966), in which it was implied that Robert Redford's character was bisexual. I remember gathering that there was something funny about him that resonated with me in an unusual way, but I couldn't quite grasp what it was. (I was nine at the time.) During my teens, I saw a telecast of *Tea and Sympathy* (1956), in which a gentle young prep-school student's lack of interest in sports and girls makes him the butt of jokes implying (without, of course, ever using the word) that he is homosexual; yet he eventually certifies himself as straight when his housemaster's wife takes him to bed. Until the se-duction scene, I identified strongly with that boy, whose story seemed to imply that a nice young man couldn't really be homosexual, or perhaps even that homosexuality didn't exist at all—that boys who aren't at-tracted to girls are just shy and need to be taken in hand by helpful older women.

Most memorable of all, however, was *Cabaret* (1972), the heroine of which, Sally Bowles (Liza Minnelli), tries to startle one of two handsome, masculine friends by telling him that she sleeps with the other friend; he tops her by coolly replying, "So do I." I was fifteen then, and I still remember how shocked I was at that line, how it lingered in my mind. It was a revelation to me that two worldly, unsissyish men could be doing such a thing together and that one of them could refer to it so casually.

Of course, *Cabaret* didn't take the relationship between the two men very far beyond that shock line, the main purpose of which was to underscore the decadence of Berlin in the years before Hitler's rise to power. This use of homosexuals as one-dimensional symbols of moral depravity and psychological instability is typical of American movies. As I discovered much later, some British films of my youth (and even earlier) tended to be less squeamish about these matters, and sometimes actually portrayed homosexuals as sympathetic three-dimensional characters. In 1961, for example, Dirk Bogarde played a married homosexual jurist in *Victim,* and in 1959 there were two very frank films about Oscar Wilde, one starring Robert Morley and the other starring Peter Finch. Unlike any American movie of the day, these films treated their homosexual subjects with understanding and respect.

Perhaps I would have found it easier to recognize myself as a homosexual had the American movies of my childhood been more like these British films. Perhaps I would have found it easier, too, had I known that such celebrated writers as Somerset Maugham, whose work I loved, had been homosexual. It might also have helped if I'd known (as I found out years later) that the flamboyant history teacher with the crazy socks wasn't the only one of my teachers who was gay and that the gossipy boy was far from my only gay high-school friend. Nowadays, I gather, the average gay high-school student lives in a somewhat more open atmosphere than I did at his age. But nonstereotypical gay teachers and students still tend not to be "out" at school; most parents and educators continue to shy away from addressing the subject; and while gay characters do appear occasionally in movies and TV shows, they tend to be marginal figures. (You can count on one hand the number of big-budget movies and network series in which the hero or heroine has been gay.)

Even today, then, young gay people are likely to feel more confusion, guilt, anger, and alienation than they have to. They are likely to feel as if they have been set down alone in a strange territory; and because parents and educators are either unable or unwilling to provide them with a map to that territory, they are obliged to find their way across it by themselves, obliged to draw up their own maps.

Having self-respecting, nonstereotypical, openly gay adults around, whether as teachers, neighbors, scoutmasters, or friends of his parents, can make all the difference to a homosexual teenager—and can mean a lot, too, to a heterosexual one. A gay young man who knew open, self-respecting homosexuals in his childhood will more readily understand and accept his own homosexuality. He won't find the idea of being gay bizarre and alien, and he won't be so scared by his fate; he'll realize that being gay doesn't mean he must either marry and live a lie or escape from the world he knows into a big-city gay ghetto. As for a child who isn't destined to be gay, knowing gays—like knowing people of races or religions other than his own—will help rid him of prejudice; he won't grow into the sort of teenager who beats up gays and calls out "hey, faggot" at limp-wristed, bouncy neighbors.

Lacking any openly gay adults in my childhood world, I subconsciously kept self-knowledge at bay for years. My defense mechanisms were first-rate. Consider this: the testimony of everyone who observed me as a child and teenager agrees that under most circumstances I was an unusually kind and considerate boy. Indeed, I was moralistic to the point of being a pain in the neck. In junior high school gym class I incurred the wrath of my sit-up partner, and confounded the rest of my gym class, by refusing to go along with the time-honored and ubiquitous custom of surreptitiously increasing his and my sit-up totals by fifty; and I quit the Boy Scouts because, to my wonder and distress, a scoutmaster refused to believe me when, on handing over my proceeds from selling Boy Scout candy, I informed him truthfully that he'd given me nineteen boxes, not twenty. Yet meticulously ethical-minded though I was, I didn't hesitate to lash out cruelly when threatened by the possibility of sexual self-knowledge.

The incident that stands out most formidably in my memory concerns an eighth-grade classmate whom I'll call Paul. Tall, skinny, and bespectacled, Paul was my best friend that year as well as the chief object of my affections; I felt a strong attachment to him, and I think he felt the same way about me. While many of my male classmates turned me off with their loud, boisterous ways, Paul's quiet, gentle manner drew me to him. Yet one day in the schoolyard, talking with a couple of my rowdier peers, I found myself referring to Paul as a "faggot." At the time I didn't fully understand why I was doing this; all I knew was that I wanted to impress those boys, who seemed to me to be *real* boys, and to distance myself in their minds from my friend. Before the day was over, naturally, word of this treachery had gotten back to Paul, who, deeply hurt, became from that moment on my bitter enemy, leading raids on my unguarded books and clothes during gym class and taunting me from across the schoolyard during recess. Paul and I never spoke to each other again except to trade insults.

In later years I was astonished at how I had managed with one word to destroy a precious friendship. What astonished me most of all was my utter lack of awareness of my own motive—namely, my immense fear of my own feelings. Terrified by my affection for Paul, I had attached to him the label—"faggot"—that I had never consciously affixed to myself but that I subconsciously dreaded might apply to me. In doing this to Paul, I had succeeded in removing him from my life forever. It would be many years before I had another friend to whom I felt so close, for whom I had so much affection, and with whom I felt such a strong sense of spiritual kinship. I often think of my brutal treatment of Paul, and of its ugly and unwitting motivation, when I hear teenage boys— or, for that matter, grown men—hurling homophobic epithets.

As I entered my late teens, I felt increasingly that I should be going out with girls; it just didn't look right not to. But I managed to find a justification for putting it off. My father had promised my mother, who hated New York, that we would move away from the city, and I told myself that if I became involved with some girl before the move, I'd just have to part from her when we left. And that wouldn't be fair to either of us, would it? So I decided that I wouldn't start being interested in girls until we moved. (We never did.)

Not that my lack of interest in girls created a major problem with friends or family. My parents didn't pressure me. My friends and class-mates didn't either, but then I was always in the "smart" class, whose members tended to be civilized, studious, and sexually behind the curve. (Several of them also proved, in later years, to be gay.) The one exception was my high-school hygiene class, in which the "smart" and the "slow" students were mixed in together, and in which some of my more street-wise classmates, pegging me immediately for a member of a different species than themselves, made certain jokes at my expense. I was shocked at what these jokes implied: heck, I might be something of a bookworm and indifferent to sports, but I wasn't a "homo."

Something similar happened in college. During my freshman year, I became mildly attached to a boy who lived down the hall from me in the dormitory. Perhaps it was just because we walked a bit too close together, or because we spoke to each other somewhat more softly than most male friends do, or because we didn't discuss sports or women, or because we were sensitive enough to each other's thoughts and moods to be able to communicate by means of a look or a smile: whatever it was, I soon found myself being kidded by our hallmates about my "romance" with this fellow student. I remember feeling at once oddly pleased and unsettled by this kidding—oddly pleased, I suppose, because the jokes made me feel that, even in a very modest way, I had a personal life like everyone else, one that was authentic enough to be noticed and acceptable enough to be joked about rather than vilified; and unsettled because my feelings were so transparent: even though our hallmates may have thought they were just kidding about this "romance," they had in fact picked up on something genuinely romantic at the heart of my feelings for my friend.

And yet, believe it or not, it still didn't sink in to me that these feelings made me a *homosexual*. I didn't even consciously consider the possibility, though (paradoxical as it may seem) I do remember being very conscious of my rationalizations. Yes, I told myself, I was attracted to boys, but (a) they were almost invariably "girlish" (delicate, soft-spoken, but *never* effeminate) boys, which surely counted—didn't it?—for *something;* (b) I didn't really think about having *sex* with them (it seemed beyond the realm of possibility that I might ever so much as touch their hands); and (c) mere attraction wasn't enough—was it?—to make me homosexual. After all, homosexuals were flamboyant, sissyish creatures with lisps and limp wrists, whereas I, though shy and indifferent to sports, was a perfectly ordinary boy whom girls seemed to find attractive and whose manner suggested to no one (except those "slow" students in hygiene class) that I might be gay.

Part of the reason why self-knowledge hovered so long just beyond my conscious grasp lay in what I can only call, to use the term literally, the utter lack of self-possession that characterized the boy I was. To put it simply, I didn't feel that I belonged to myself. Deep down, I couldn't accept that my own feelings, overpowering though they might seem to me, had any significance, or even any reality, in the world outside my-self—the world of my family, school, and friends. At the profoundest level of my subconscious, I saw myself as belonging to my parents in mind and heart and soul, and believed (absurd though it sounds) that if I were gay they would have known about it first, and told me about it. For this reason, it would have seemed to me, as a teenager, impertinent and self-dramatizing to pronounce the words "I'm gay" to myself, to my parents, or to anyone. Not the least of the wondrous corollaries of my eventual recognition of my homosexuality was the recognition that I was capable of discovering something momentous about myself of which my parents weren't aware—the recognition, in short, that I *did* belong to myself, that my emotions had an objective existence, that I knew myself better than anyone else did.

When I finally did realize that I was homosexual—a psychological event that happened instantaneously, with the force of a thunderclap, when I hugged a college friend goodbye one year on his departure for the Christmas holidays and suddenly knew that I was in love with him—the abrupt, staggering sense of self-knowledge was extraordinarily joy-ful. I felt like Helen Keller when she made the connection between the word "water" and the liquid that poured out of the backyard pump. It was as if the undercurrent of confusion and alienation that I'd always sensed within myself had suddenly been explained to me—and as if the answer had been right there before my eyes all along, like the pur-loined letter in Edgar Allan Poe's story, for which investigators conduct a comprehensive search in a government minister's apartment but that no one notices in full view, stuffed into a card rack dangling from the mantelpiece. Once I realized that I was gay, in short, I felt like smacking my forehead and saying: "Of course!"

That's what recognizing your homosexuality comes down to: it's a matter of making the equation between yourself and that strangely im-posing seven-syllable word; a matter of realizing that you *are* different, that to most of society you *are* from the moon. The realization can be discomfiting. But it can also be a comfort, in a peculiar way, because you've always felt an odd, seemingly indefinable sense of being estranged in some way from the world that's familiar to you. To realize you're homosexual is to have, at long last, an explanation for that feeling: it is to realize that you're living in a world in which a fundamental aspect of who you are is considered by many to be bizarre, wrong, wicked.

Though my subconscious mind had for years fought off the idea of my homosexuality, now that it had presented itself to my conscious mind I didn't experience any of the emotions that homosexual men often mention when recalling their first awareness of their own sexuality. I didn't feel so much as a shadow of regret, fear, guilt, or disgust; it didn't occur to me for a moment to think that there was anything wrong or unnatural about my homosexuality. On the contrary, nothing in my life had ever felt as right and natural as this. All that I felt was joy, excitement, hopefulness—a mixture of emotions so energizing that, in the first minutes after realizing that I was homosexual, I ran thirteen blocks without stopping through the streets of midtown Manhattan.

I've talked to men who say that they knew they were gay when they were as young as six or seven. In my experience, such men tend to have been "sissy boys" who always identified with women rather than men, whose difference from other boys was manifest in their childhood not only to themselves but to others, and who as teenagers longed for older, more masculine men to take care of them—a longing that I have never experienced. For many such people, and for many a heterosexual reader as well, it may sound incredible that it could have taken me as long as it did to realize I was gay. But in fact many homosexuals take a lot longer than I did to recognize the truth about themselves. I once considered this an inimical phenomenon, but now I view it as a blessing—a manifestation of a valuable defense mechanism that protects young people from the truth about themselves until they're ready to accept it.

For a young gay person to recognize himself as homosexual is a genuine discovery. It makes all the sense in the world for such a young man to say to himself, "I now know something important, something *essential,* about myself." But it's a mistake for him to say, "Now I know who I am," as if there were nothing else to know. To make his first visit to a gay bar can, of course, be a great relief, because for the first time in his life he is in a public place where he doesn't feel that he has to hide a side of himself that he's been hiding for a long time; he feels as if he can finally look at other young men in the way that straight men look at young women, and can do so without worrying that he might get beaten up for it. In such circumstances, it's understandable for a young man to survey his fellow gay-bar patrons and think, *These are my people! This is where I belong!* It may take him a few months, or even years, to realize they are "his people" only in terms of sexual orientation, and that his fellow patrons can in fact be as brutal and unfeeling as anyone else. If he's unattractive, they may ignore him completely; if he's beautiful, some of them may try to take advantage of him. It can take a while, too, for the gay-bar neophyte to realize that while he may not have to hide his sexuality in a gay bar, he may feel obliged there to hide other, equally important sides of himself.

To recognize the truth about your sexual orientation is one thing; to share the news with your friends, family, and co-workers—to "come out"—is quite another. First, it should be said that the term "coming out" poses certain difficulties. For one thing, it reduces a complex psychological and social process to a simple cut-and-dried one-time ritual. For another, it implies that the proper way to deal socially with the discovery of one's homosexuality is to tell everybody in one's life about it, in so many words and as soon as possible. And finally, it implies a moral judgment of those who choose to keep their homosexuality to themselves or to tell only selected friends. Such individuals are described as being "closeted," a word that implies deception and shame; by contrast, those who have told everyone about their homosexuality are referred to as being "out," a word that implies candor, self-knowledge, self-assurance. If until very recently these associations appeared to be decidedly unfair to closeted gays, the phenomenal escalation of the public debate over homosexuality in recent months has made more and more gays realize that the best way to correct the misunderstanding of the subject—and to counter the heinous, large-scale disinformation campaigns by anti-gay crusaders—is to come out *now*. These rapid changes have also made them increasingly (and, I think, properly) impatient with comfortable, privileged, seemingly well-adjusted gays who continue to refuse to challenge the prejudices of their straight friends and colleagues.

Like the gay subculture itself, the existence of such a phenomenon as "coming out" is characteristic of a society in transition. Two or three generations ago there was no such thing as coming out; virtually all homosexuals felt obliged to remain more or less closeted in order to survive. Nor would there be such a thing as coming out in a society where sexual orientation was a matter of indifference, taken no more seriously than the difference between left- and righthandedness; in such a society *every* gay person would be "out." It is only because homosexuality is still considered a problem that there is such a thing as coming out.

In recent years the issue of "out"-or-"in" has gained increasing urgency. A gay newsweekly called *Outweek* lasted for a few months a couple of years ago; a glossy periodical called *Out* debuted in 1992. There is even a National Coming Out Day every October—a manifestation of the subculture's failure to recognize that coming out is not a one-day event but an ongoing process, and that it should begin not when some subculture-designed calendar says it should but when the individual in question is psychologically, socially, and financially prepared to face the consequences. "Outing"—the forced publicizing by gay activists of a prominent individual's homosexuality—seems poised to become one of the major gay issues of the 1990s. At the first annual convention of gay journalists, held in San Francisco in 1992, the debates focused largely on the ethics of outing, with mainstream figures like *New Republic* editor Andrew Sullivan and *San Francisco Chronicle* reporter Randy Shilts attacking it (Shilts criticized pro-outing gay journalists as "lavender fascists") and writers for subculture publications like Michelangelo Signorile of *The Advocate* giving it their thumbs-up. Outing peaked in the wake of the 1992 Republican convention, when gay magazines "outed" major GOP figures whose professional association with gay-bashers they considered hypocritical.

Though the outing of homosexuals who have deliberately furthered anti-gay policies (as did, say, the late Roy Cohn and J. Edgar Hoover) seems justified as an exposure of outright hypocrisy, subculture-oriented gays often define as "anti-gay" any criticism, whether by heterosexuals or homosexuals, of the subculture's canons or of its equation of homosexuality with the subculture. The desire to "out" gay celebrities for no other reason than that they have failed to come out to the general public, moreover, cannot be regarded as anything but authoritarian. Indeed, the subculture's tendency to paint the issue in simplistic, black-and-white terms is at once ignorant, dishonest, and brutal. It ignores the differences that exist among the millions of men and boys who happen to be gay—differences in personal temperament, in the nature of their relationships with family and friends, in their cultural backgrounds and social circumstances and professional contingencies and financial problems, and in their understanding of the meaning of homosexuality.

. . .

And those differences are vast. Some realize they're gay at six, some at sixty. Some can't keep it to themselves for a moment; some can't ever bring themselves to speak of it to a living soul. Some are by nature more private and less confrontational than others. Some have grown up in families where people are polite to one another but don't speak about personal matters, some in families where all subjects are discussed frankly and maturely, and some in families where almost everything is an occasion for explosive arguments, threats, and imprecations. Some have reason to believe that their parents would never be able to understand and accept their homosexuality, and some have reason to believe the opposite. Some know that their parents are already aware of their homosexuality and are willing to turn a blind eye to it, but would angrily resist any attempt at a discussion. Some simply can't bring themselves to come out to their parents because they feel that their parents are too weighted down by other things—illness, divorce, financial troubles—to make a coming-out scene seem anything but a rude imposition. Some work among people whom they can count on to be tolerant of their sexual orientation, and others work in places where they know that coming out would result in ostracism and harassment, if not termination. Some gay people have it in them to let insults roll off their backs, while others want desperately to be loved and accepted. Keeping one's sexual orientation a secret imposes one kind of pressure; making it public imposes another kind; and some are simply designed to endure one of these kinds of pressure much more capably than the other.

Most homosexuals, who in society as it is currently constituted face the choice of either seeming defiant or being deceitful, spend some time—if only when they are young and first aware of their sexual orientation—hiding their homosexuality from others. Out of necessity, they become experts at keeping secrets, at deceiving loved ones, at talking around the truth about themselves, at communicating subtly with other homosexuals by means of the briefest of glances on a crowded sidewalk. They are likely to feel guilty about lying and to feel resentful toward both their loved ones and society at large, whose attitudes toward homosexuality may make them feel that they have no easy alternative but to lie. Few heterosexuals can imagine the stress that is involved in having to lead this kind of double life. One comes to be very good at repression, suppression, deception. I have mentioned the joy with which I realized that I was gay and in love with my best friend. Yet that joy was followed by two years during which I never so much as spoke the word "love" to him, though we were together almost daily for hours at a time. Once in a long while our eyes would meet and our hands would touch, and there would be no question as to what was in our minds and hearts; yet neither of us could bring himself to speak so much as a word about what we felt. Guilt-ridden about his feelings for me, my friend actively resisted them, throwing himself into relationships with women that seemed never to last more than a week or two; in order (I realize now) to pay him back, I also became involved with a couple of women. On both our parts, it was a shameful, cowardly exercise.

There is no psychologically easy or socially tidy way of making a break with this kind of silence. Some do so dramatically, and begin telling everyone they meet that they're gay. Some move out of the closet step by tiny step, telling some people but not others. Some don't tell anyone and spend their lives lying to everybody, perhaps even themselves. Yet for all the differences that exist among individual human situations, "coming out" has become a transcendent, monolithic gay-subculture concept. "Coming out" is to the subculture what conversion experiences are to religion; scenes in which young protagonists burst proudly out of the closet occupy a central place in contemporary gay novels. "When did you come out?" people ask, as if there were always a simple answer, as if there were a distinct boundary between "in" and "out," as if they were asking something as cut-and-dried as "When were you born?" or "When were you graduated from high school?" Most gay men, I suspect, could not answer the question accurately without writing an autobiography.

I, for one, let years go by before I told some of my nearest and dearest my most intimate secret. Worst of all, in a few cases I wasn't even the one who initiated the revelation. For example, a couple of years after realizing I was gay, I visited a cousin and childhood playmate of mine, two years my senior, who had recently moved to New York from his Southern hometown. His first words to me were: "I'm gay. Are you?" "W-e-l-l," I said, taken aback (to put it mildly), and he exultantly replied, "I thought so!" and handed me a gin and tonic. At lunch in Los Angeles a year or two after that, an old friend of my father's was talking to me in a general way about women when he asked something like

"Hey, that's why we enjoy sleeping with them, isn't it?" Again, I said, "W-e-l-l," and when he followed up with a question about my sexual orientation I acknowledged that, yes, I was gay.

What these and other coming-out experiences drove home to me is that people are so dissimilar, life so complicated, and real-life human situations so unpredictable that in some cases a certain messiness cannot be avoided. Perhaps the easiest way to handle coming out is to follow my cousin's example: the moment you meet somebody, say "I'm gay." But many a young gay person may find such a strategy inconsistent with his temperament or inappropriate to his individual circumstances. When I think of the friends and relatives with whom the subject of my sexual orientation was broached at some point or other, one fact that stands out is that these friends and relatives have different views of the world, relate to different sides of me, and have different understandings of what it might mean to be homosexual. One is a black lesbian English professor, one a conservative Jewish number cruncher, one a Hollywood screenwriter, one a former phone-company hardhat, and so on. It should not be surprising that addressing the subject with each of them took a different form. With some, directness seemed the way to go; with others, a certain obliquity of approach helped avoid a feeling of awkwardness on either part. I know that with some friends I miscalculated badly. In at least a couple of instances, I assumed that I'd indirectly communicated the fact of my homosexuality when in fact I hadn't communicated anything at all. As it turned out, I caused one of these friends a lot of unnecessary pain by not telling her explicitly until a year after our first meeting. Many gays would say that I copped out—and perhaps, in some cases, I did. They would say that as soon as possible after realizing I was homosexual I should have taken aside each of my friends and relatives, told them that I was gay, and demanded that they accept me as I was.

I didn't do that, and here's at least part of the reason why. Years of writing have taught me how mysterious the mind is, how much work it does when one is not looking. I can be blocked on a piece of writing for a long time, and then start typing one day and find it all there, worked out by my subconscious. The subconscious mind works out a lot of things that way, and with some of us it takes longer than others. One of the things that the subconscious has to work out, in a society where homosexuality is viewed as a terrible problem, is an acceptance of one's own, or a loved one's, homosexuality; and one simply must give the mind time to do its work.

I didn't mention my homosexuality to anyone until I felt pretty confident that I could deal with the consequences. If asked, to be sure, I didn't lie. And nobody asked unless they suspected and were ready to know. I didn't *want* to "make a scene" in any sense of the phrase, didn't want to look as if I were seeking attention on the grounds of my homosexuality. Accordingly I introduced my parents to the school friend with whom I was in love—but didn't mention the love part. Nonetheless they saw us together, and that was enough to get their subconscious minds to work preparing to deal with it. For any of us to have forced a discussion of the matter at that point could, I think, have been damaging rather than helpful. When I eventually told my father that I was gay, he already knew, and had had time, just as I had, to live with the fact and get used to it; for much of that time, I'm sure, the awareness hovered just beyond the fringes of his consciousness, just as it had beyond the fringes of *my* consciousness. In any case, when I finally told him, he was more prepared than he might have been otherwise.

I came out to my straight friends in various ways. Two of them found out that I was gay when I invited them to dinner one evening with a new gay friend with whom I had a date later that night to go dancing. My two straight friends ended up joining us, and the four of us had a very good time. Neither of my straight friends mentioned the word "gay" or "homosexual" that night, but the next morning one of them phoned me to say that he hadn't realized I was gay and to apologize for having made fag jokes over the years. Neither he nor my other straight friend acted differently toward me after that night.

So it went, more or less, with all my friends. I made my status clear, but also made it clear that there was no immediate need to address the subject head-on. Life is not the *Oprah Winfrey* show. The matter-of-fact tone I took implicitly invited them to take the same attitude.

I must say that most of the coming-out scenes I ran across in novels bothered me. It seemed to me that the very act of staging such a scene constituted an announcement that sexual orientation is a Big Deal. It invited—indeed, welcomed—argument. It turned homosexuality into an issue. And I rebelled against that. Damn it, my sexual orientation *wasn't* an issue. Why should I be put in the position of defending it? Why should I give other people an opportunity to reject me, to say "I'm sorry, I don't approve"? The hell with that. Nor, come to think of it, were coming-out scenes necessarily fair to those other parties. When a gay person comes out to his parents or friends, he's not only putting himself on the line; he's putting *them* on the line. And the playing field is uneven. He sets the timetable. He's ready; they may not be. For years he's been preparing himself subconsciously to tell his loved ones. The problem is that those loved ones may or may not suspect the truth. It may come as a surprise to them, or it may not. If they're his parents, they may have been aware of his homosexuality for a long time, on some conscious or unconscious level. Like him, they may have been preparing themselves for this revelation; but their understanding of what it means for him to be gay will almost certainly be very different from his own. They may have grown accustomed to the idea of his homosexuality—but they may also have grown accustomed to, and emotionally dependent upon, the silence that surrounds it. It may not be the fact of their child's homosexuality but the confrontation itself that comes as a shock to them. And make no mistake: more often than not a coming-out scene *is* a confrontation, even if no one means for it to be; in most cases, confrontation is inevitable, given the place of homosexuality in our society.

Whatever the case, the gay person often expects his family and friends to be ready at a moment's notice to hear about his homosexuality. He's not only asking for understanding; he's administering a test. Will they respond properly? Will they say the right things? Will they be stunned, disturbed, ill at ease? Will their body language or facial expressions betray discomfort? If they don't pass with flying colors—if, that is, they're taken aback and respond in a way that they may well regret · afterwards—the bad feelings on both sides could end up doing irreparable damage to a precious relationship.

For the gay person may have unreasonable expectations—may, for instance, expect his loved ones to say or do something that will dispel his own irrational feelings of guilt. Or he may, in his insecurity, make a self-righteous drama out of his declaration: "I have something special about me and you don't." The pain of the silence and confusion that most gays experience in their youth, and the resentment that such pain can breed toward parents who failed to prepare them for the possibility of their own homosexuality, or toward friends whose gay jokes they may have listened to for years without comment, can cause young gay people to enter into coming-out scenes already contentious, already expecting and itching for a fight. Secrets are powerful; and every gay young man needs to be on guard against the temptation to use the power of his own biggest secret to hurt his loved ones, to settle scores that are real to him but of which they may not even be aware.

These days, "openness"—that is, the willingness to bare your heart at the drop of a hat to strangers, whether on the street, in the pages of *Vanity Fair,* or on the *Oprah Winfrey* show—is celebrated as a paramount virtue. But civilization relies on a certain degree of restraint, of discretion. This is not to suggest that it is wrong for gays to be every bit as open about their relationships as straight people are about theirs; it is simply to point out that the gay subculture's cult of openness, as manifested in outing and in some of the more unseemly displays on Gay Pride Day, is often little more than an excuse for exhibitionism, reflecting a lamentable antagonism toward the value of privacy, toward the idea of propriety, and toward the notion that life should be divided into private and public realms. In short, coming out is a vital and a moral act; but it should not be confused with narcissistic display.

Coming out isn't a straightforward matter. In certain circumstances, you just can't win. If you come out, it may be seen as an inappropriate gesture or even as a come-on; if you don't, it may be viewed as a sign of shame or deception. If you do, it may hang over the relationship as an unspoken fact that makes the other person uncomfortable; if you don't, you may find yourself constantly waiting on pins and needles for the stray anti-gay comment or pointed question that compels you to come clean. There's no simple answer. At what point, if the fact hasn't emerged naturally in the course of conversation, is one close enough to another person to feel that mentioning one's homosexuality out of the blue would not be seen as inappropriate? Should one make a point of it—as if to acknowledge one's awareness that it might cause distress— or just start dropping in references to one's companion as if it were an established fact? If the other person has a conspicuous problem with one's homosexuality, how should that be handled?

It is an essential part of the subculture philosophy that coming out is necessary because it helps transform young gay people's self-hatred into self-esteem. Yet this can be a dangerous teaching. A gay person should, I believe, have a certain degree of self-esteem and emotional security before he even begins to consider telling his parents and friends about his homosexuality. As Joseph Steffan observes, "people are very sensitive to your own sense of self-worth, to your own self-image. If you feel ashamed or afraid, regardless of whether you overtly show it, they can sense those feelings. People will inevitably treat you as you feel you should be treated. If you don't respect yourself, if you don't trust yourself, you will never be able to inspire that trust and respect in those around you." Exactly. A gay person must be ready for anything when he comes out; reactions can be wildly unpredictable. He must be prepared to learn that his assumptions about others might be as mistaken as are theirs about him. People who he assumes will take his homosexuality in their stride may become very uncomfortable and never speak to him again; people who he thinks will be bothered by it may have no trouble with it at all and wonder why he's making such a fuss over the whole thing. In any event, the gay person must realize that acceptance, like coming out itself, is a process. Parents may say all the right *Donahue* show things—"I still love you," "I accept you"—but may take years to stop viewing his homosexuality as a phase that will pass or as a problem that must be fixed; alternatively, they may reject him unmercifully only to come around eventually to remorse, apology, and acceptance.

None of this should be taken as a suggestion that it is either psychologically beneficial or socially responsible to keep one's homosexuality secret forever. Accepting the gay label is an inextricable part of dealing morally with one's sexuality. Being honest about one's homosexuality, moreover, helps to eliminate prejudice. I know that several of my friends were astonished when I came out to them, and had their eyes opened by the fact that I was gay. As Steffan writes about his own straight friends, "They simply could not reconcile their stereotyped understanding of homosexuals with someone they had grown to know and like over a period of years." That's precisely how intolerance is eradicated—one person at a time, through the victory of the familiarity and trust implicit in close personal relationships over tenacious and misbegotten prejudices. This is, indeed, one good reason why a gay person might not want to rush into telling new friends or co-workers about his homosexuality: the news might in some cases make friendship impossible, whereas to put it off for several months, until friendship has already been firmly established, is to mount a more formidable challenge to prejudice.

Thousands died of AIDS before Rock Hudson did, but it was not until his passing that the mainstream news media focused on and heterosexuals in general paid serious attention to the epidemic. The lesson homosexuals should take from this is not that human beings are all shallow and celebrity-oriented, or that heterosexuals hate homosexuality so much that they don't mind seeing gay people die, but rather that it is only human nature to be moved by the suffering of somebody that one knows (or feels as if one knows) and to be left cold, relatively speaking, by statistics. For heterosexuals to sympathize with AIDS victims, in short, they first had to know and care about somebody who was suffering from AIDS; in the same way, for them to stop fearing and hating homosexuals, they first have to know and care about someone who is gay. It is for this reason that, in the war against homophobia, a million gays marching on Washington would have less impact than a million gays being honest about their homosexuality in their respective homes and workplaces and houses of worship. Homophobia will not end until every heterosexual knows and cares about one gay person.

It is vitally important for a gay person to accept his sexuality. But such is the nature of the human mind that gay people can be very good at fooling themselves and others on this score. Those who trumpet their homosexuality the most loudly are often the most insecure about it, the most emotionally unstable. In this connection I cannot help thinking of the first openly gay person I ever knew, a boy whom I'll call Allen. He was a fellow student of mine in college, a junior when I was a freshman—and when, I might add, I still didn't realize I was gay. That year, Allen lived down the hall from me in our dormitory. We weren't close friends by any means—we didn't study together or go out drinking or share our gripes and dreams—but every week or so, after taking a shower in the evening, he would stroll into my room in his briefs, sit on my roommate's bed, and wordlessly dry his hair with his electric hair dryer while I sat writing at my desk. I never asked why he did this; I thought that perhaps there wasn't a handy socket in his room into which he could plug his hair dryer, or that perhaps he simply liked company while he was drying his hair and had settled on me because I could always be relied upon to be at my typewriter. It was only years later that it occurred to me that perhaps Allen had recognized my homosexuality before I did, and that he had spent those evenings drying his hair in my room not because he was out to seduce me (there was never anything of that sort in the air) but simply because, sensing I was gay, he felt comfortable in my presence.

My most vivid memory of Allen, however, is of an evening when I was, as usual, at my typewriter and he was standing with several other boys near the open doorway of my room, talking about an undergraduate club to which he belonged. The club was called EROS, and its purpose was to provide students with information about sex and to advise them on sexual problems and conflicts. I was not taking part in this conversation, but I was listening in, and when Allen nonchalantly mentioned that he was gay, I turned and looked at him.

I don't know which astonished me more: that Allen was gay or that he had been so frank about it to a group of male college students. Certainly our dorm was not the safest place in the world to be frank about such things. There were fag-baiting types on our hall, and Allen was short and slight. Later in the term, indeed, a couple of jocks started pushing Allen around in the hallway and would probably have beaten the hell out of him if half a dozen or so of our hallmates, under the leadership of our residential assistant, hadn't put a stop to it. Allen walked away from this encounter with what seemed like equanimity. I remember being in awe of his composure, maturity, and self-esteem; he seemed eminently well adjusted.

Then something happened. Allen's mentor, a professor in his major department, discovered that Allen was gay and told him he wanted no more to do with him. Allen sunk immediately into a depression. For a few weeks he was at home more than he was in his dorm room. Then, one day in February, he killed himself. Along with a dozen or so of my hallmates, I spent an unusually warm and sunny winter day at his funeral and burial. It wasn't until years later that I discovered how common a story Allen's was. A 1989 study for the Department of Health and Human Services concluded that 30 percent of teenage suicides were related to "sexual identity problems" and that as many as a third of all gay teenagers attempt suicide.

Allen's death made me realize how callous people can be in their rejection of gay friends and how destructive that rejection can be. It also made me realize that the compulsion to announce one's homosexuality at an early stage in one's sexual self-awareness—a compulsion which may be read by some as a sign of strength and self-esteem—can, on the contrary, be the manifestation of a terrible vulnerability, insecurity, and sense of guilt about being gay. It seems to me, in other words, that many a young gay person proclaims his secret to his loved ones and even to relative strangers in the unrealistic hope that they will, without any reservation or mockery or show of anguish, accept the truth about him and, in so doing, help *him* to accept it. Consciously or unconsciously, what such a young person yearns for is approval so unconditional that it will eradicate his own self-disgust. If this doesn't happen—and in most cases it's rather unlikely that it will—disaster can result, especially if he lacks a network of supportive friends to fall back upon. I must say that sometimes, when I see young gay people audaciously declaring their sexual orientation to the world—whether with their voices or T-shirts or buttons, whether in a classroom or a place of business or at a Gay Pride Day march—I think of Allen.

A Gay Studies scholar named Jeffrey Escoffier has written that coming out "is a moment of personal transformation that continues to demonstrate that for lesbians and gay men the personal is, in the widest sense of the term, the political." This sentiment is widely shared in the gay subculture. But the more one thinks about it, the more problematic it seems. For one thing, as I've noted, coming out should not be seen as a single extraordinary "moment" but as a long-term, day-by-day process. Also, in describing coming out as "a moment of personal transformation," Escoffier would appear to be suggesting that when a homosexual comes out, he becomes, in some sense, a different person. But to say this is to get things completely wrong; for if coming out is about anything, it is not radical change but consistency, integrity, reconciliation. Coming out is, after all, the culmination of a long process during which a young person discovers that, at the most fundamental personal level, self-transformation is impossible—that, in other words, he's gay and he's going to stay gay, and whether he likes it or not he'd better start learning how to live with it. For this reason, it seems to me that discussions of coming out should emphasize not that one is some "transformed" creature but that one is *oneself*—the very same individual that one's family and friends have always known. What one is telling others is not that one has changed into a different person but that one has discovered something about oneself that was always there, an integral part of the person they've always known and cared about.

But of course to speak of the situation in such a way is to take an apolitical view at odds with the philosophy reflected in Escoffier's remark. For when he refers to "coming out" as an act of transformation, what he means is that it is a veritable rebirth into leftist confrontation. In short, as he puts it, "the personal is . . . the political." But to politicize one's sexual orientation is to *deny* the personal. After all, every personal relationship is different; each is an emotionally and morally complex affair with its own history and social context. To say "the personal is the political" is to impose, often unfairly, the idea of a partisan cause on a personal matter, to privilege one's own position, to presuppose antagonism instead of focusing on factors that might make for comprehension, empathy, acceptance. Rather than trying to achieve understanding and conciliation, a gay person who consciously "makes the personal political" turns a friendship or a family relationship into a battleground, the setting for a power struggle. To make the personal political is ultimately to rob oneself of one's own individuality, of those multitudinous characteristics that connect one to other people who happen, unlike oneself, to be straight and that make one different from other people who happen, like oneself, to be homosexual.

Coming out can call for extraordinary courage—and can involve a great deal of drama. But a young gay person, while thrilled by his feeling of self-discovery, may also be inclined to feel guilty, to blame that feeling of guilt on his parents, and to transfer to them whatever other negative emotions he may be experiencing; given all this, the temptation may be strong to behave as if he is more virtuous than he really is, to tell his family things about his sex life that a young heterosexual wouldn't be likely to tell his parents about his sex life, and to interpret any discomfort on his parents' part as hostility. Even if parents do react by saying stupid or hateful things, the brave thing can be *not* to reject them, not to make ultimatums, not to be militant, but rather to endure the pain of rejection, to give them time to understand, to return love for contempt, and to have patience—patience in the sense not of complacency but of quiet, steady perseverance. The bottom line is that prudence in these matters is not always evil, and stridency not always a virtue; and that a young gay person who is only beginning to be comfortable with his own homosexuality should hardly expect his loved ones to be comfortable with it immediately. If it is wrong for parents, in their refusal to accept a child's homosexuality, to demand of him something (that is, heterosexuality) of which he is constitutionally incapable, then it is equally wrong for that homosexual child to expect of his parents a comprehension that, owing to their own limited education and experience, may simply be beyond them.

Different parents may react differently to a child's disclosure of his homosexuality. Some may have already figured the situation out but prefer not to be told about it ("That's OK," they may say anxiously when they sense that the dreaded word is coming, "you don't have to tell me"); others, when they do hear about it, may refuse to believe it ("No, you're not gay; it's just a phase"). After the gay sailor Allen Schindler was murdered by a shipmate, supposedly for being gay, his mother told a newspaper reporter that "she still doubted that her son was gay, even though he told her so in 1991." This sort of denial is a frequent parental reaction to the news of a child's homosexuality. It can, after all, be difficult for a parent to reconcile her image of a beloved child with the images she may have of homosexuality. What such a parent doesn't realize is that in denying an essential part of her child's identity she is refusing to know him fully, choosing to embrace a fictional version of him rather than acknowledge, and love, the person that he really is. (It should be said that Schindler's mother, a devout Salvation Army member, eventually accepted his homosexuality; during his murderer's trial she spoke out bravely against gay-bashing, and at the March on Washington she delivered a moving address in favor of gay rights.)

In many cases, of course, a young gay man's family is not only uncomfortable with the news of his homosexuality but cruel and rejecting. It is still far from unusual for teenage boys who have announced their homosexuality to their parents to be kicked out of the house and forced to fend for themselves. The gay subculture frequently serves as a lifeline for such kids. But in trying to help them, the subculture can often do things to their self-images that are potentially as harmful in the long run as their parents' rejection. A representative example: in 1991, the *New York Times Magazine* ran a generally glowing article about Harvey Milk High School, a public institution in Manhattan for troubled gay students. One couldn't help sympathizing with the teenagers who (as a consequence of their parents' and teachers' prejudices) had ended up in this school, and admiring the people whose compassion and enterprise made the institution possible. But the picture painted by the article raised one's concerns about the ways in which these students were being taught to think about their homosexuality. Rather than help them to free themselves from stereotypes, the school seemed to encourage them to embrace stereotypes.

Apparently assuming, for example, that self-esteem is an outgrowth of freedom of self-expression, the teachers appeared to be very permissive in such matters as dress and punctuality. This laxity would seem, intentionally or not, to communicate to students the idea that being gay means having, or being permitted to have, less self-discipline. Consider one teacher's joke to the effect that it's all right for students to be late to school because they're on "Gay People Time"—a variation, of course, on the black in-joke about "Colored People Time." It's understandable, to be sure, that these emotionally bruised young people escape into stereotypes in order to protect themselves from what seems to them a hateful world; but those stereotypes are a prison, and if there is any justification for such a thing as special gay education, it appears to me that an essential part of its responsibility should be to help such students to release themselves from that prison, not simply to decorate the walls of their cells.

The Harvey Milk School is the only facility of its kind in the world, and its few dozen extremely troubled students form an infinitesimal percentage of the millions of gay American teenagers attending high school at any given time. But the Harvey Milk School can hardly be considered an anomaly, for it reproduces, in miniature, the gay ghetto that exists in every large city; and the assumptions on which it is founded are the assumptions that underlie the existence of each of those ghettos. Indeed, the main problem with the school, to judge by the *Times* article, is that it aims to prepare students not for life in the world but for life in those ghettos.

Paul Monette's 1991 memoir *Becoming a Man,* which was lodged at the top of gay bestseller lists for several weeks and received the National Book Award—the first nonfiction book with a homosexual theme ever to win so important an American literary prize—has been viewed as the archetypal gay coming-of-age story for our times. In fact this book, which is beautifully written and often extremely moving, and which I can imagine few gay men reading without an occasional shock of recognition, also provides a very good window on the way in which many subculture-oriented gays see themselves and their relation to mainstream America. Monette thinks that the book is about a proud and loving gay man's triumphant liberation from the oppression and self-hatred that marked his years as a scholarship student at Andover and Yale. Yet what he sees as a time of terrible suffering often sounds like a pretty typical (if highly privileged) youth. For example, he bemoans the "tragedy" of how he "threw away" his teenage years by not having plenty of sex; yet it seems excessive, to say the least, to describe such circumstances as tragic. (As if most preppies got plenty of sex in those days, or should have!) He complains that "still the fury boils inside you because the liars made you grow up in a cage." What he appears not to realize is that we *all* grow up in cages—which is to say that almost all of us have obstacles to overcome and things to discover about ourselves, that we all have to learn the meaning of the words "delayed gratification," that only a very few of us are given exactly the life that we think we want, and that the lonely, lovelorn adolescence he recalls is par for the course for intelligent, sensitive teenagers, straight or gay.

Indeed, the unacknowledged truth at the heart of *Becoming a Man* is that, until AIDS came along, Monette was very fortunate: being a smart, slim, attractive, affluent, healthy, non-handicapped, white New England male, he was someone who, but for his homosexuality, would probably not have known any socially debilitating "differentness" at all and who, even with his homosexuality, was still better off than most people in terms of being "caged" or free. Yes, Monette may have a genuine grievance against his parents and teachers; yet he seems never to have learned that part of becoming a man is putting behind oneself the anger at the imperfect grownups who (perhaps because they had *their* problems, too) may not have recognized immediately who one was and what one required of them. Reading Monette's attacks on the adults who failed him, one keeps thinking of Sylvia Plath, and then suddenly there she is on page 138, where Monette speaks of "using Sylvia to tap into a rage I couldn't name." One can't help thinking that Monette, like Sylvia, was blessed with decent enough parents and a first-rate education, a fine talent and a rare chance to develop it. Like Plath, however, for all the attention, approval, and opportunity he received as a child, Monette looks back on his early years as a time of imprisonment and employs Holocaust metaphors in an attempt to convey the measure of his torment. One minute he'll sound sensible and sensitive; the next he'll make an outrageous statement to the effect that genocide is "the national sport of straight men, especially in this century of nightmares." He laments that he "didn't have a scintilla of political consciousness to save me. Didn't know about the exchange of power, the wild circle of top and bottom, the challenge two men fucking made to the slave laws of the patriarchy." And he speaks of his three live-in relationships as "my white-knuckle grip on happiness, hoarded against the gloating of my enemies, against the genocide by indifference that has buried alive a generation of my brothers." Yet for all his bitterness toward his "enemies," the heterosexuals who don't want him to love another man, such bigots are hardly in evidence in this narrative; on the contrary, the heterosexuals to whom he comes out are mostly very understanding. (Besides, if one is going to talk about "genocide by indifference," how many African children die of hunger every day because of Monette's indifference?)

Monette makes a heroic act, in short, out of his own horniness, equating his obsessive quest for sexual pleasure with the real heroism of men and women who have struggled selflessly against real slavery. For him, "the point of life outside the closet" was "that you had to seize it and waste no time, because Now was all there was. . . . The erotic can be a window into the deepest core of feeling." It can also, alas, be a one-way ticket to palookaville. All too often, Monette comes across as a stereotype of the promiscuous gay man who serves up pretentious rhetoric about "existential sexuality" and such as a way of justifying his own irresponsibility. What's disturbing is his apparent failure to realize quite how irresponsible he has been—for example, in his relationship with a confused, emotionally needy (and straight) prep-school student of his named Greg, who gave himself sexually to Monette. For this boy whose hunger for love he exploited, Monette ended up having nothing but contempt; yet later, when he slept with an older homosexual drunk, Monette decided that "for better or worse this boozy guy was one of my own, and Greg most definitely wasn't"—meaning that other homosexuals are his "brothers" (a locution that Monette routinely employs) and heterosexuals are not. Monette doesn't seem to realize how arbitrary it is to draw such lines; he doesn't seem to realize that both Greg and the boozer were "his own" because they were both *human*, and that, if anything, he had more responsibility toward Greg because the boy was young and impressionable and in his professional charge.

Monette talks about his "enemies." But in the end, his biggest enemy would seem to be within himself. He admits as much, speaking of "my own homophobia" at age twenty-two and of the "narcissism of self-hatred." As a young teacher he was thrilled to be able to "pass" as heterosexual and strove to be as straight-seeming as his student Scott, for whose approval of his efforts in this regard he was pathetically desperate. Monette's means of ultimately accepting his own homosexuality was that of many a subculture-oriented homosexual—that is, he plunged into identity politics, made his homosexuality an obsession, clung to his resentment toward the adults who failed him in his youth, and transferred his hatred for himself to an army of imagined enemies. In the book's last sentence he proclaims victoriously that "no one would ever tell me again that men like me couldn't love." Yet throughout the book, the only voice telling him such a thing is his own. In the end, I think, what vexes Monette is that he came so close to having a perfectly comfortable, privileged life that the solitary affliction of his homosexuality (and he *does* write about homosexuality as if it's an affliction) weighs him down inordinately. It might make sense, then, to see *Becoming a Man* as a study not in the triumph of gay pride but in the disappointment of another kind of pride—as, that is, the story of a middle-class boy whose homosexuality foiled forever his desire to slip smoothly into the glittering elite world of regattas, cotillions, and debutante balls in which he moved enviously as a student, and whose resentment over the defeat of this ambition made him unable, in his youth, to live gracefully with his homosexuality and rendered him pointlessly rancorous, in his later years, toward the heterosexual world.

What makes Monette's coming-out story typical of much gay-subculture thinking is, however, not his frustrated snobbery but the way in which, instead of accepting the part played by his own individual quirks of character in the various emotional torments of his youth and adulthood, he forces upon his story the approved subculture interpretation, thundering self-righteously about his heterosexual elders' victimization of him but refusing to take responsibility himself for his own victimization of Greg. Yes, homophobia is a very real phenomenon and a blight upon the life of virtually every gay person; but it is only one of the many forms taken by man's inhumanity to man, and is certainly not by itself sufficient to explain why Monette's life took the course it did. As in many such subculture-oriented testaments, Monette's focus on homophobia comes off as a way of avoiding his own culpabilities, of emphasizing his own victimhood, and of making his story seem more heroic and politically meaningful than it would otherwise.

Of course, Monette's hyperbolic rhetoric about his early years is understandable. His youth may not have been as terrible as he thinks it was, but his recent life has been genuinely tragic. His 1988 book *Borrowed Time* is a poignant account of the last years of his companion Roger, who died of AIDS and to whom Monette was devoted. After Roger's death, Monette tried to make a life with yet another companion, only to lose him as well to AIDS. In the wake of all this suffering, it only makes sense that Monette would look back with bitterness at his early years, when self-hatred drove him to embrace the sexual mores that helped hasten the epidemic which would eventually rob him of his hard-won happiness. To say what needs to be said about his all too representative excesses in rhetoric and failures of self-knowledge does not preclude saying as well that one can quite understand how he came to write some of the more vitriolic passages in *Becoming a Man,* can sympathize with him in his grief, and—knowing, as all devoted gay lifemates do, how extraordinary it can seem to find someone in this world—can appreciate the deep and bitter irony of his devastating loss.

Not long after my companion, Chris, and I moved in together, a straight woman friend of ours came to dinner and said: "You two have really turned this place into a home."

Another heterosexual friend once told us, "You two are more devoted to each other than most of the married couples I know."

These are words we prize and remember, far more than we do the praise of employers or book reviewers. Why? Because it means a great deal to us to know that a person whom we love, and who happens to be straight, can recognize our relationship as a blessing, as something touched by grace. It means a great deal to us when such a friend dares to call our house a "home" and to liken our relationship to a marriage. The word "home" is deeply important to both of us. When we moved in together, we were very conscious of the fact that we weren't just sharing an apartment: we were making a commitment, creating a family of two, establishing a *home.* To both of us, it seemed a miracle that such a thing was possible. If anyone had told me the day before we met that within a year I would be sharing furniture and kitchen appliances and bathroom towels with another man, I'd have said it was impossible. I couldn't imagine such a thing. That's the way it is for a lot of young gay men: many of us feel that to be gay is, by definition, to be alone. Most gay people grow up learning to divide their lives into two strictly separated compartments: the life of family, school, work and straight friends; and the life spent among other gay people, often in bars, some-times in bed. One reason why some gay people spend immoderate amounts of time in gay bars and in bed may well be that those are two of the few places where they can feel as if they are being completely honest about who they are.

For years my life as a gay person was something that existed utterly apart from my life with my family and my straight friends. For the most part, that gay life, such as it was, took place three or four evenings a month, in and around the gay bars where I would drink, chat with friends, and watch music videos for a few hours. At the time, I couldn't imagine the two lives ever becoming one; and so it was remarkable to me, after I met and fell in love with and eventually moved in with Chris, to watch my life as a gay person become a part of my other life—to see this man whom I'd met in a bar become a member of my family and to see myself become a member of his.

So accustomed are many gay men to the notion of their homosexuality as something that must remain forever separated from the rest of their lives that the idea of a committed relationship seems to them as absurd as homosexuality itself seems to many straight people. That gay cousin of mine who moved to New York in the early 1980s once mentioned to me that a gay couple of his acquaintance had recently held a wedding ceremony. He said he would never do such a thing. "I'm gay," he told me, "but I'm not *that* gay!" We both laughed: at that time the idea of gay marriage seemed bizarre to both of us. This was, I guess, about ten years ago; since then, each of us has become domesticated. What now seems bizarre to me is that ten years ago my cousin and I laughed at the idea of gay marriage but took for granted the idea of gay bathhouses.

It's easy to understand why the gay movement long emphasized sexual freedom rather than domestic-partnership rights. From childhood, most gay people are (like their heterosexual siblings) raised to think of homosexuality as something that automatically excludes one from the ordinary social structures. The role of bachelor is a socially accepted one; in many circles, what a bachelor does in bed, and whom he does it with, is not considered anybody's business. But the role of gay spouse is far from a generally accepted one; many people with bachelor friends whom they assume to be gay are outraged by the idea of a gay couple. Some, as I've noted, are offended at the thought that gay lovers might actually consider their relationship to be "morally equivalent" to a heterosexual marriage. And some feel that when two gay people make a home together, they are "flaunting their sexuality."

All other things being equal, the gay man who lives alone and makes regular trips to a pickup bar is confronted with considerably fewer social and professional problems than one who lives in a committed relationship with another man. The regular bar-goer can compartmentalize his life very easily; all he has to do is keep his pickups a secret from family and friends and co-workers. But a member of a gay couple is automatically confronted with moral problems. When co-workers talk about their spouses, what does he do? Keep quiet? Lie? Mention his companion as matter-of-factly as they mention their spouses? If he keeps it a secret, he may be disgusted with himself for behaving as if his love is something of which to be ashamed. What hope is there for a committed, loving relationship between two people when it is hidden in this way? On the other hand, if he does mention his companion, he is liable to come up against some who find his homosexuality anathema and who are in a position to threaten his livelihood. Even if he doesn't mention his relationship, the people he works with will probably find out eventually; it is difficult to live with another person for long without one's co-workers knowing about it. And other problems may arise. Though he and his companion may have been living together for years, for example, they may feel obliged, when looking for a new apartment, to tell a realtor that they're just friends who are "sharing." (Despite legal protections in certain cities against housing discrimination, after all, landlords can still find other excuses to reject a rental application.)

When two straight people decide to marry, everyone celebrates their commitment. When two gay people decide to move in together, they commit themselves to insult and discrimination and attack. At one apartment building in which Chris and I lived, the superintendent spit at me one day without provocation; at our next address, members of the building staff, not knowing that I understood Spanish, joked with one another in my presence about the *maricones* (faggots). Living alone, most gay people can conceal their sexuality; living together, a gay couple advertise theirs every time they step out of the house together. Is it any wonder, then, that so many gay men have historically been promiscuous, shunning long-term relationships in favor of one-night stands?

One yearns to have one's relationship respected, but even very sympathetic heterosexual friends will often draw unconscious distinctions between gay and straight couples. I have longtime professional associates who routinely ask other men "How's the wife?" but to whom it never occurs to ask me "How's Chris?" Recently, when a gay friend of mine was singled out to work on a holiday, he had to call off plans with his companion. But a co-worker explained: "It's only fair. *We* all have families to go home to." No insult was intended: it's just that none of my friend's co-workers could quite grasp the idea that to my friend, his companion *was* family; they couldn't see that by relegating his relationship to a lower level than their own marriages, they were placing him, his life, and his feelings on a lower level than themselves, their lives, and their feelings. The same might be said of the longtime friend of my family who, when Chris and I spent a week with my mother not long ago, was astounded that she let us share a bed. Dining with married friends who appear to accept us as a couple, Chris and I sometimes wonder how they would vote in a referendum on gay marriage. Some, I know, would cast their ballots against it. In their minds, accepting us seems to be one thing; accepting the *idea* of us, another.

Despite the problems that afflict gay couples, Chris and I never considered *not* living together. We loved each other; we wanted to be a family. We both valued the idea of family; for all our professional gratifications, life without a home—a home that centered on a strong and stable and loving relationship—seemed to both of us an empty, meaningless prospect. If the phrase "family values" means anything, that's what we had—and have. The home we've created out of our love for each other is precious to us; and few things please either of us more than the occasional indication that one or another of our straight friends recognizes what we have together and respects it for what it is. Why? Partly because when straight friends show that kind of recognition and respect, it gives one hope for the world in general. And partly because if they didn't feel that way, they wouldn't really be friends; however hard one tried, one wouldn't really be able to think of them in the same way anymore.

In some sophisticated urban circles, a strange kind of tolerance of homosexuality obtains. Many a society woman with a busy husband and a crowded social calendar keeps an urbane, presentable homosexual man on call as her regular escort or "walker." She knows he's gay, and so does everybody else, and no one has a problem with it—indeed, it's considered a rather chic touch; but for him to so much as mention his private life to her or anyone would be considered utterly déclassé. What could be more offensive, more patronizing than subjecting any adult to this kind of treatment? Either homosexuality is wrong, in which case such a woman shouldn't associate with gay men at all, or it's not wrong—in which case the unwritten rules that forbid any mention of his private life, while allowing her to talk as much as she wants to about hers, are just plain inequitable.

"My friends," a famous hostess and political wife has reportedly commented apropos of this double standard, "don't talk about their sex life at the dinner table." But the average homosexual doesn't want to sit down at somebody's dinner table and say "Hi, I'm gay, and this is what I like to do in bed." What he wants is to be able to bring the man he lives with to dinner, just as a heterosexual guest would bring his or her spouse; he wants to be able to introduce his companion to the other guests and to have their relationship treated as respectfully as anyone else's. The society hostess's rules are based on the belief that a homosexual's private life is by definition a dirty little secret and that the only respectable social role for which he is suited is that of bachelor escort, the contemporary equivalent of a court eunuch—or, as Paul Monette puts it, an "emasculated courtier." Monette himself lived the courtier life for a couple of years, providing "the ladies of the suburbs" with

> their regular fix of my laser wit and gossip over cappuccino. . . . I should have been finding a boy of my own instead of talking to Cilla Fitzgerald about which one of her many suitors for the Junior Prom she ought to accept. That was the most sinister aspect of my courtier's self-denial: the sizing up of straight men for a mating dance I had no part in. And then later to be a shoulder for Cilla to cry on, after she'd dumped the beast in question. . . . The better you get at being a shoulder, the more unsexed you become.

For a homosexual to go along with such thinking, and to accept such a role, is to acquiesce in the idea that he deserves no better than second-class social status.

Yet, as if to form a grotesque contrast to the out-loud-and-proud stance of many subculture-oriented gays, some non-subculture homosexuals have made a virtual career of allowing themselves to be treated this way, and have raised discretion in these matters to an art form. Gliding through heterosexual society, these gays take a certain pride in wearing their sexuality close to the vest. It's not as if their homosexuality is exactly a secret: sitting side by side at the opera in tuxedos, sipping martinis and chatting wittily about the soprano, such gays are hardly hiding their sexual orientation; but by the same token, they would never be so gauche as to discuss at a dinner party the question of gay-friendly curricula in schools, say, or gays in the military. They don't want to be seen getting exercised over gay political issues, one way or the other: in their view, their homosexuality is something that places them above the herd, above the tiresome problems of the hoi polloi, and its very cachet depends on its not being referred to directly. As Darryl Pinckney has written, "elitist tendencies are strong in the American homoerotic tradition—the chic of going where others do not go, the vanity in knowing what others do not know." In such circles, writing a book like the present one is the most unsophisticated thing that anybody could do. It's bad form; it reveals that people's attitudes about homosexuality *matter* to you. Among such homosexuals, the approved attitude toward bigots is one of condescension: look down on them, feel superior to them. The bigots, after all, are morons, servants, proles; they're the ones who deliver your groceries, repair your car, take your ticket at the theater or the movies or the ballet. Who *cares* what they think? The philosophy of such homosexuals can be summed up in one sentence: "How can you possibly insult me when I hold you in no esteem whatsoever?"

This gay elite might be referred to as the *other* gay subculture. Its members, some of whom are much more deeply closeted than others and many of whom hold key positions in business, politics, the media, and the professions, are often extremely snobbish and politically conservative. They live in places like the East Side of New York; they collect antiques and rare books and etchings and *objets d'art*; and they can be found exchanging witticisms in small, tightly knit groups at the opera and the ballet, on Cape Cod and Fire Island, and during coffee hour at fancy urban churches. They live among sophisticated, tolerant people who often are aware of their homosexuality and have little or no problem with it, especially since these men's cardinal rule is never to mention the subject to outsiders. They don't like the word "gay" (much less "queer"), and tend to avoid the word "homosexual" even among themselves, instead referring to homosexuality as, say, "Topic A." When they want to tell a gay friend that someone else is gay, they'll say, "X is a friend of ours." Yet while avoiding the subject entirely among straight friends, among themselves (and even with other gay men whom they hardly know) many of them will talk crudely and incessantly about sex.

If these men are often among the strongest opponents of gay rights and the most fervent supporters of the closet, it is partly because the closet is, for them, a very comfortable clubhouse—and partly because, under their self-possessed veneers, they profoundly dread the contempt of their heterosexual friends and the loss of privilege and prestige that, they fear, greater openness would bring. When I suggested to a writer who moves in such circles that it was important for gays to come out of the closet, he disagreed, insisting that he preferred the closeted life. "The closet keeps tensions on both sides at a minimum," he argued. "Besides, living in the closet makes being gay romantic and exciting. It's like belonging to a secret society, an exclusive gentlemen's club."

"But I don't want to belong to a secret society," I replied. "I want to belong to my family." So do most gay men, for whom viewing a committed personal relationship as some sort of covert club activity is a pathetic substitute for seeing it become a fully integrated and accepted part of family life. In any event, most gays do not have the option of belonging to the "other subculture"; toward them, its members tend to have little sense of responsibility. Nor do they feel an obligation to society at large, whose misunderstanding of homosexuality many of them are in a splendid position to help correct. However widespread homophobia may be, and however much other gays may suffer from it, these men see themselves as being too highly positioned, and too well protected by the secrecy of their "secret society," to be seriously affected by the words or deeds of vulgar hatemongers. And so, looking down on everyone else, straight and gay alike, the members of the "other subculture" pursue their clandestine—and often promiscuous—lives. (For, after all, the idea of homosexuality as a "secret society" and the notion of emotional commitment and domestic stability do not go together very easily.)

Among the literary works that reflect the "other subculture's" view of itself is James Merrill's poetic trilogy *The Changing Light at Sandover,* which received the 1982 National Book Critics Circle Award. The poem relates Merrill's supposed adventures with a Ouija board, by means of which he and his companion, David Jackson, communicate with various spirits and learn about the hereafter. One thing they learn is that heaven's most esteemed inhabitants tend to be the spirits of privileged gay men, mostly poets. Their supernatural interlocutors explain, moreover, that it is Merrill's and Jackson's homosexuality that renders them deserving of communication with the Beyond. Why should this be the case? Because, they are told, gay men, on earth as in heaven, constitute the race's intellectual aristocracy. Heterosexuals—most of whom apparently fall under the category of "THE DULLWITTED, THE MOB, THE IDIOT IN POWER, THE PURELY BLANK OF MIND"—almost never figure in the poem, and when they do, they appear as servants: cleaning ladies, oil deliverymen, lift boys, porters, chambermaids.

A story. Shortly after we moved into our first apartment, Chris and I had a party. For us, the highlight of the party was that it brought together two friends of ours—a fellow I'd grown up with and a woman with whom Chris had gone to college. They hit it off immediately, and before long were dating each other steadily. Soon they were living together, and four years after their first meeting they married. I was asked to be the best man and Chris was invited to be a member of the wedding party. We were touched by this gesture, and indeed surprised by it: though we were both friendly with the bride—especially Chris, who had been very close to her in college and during their first years together in New York—I was not quite as close to the groom as I had once been. Yet Chris and I felt that we had a special connection to them both, and that their wedding held a special significance for us, because our love had, in a very real way, made possible their love.

We were, to be sure, wary about the wedding. Weddings can pose numerous difficulties for a gay person, and even more difficulties for a gay couple. At weddings, relatives and friends come together, and almost any such group exhibits a wide spectrum of attitudes about homosexuality. Consequently a gay person finds himself socializing with people whom he would ordinarily never have anything to do with and who would ordinarily have nothing to do with him. Also, weddings are celebrations of heterosexuality. At our friends' wedding, I remembered a man who had complained on some TV show that homosexuals "shouldn't throw their homosexuality in my face" because "I don't throw my heterosexuality in their face." But if a gay couple walking hand in hand could be accused of throwing homosexuality in people's faces, certainly a wedding ceremony such as the one we attended—with its 125 guests and three crowded days of dinners and breakfasts and receptions, the whole point of which was to celebrate the union of a man and a woman—could only be described as a colossal act of throwing heterosexuality in people's faces. And since they *are* celebrations of heterosexuality, weddings tend to occasion jokes not only about sex and marriage—jokes told, moreover, from a point of view that assumes everyone in the teller's presence to be heterosexual—but also about gays and, these days, AIDS. Guests who don't know that a fellow guest is gay may even make hostile remarks about homosexuals in his presence. Under other circumstances a gay person might walk away from such people or confront them, but what can one do when one is close to the bride's or groom's family and doesn't want to ruin their big day by "creating a scene"? So it is that one may find oneself listening quietly to remarks that one would ordinarily never tolerate.

There is nothing like a wedding, moreover, to remind a gay couple that they live in a society whose institutions don't recognize their orientation or acknowledge their relationship. Almost every element of a wedding ceremony, from the bachelor party and bridal shower to the procession and the tossing of the bouquet, is organized along gender lines and assumes the heterosexuality of the participants. It is possible for sensitive wedding planners to avoid situations that insult gay guests or that make them uncomfortable—but all wedding planners aren't sensitive, particularly in this regard. A gay man very close to me once lost a friend because she insulted him in a way that he might forgive but could never forget. The friend was the bride, and a week before the wedding she phoned him and said, "I'm so glad you're coming to the wedding. Um, I know that you wouldn't try anything funny in the men's room, but I just wanted to tell my parents that of course you wouldn't." Let it be understood that this gay man had never been known to "try anything funny" in a men's room; the bride, or her parents, or somebody, simply had the idea that it was in the nature of gay men to try something funny in men's rooms. My friend was so thrown off that he simply said, "It's ridiculous, of course I wouldn't try anything funny in the men's room," and hung up, and naturally didn't go to the wedding. He never called the bride again, and she never called him.

Chris and I didn't think there would be any problems with our friends' wedding, though: we knew the bride and groom well—or thought we did—and took it for granted that they respected our relationship as much as they did their own.

We had to fly out of town for the wedding. From the beginning it was unpleasant. Over an informal, convivial dinner the night before the ceremony, several of the couple's other friends, who were strangers to us, kept starting to tell fag jokes and then catching themselves, their wide grins turning into nervous glances in our direction.

The next day, at the picture-taking, the wedding party posed for (it seemed) every possible combination of photographs: the bride and her family, the groom and the bridesmaids, the bride and groom with their two sets of parents, and so forth. Last of all came the "couples" pictures: portraits of each of the ushers and bridesmaids with his or her significant other. One by one, as their names were called, the ushers trotted up to the front of the room with their wives or girlfriends, and the bridesmaids with their husbands or boyfriends. But one couple was excluded. As it happened, the list that had been given to the photographer did not include the names of the couple in whose home the bride and groom had met—Chris and me.

The reader may not be surprised at this omission, but I was. This bride was my friend, and the groom and I had grown up together; as I would later say in my toast, he had been the closest thing I had to a brother. Chris and I had dined with them countless times and had joined them on day trips; every August the four of us got together to celebrate the birthdays of Chris and the bride, and every October we celebrated the groom's birthday and mine. The bride had helped Chris and me through the growing pains of our relationship, and we'd helped her through hers. We were four friends: two couples.

Later the groom took me aside and told me that he'd just realized the photographer hadn't taken our picture; he said that he'd put our names on the list and that there must have been a mistake. I wanted to believe this, but the fact was that the photographer had shown himself to be a well-organized professional with an assistant whose primary job was to check off the photo subjects one by one. If the groom had indeed put us on the list, then someone—the bride? her mother?—had deliberately taken us off.

But the picture situation wasn't the worst of it. That came at the wedding itself. After walking in procession to the stage with the rest of the wedding party, Chris and I stood side by side near the bride and groom as the judge began reading the ceremony that the bride had written in consultation with him. The first few sentences were harmless enough. But then came this line: marriage between a man and a woman, the judge said, was "the only valid foundation for an enduring home."

I turned and looked at Chris. He turned and looked at me. In his face I read the same shock, disappointment, and anger that I was feeling. Afterward, at the cocktail reception, we talked privately about what had happened, and struggled to keep our cool.

For Chris, whose friendship with the bride had been intimate and mutually dependent, the experience was traumatic. Here, he thought, had been one person who surely understood, cared about, and respected our relationship. He later told me how he'd felt at the moment when the judge had read that line: "My jaw tightened. I felt like an idiot. I was on the verge of tears. Not because of all the money we'd spent to go there: if I'd gone across the street and been treated like that, I'd have felt the same way. I felt patronized, as if nothing about our life meant anything to her. I couldn't figure out how someone I'd considered so close a friend could be capable of this. It wasn't as if she looked down at us; it was as if she didn't even *look* at all. As long as I live, I'll never forget how it felt to hear those words."

Were we making too much out of mere words? I don't think so. Words mean something to Chris and me. We both work with words and value them. When we say something, we mean it. When someone else says something, especially in the meticulously drafted text of a brief wedding ceremony, we assume that he or she meant it too. Certainly the bride, a lawyer specializing in intellectual property, had always been proud of her mastery of the English language. If she didn't believe that marriage between a man and a woman was "the only valid foundation for an enduring home," then why had she allowed such language in the ceremony? Both Chris and I had attended plenty of weddings—Protestant, Episcopal, Catholic, Jewish, secular—and he'd played the organ at dozens of them. Neither of us had ever heard such exclusionary words.

Who was responsible for the offending passage? The judge or the bride? If she'd written it, had she done so on purpose—to wound Chris and me for some inexplicable reason—or had she done it thoughtlessly, inadvertently? No sooner did we voice these questions in hushed tête-à-tête than we realized that the answers didn't matter. Even if she hadn't written it but had only approved it, or if she'd written it without any intention to wound, the simple fact was that she'd seen it, she'd examined it carefully, and she'd allowed it to stand. If she had appreciated and valued my relationship with Chris for what it was, those words would have jumped off the page the moment she saw them. But they didn't; and this suggested to Chris and me that, in her view, our relationship *wasn't* comparable to her marriage.

This episode reminded me of something Chris had said to me once— namely, that some straight people consider a close friendship with a gay person to be a part of their wild and colorful youth, along with taking drugs and sleeping around and being financially irresponsible. Then they reach a certain age and decide to settle down; they find responsible jobs, get married—and kick the gay friend in the teeth. Suddenly, to the friend's surprise, he's out in the cold, like Falstaff when he's rejected by his old chum Prince Hal at the end of *Henry the Fourth, Part Two.* I'd never experienced such a renunciation before—and I hope never to experience it again.

What could Chris and I do about this insult? If such a line about marriage and enduring homes had cropped up in casual conversation, I would not have hesitated to challenge it. But this was different. We were at a wedding with 125 other guests. An hour later it would be my job to stand up at dinner and toast the bride and groom. What we both longed to do was take the bride aside as soon as possible, tell her what we thought of her wedding vows, bow out of the toast, and make an exit. But there were mitigating factors: I was close to the groom and his parents, who'd had nothing to do with the preparations for this wedding and who'd always been kind to Chris and me; I didn't want to do anything to hurt or embarrass them. Besides, if either Chris or I said anything now, we'd risk being dismissed by our friends and many of their other guests as "touchy fags" who were acting out of simple envy and resentment. It would be impossible, under the circumstances, to explain our grievance in such a way that they might understand.

Yes, it was the wedding couple's right to consider marriage "the only valid foundation for an enduring home," and to say so in their ceremony. But to incorporate such language in their ceremony while at the same time including a gay couple in their wedding party was at best thoughtless, at worst cruel. Chris and I had been asked to join the wedding party, after all, in what we took to be a spirit of acceptance of our relationship. What we'd received instead was a patronizing tolerance, which (as I've observed) is most assuredly *not* the same thing as acceptance. Chris and I had always assumed that the wedding couple thought of our relationship in the same way that they thought of theirs. To both of us, our omission from the "couples" pictures and the callous wording of their marriage ceremony constituted a clear declaration that this was not the case, at least on the part of the bride. With those two actions, she drew an unmistakable line of demarcation between their relationship and ours.

As I've said, it is not always as unpleasant as this to be the gay guest at the wedding feast. People *can* be accepting. Chris and I have had wonderful times at the weddings of several of our other friends; though most wrote their own ceremonies, none considered it necessary to include exclusionary language in the vows, and it did not occur to any of them to treat us as anything other than a couple. So I can't say that our terrible experience at the wedding I've described was representative. But it did dramatically underscore for me the frustrations attendant upon the legal and social nonrecognition of gay unions. And it reinforced my conviction, which has grown steadily over the last few years, that the cornerstone issue of the gay-rights movement should be the legal recognition of gay unions. Call them what you will, marriages or domestic partnerships or whatever: the point is that acknowledging and endorsing them, rather than rejecting and discouraging them, would be a socially positive act, conservative in the best sense of the word.

I don't fool myself, however, about the possibility that this will happen anytime soon. Even people who consider themselves very tolerant and who have many gay friends often stop short of accepting the idea of gay marriage. The attitudes of many were summed up by a man who called in to the *Larry King* show after the first presidential debate in 1992. A family, the man insisted, consists of two people who are married, with or without children. It does not consist of unmarried people, whether of the same sex or different sexes, because in such cases the parties have made no legal commitment. What that man, and many like him, aren't willing or able to recognize is that most homosexual couples *want* the right to make a legal commitment to each other. The irony is almost grotesque: heterosexuals deny gay couples the right to make legal commitments, then fault them for not making such commitments.

It's not just heterosexuals, however, who are uncomfortable with the idea of homosexual marriage. In fact, gay couples find themselves trapped between antagonists of the right and left. On one side are heterosexuals who—even though they may tolerate homosexuality on a personal level, recognize that it is not going to go away, and acknowledge the value of monogamous gay relationships—balk at the idea of granting such relationships the same official recognition that is afforded to heterosexual marriage. On the other side are leftists, both gay and straight, who view homosexuality as a form of social rebellion and who thus have little interest in promoting so bourgeois an institution as gay marriage. For gays to marry each other, in the eyes of such people, is to betray their own nature and obligations as homosexuals. Yes, there *are* subculture-oriented gays who live in deeply committed long-term relationships. But the subculture as a whole is not at all comfortable with the idea. The gay minister Troy Perry has described how the organizers of the first gay March on Washington, who countenanced an extraordinary range of radical politics and irresponsible hijinks on the part of participants, were nevertheless quite uncomfortable with the idea of homosexual unions.

If AIDS broke out in the United States before it did in the Soviet Union or China, it's because a homosexual man, beginning in the late 1960s and early 1970s, had much more freedom here than in most other countries. But in a sense he didn't have enough. He had the freedom, that is, to have indiscriminate homosexual sex without fear of arrest and imprisonment; he could even cruise gay bars after work and return to the office in the morning (or, in many cases, to his wife and children later that night) without anyone being the wiser. Even if co-workers suspected, many of them wouldn't care very much, so long as he kept his private life to himself; they understood that he was "made that way." But if he were to settle down into a stable, loving relationship with another man, some of those same co-workers would turn on him.

Polls confirm this. They've shown that straight people are more tolerant of homosexuals than they are accepting of homosexual unions; they're less hostile, in other words, to promiscuous gays than to monogamous ones. On what grounds? Well, they tolerate homosexuals for libertarian reasons—"to each his own"—and disapprove of homosexual unions on moral grounds: "how dare they pair off as if they were legitimate married couples?" The bottom line would seem to be that most heterosexuals, for all their discomfort at the idea of homosexual intercourse, have less trouble dealing with the idea of gay sex than with the idea of gay love. Many people seem to figure that a sex drive is something you can't resist, so you may as well go ahead and do what you have to—but actually to *love* someone of your own sex is, well, just plain disgusting. Besides, if you live alone and succumb every few nights to the temptation to have sex with a stranger, you can put your clothes back on in the morning and go home and repent until it happens again, and thus be virtuous most of the time; but if you move in with someone and call yourselves a couple, you're in a state of sin 100 percent of the time. Thus what in heterosexuals is admired as constancy is in homosexuals viewed as stubborn unrepentance. Such an attitude makes little sense, certainly little *moral* sense, but homosexuals know very well that this is how many people feel.

I can't imagine that even the editors of the *American Spectator* would deny that homosexuals, like the poor, will always be with us. This being the case, the sensible—and truly conservative—way of dealing with the fact of homosexuality would be to arrange society in such a way that homosexuals can grow into well-integrated and productive members of it as easily as their heterosexual counterparts. Instead, most conservatives fight to preserve a system that forces most homosexuals to treat their private lives like a dirty little secret and drives many others toward a subculture that encourages them to view themselves as extremists, subversives, outsiders. The idea is to keep homosexuals out of sight; but to keep members of a minority group out of sight is to push many of them to the edges, to foster the radicalization of people who might otherwise be conservative themselves.

Conservatives have done all this in the name of "the family," to which homosexuality supposedly poses a threat. We all know the sort of family that people who speak of "the family" have in mind; indeed, I happen to know some members of just such a family. Until recently, they lived in a small Southern town. Mom was a pretty, perky housewife in her late thirties; Dad, a respected local businessman, was active in local politics, in the church to which they belonged, and in community volunteer work. Married to each other since they were teenagers, Mom and Dad were the devoted parents of six smart, handsome, well-behaved sons; during their years together, neither of them ever strayed.

To the casual observer, they would look very much like the perfect American family. But there's one little difference: Dad is gay. Raised to think that homosexuality is evil, he kept it hidden for years. During that time he did everything to fight off his homosexuality: he joined a fundamentalist denomination that was virulently homophobic; he married very young; he lectured on the evils of homosexuality; and he secretly consulted with several ministers and psychotherapists in an attempt to eradicate his homosexual urges. But nothing helped. Finally, not long ago, Dad realized that he couldn't fight off his homosexuality any longer.

What to do? Dad loved Mom and their boys and didn't want to leave them; she loved him, too, and didn't want him to go. But he *had* to go. Either that, or they'd have to work out some kind of shabby arrangement, foreign to both their characters, whereby they could stay together with their sons and have lovers on the side. Watching this family crisis from the sidelines, one hardly knew whom to pity the most: Mom, who had discovered the last twenty years of her life to have been a lie? The boys, who were traumatized by the discovery that their father wanted to leave Mom and live with a man? Or Dad himself—who, had he not been raised to think that homosexuality is evil, might have spent the last twenty years residing happily with another man, and who had instead lived with unimaginable guilt, anxiety, and self-hatred, all of which he felt obliged to keep to himself? Dad's twenty-year attempt to go straight had made him into a well-nigh tragic figure.

But not quite. So far, the family is surviving, though it no longer looks anything like a traditional family. Mom has found a boyfriend, with whom she and two of the boys have started a new life in another state. Meanwhile, in a therapy group for husbands who have recently discovered their homosexuality, Dad has met and fallen in love with a man; together, the two of them have bought a house. Though Mom, for all her anguish, continues to love Dad and to understand that their circumstances are not his fault, Dad's parents, siblings, and older sons have given him a very hard time. Likewise, he has been repudiated by many people whom he thought of as friends, and as a result has suffered serious business losses and has had to withdraw from involvement in local politics.

The story of this family, which is not at all an unusual one, returns us to the question: in what way can the mentality that forced this man to deny his homosexuality for twenty years be said to be good for "the family"? The truth is that such an attitude toward homosexuality is terribly destructive of families; what would be a blessing to "the family" would be to recognize homosexuality as a part of nature and to offer homosexuals every opportunity that heterosexuals have to lead responsible monogamous lives—to allow them, quite simply, to regard as their families the loved ones to whom they have dedicated their lives.

For it is, in reality, not homosexuality but the stigmatization of homosexuality that is inimical to the institution of marriage. Either because they don't yet realize they're gay, because they can't accept being gay, or because they feel pressured to marry, young men who would otherwise pair off in households with other men marry women and father children. Some live a lie all their lives; some, worn down by years or even decades of stress and guilt, eventually accept their homosexuality and leave their families.

The reality of such men's predicaments is vigorously denied by people like Ralph Reed, Jr., of the Christian Coalition, who in November of 1992 insisted on a public-affairs program that being homosexual is a matter of choice. The interviewer quoted the conservative activist Phyllis Schlafly's gay son, John, to the effect that homosexuality *isn't* a choice, that being gay is like being born lefthanded rather than righthanded. Reed countered that the analogy wasn't a good one: he'd never known a person to change his handedness, but he'd known several people who had given up the "homosexual lifestyle" and were now "happily married." My first thought, as I listened to Reed that morning, was that Chris and I pass men like that on the street all the time. At first, seeing a young man walking toward us, arm in arm with his wife, one of them pushing a baby carriage or stroller or carrying an infant, we'll think we're looking at a nice ordinary happy little family. But then, just as this family is about to pass us by, the young husband's eyes will suddenly meet mine or Chris's in a fleeting, painful, haunted stare, and all at once we'll both realize that the picture is a lie, a forgery, and that this family's home is built on quicksand. As they move away from us, Chris and I, without exchanging a word, will look at each other pensively, ruefully, and shake our heads. There but for—what?—goes one or both of us.

It never ceases to amaze me how many people live such lies. A woman friend of mine, for example, has a boyfriend who used to be involved with another man but now claims to be straight. My friend recently discovered that he's been sneaking off every week or so to his ex-lover's house, where (she has learned) he still keeps some of his clothes. "We're just friends now," he insists. "I'm not gay. I *hate* gays." A professional acquaintance of mine works in New York City and lives with his wife in the suburbs. Once or twice a week he stays late in town and meets friends in gay bars, where he flirts shamelessly with young men. Why do these gay men lead these deceitful lives? Because the attitudes of people like Ralph Reed made them feel obliged to marry despite what is in their hearts. Paul Monette writes in *Becoming a Man* about how he once considered doing "what closeted WASPs had been doing ever since they trundled off the *Mayflower:* a sociable match with a proper lady, passion kept to a minimum, and lots of gin martinis as they pored over their Greek vases, fantasizing about the coachman."

In Mary Renault's novel *The Charioteer,* the young homosexual soldier Laurie experiences a moment of temptation. A sweet, innocent young female nurse is in love with him, and when he kisses her he realizes that he could marry her and carry off the charade of being an ordinary husband and father. Yet he is too honorable to do such a thing. Kissing her, Renault writes, "he knew . . . that he was already beginning to exploit her, and that this was only the first of many excuses with which he would be able to furnish himself, if and when he wished." Most gay people understand Laurie's predicament all too well: they have known the temptation to exploit, to deceive. The proper aim of the gay-rights movement is to help create a world in which no one is so tempted, and such deceit is unnecessary; in which all gay teenagers can understand, accept, and respect themselves, and have no more trouble making a life for themselves than young straight people; and in which every heterosexual can look at a gay couple and say: "What they feel for each other is a good thing. Let us rejoice in it."